FIGHTING THE
INVASION

The German Army at D-Day

by
**Günther Blumentritt, Wilhelm Keitel, Alfred Jodl,
Walter Warlimont, Freiherr von Lüttwitz et al**

Edited by
David C. Isby

Skyhorse Pu

Copyright © 2000 by Greenhill Books
First Skyhorse Publishing 2016
Introduction © 2016 by Skyhorse Publishing, Inc.

Skyhorse Publishing books may be purchased in bulk at special discounts for sales promotion, corporate gifts, fund-raising, or educational purposes. Special editions can also be created to specifications. For details, contact the Special Sales Department, Skyhorse Publishing, 307 West 36th Street, 11th Floor, New York, NY 10018 or info@skyhorsepublishing.com.

Skyhorse® and Skyhorse Publishing® are registered trademarks of Skyhorse Publishing, Inc.®, a Delaware corporation.

Visit our website at www.skyhorsepublishing.com.

10 9 8 7 6 5 4 3 2 1

Library of Congress Cataloging-in-Publication Data is available on file.

Cover design by Rain Saukas

Print ISBN: 978-1-5107-0357-5
Ebook ISBN: 978-1-5107-0366-7

Printed in the United States of America

Contents

Contents

Illustrations

Note: The maps on pages 52, 56, 176, 206 and 234 are reproduced directly from original and surviving maps and sketch maps held in the National Archives.

Contributors to this Volume:
Positions Held on D-Day

General der Infanterie Günther Blumentritt: Chief of Staff to Commander-in-Chief West

Oberstleutnant Friedrich von Criegern: Assistant Chief of Staff (Ia*), LXXIV Korps

Grossadmiral Karl Dönitz: Commander-in-Chief, German Navy

Oberst Paul Frank: Chief of Staff (Ia), 346th Infantry Divisison

Generalleutnant Edgar Feuchtinger: Commanding General, 21st Panzer Division

Generalmajor Rudolf, Freiherr von Gersdorff: Chief of Staff, Seventh Army (at end of July)

General der Panzertruppen Leo, Freiherr Geyr von Schweppenburg: Commanding General, Panzer Gruppe West

Oberstleutnant Dr Friedrich, Freiherr von der Heydte: Commanding Officer, 6th Fallschirmjäger Regiment.

Oberstleutnant Günther Keil: Commanding Officer, 1058th Infantry Regiment

Generalfeldmarshall Wilhelm Keitel: Chief of Staff, Wehrmacht High Command

Generalmajor Fritz Krämer: Chief of Staff, I SS Panzer Korps

Generaloberst Alfred Jodl: Chief of Operations, Wehrmacht High Command

General der Panzertruppen Heinrich, Freiherr von Lüttwitz: Commanding General, 2nd Panzer Division

Generalleutnant Max Pemsel: Chief of Staff, Seventh Army (until replaced by von Gersdorff)

General der Flaktruppen Wolfgang Pickert: Commanding General, III Flak Korps

Generalleutnant Joseph Reichert: Commanding General, 711th Infantry Division

Generalleutnant Richard Schimpf: Commanding General, 3rd Fallschirmjäger Division

Generalleutnant Karl Wilhem von Schlieben: Commanding General, 709th Infantry Division

Captain Herbert Schoch: Training Officer, Division Staff, 243rd Infantry Division

Major Dr Percy E. Schramm: Staff Officer at OKW, responsible for the War Diary

Generalleutnant Dr Hans Speidel: Rommel's Chief of Staff

Oberst iG Anton Staubwasser: Chief of Intelligence, Army Group B Staff

Generalmajor Gerhard Triepel: Commanding Officer, 1261st Coast Artillery Regiment

Konteradmiral Gerhard Wagner: Chief of Staff to Commander-in-Chief German Navy

General Walter Warlimont: Jodl's Deputy Chief of Operations

Generlleutnant Gustav Wilke: Commanding General, 5th Fallschirmjäger Division

Oberstleutnant Fritz Ziegelmann: Assistant Chief of Staff (Ia*), 352nd Infantry Division

Generalloberst Bodo Zimmermann: Assistant Chief of Staff, OB West

Foreword

Success or failure on D-Day was about which side would win the race to dominate the Normandy foreshore at the end of the first day, and hold it. Cornelius Ryan's epic account of *The Longest Day*, suggests the D-Day battle was won within the first twenty-four hours. This is too simplistic an assertion. General Bernard Montgomery, who commanded the Allied ground forces, identified potential crisis points in his invasion-planning parameters. He could only mount a joint airborne and amphibious assault with ten divisions, which he anticipated would clash with five German divisions on the coastline. There could be ten German divisions in situ by the end of the day and as many as fifteen at the six-day point and eighteen inside eight days. The Allies could land fifteen divisions in six days and maybe eighteen by D+8, when the Germans might counterattack with as many as twenty-four divisions. D-Day could not be judged a success until a stalemate of sorts was achieved.

By the 14th of June, both sides were bogged down in village fighting along the coast. At this eight-day point, German aims reflected in the preamble to surviving copies of attack orders were less concerned with 'throwing the enemy back into the sea' than with creating conditions for a counterstroke. At this stage the fight for D-Day beaches was over; the battle of Normandy was about to begin.

David Isby has brought together a virtual treasure-trove of firsthand German documentary material. Two-thirds of it relates to the strategic and operational level of command and preparation for the coming invasion, and the operational deployment of formations employed along the coast. The final third of the book covers the divisions on D-Day, with a smaller section about subsequent counterattacks. Of particular interest is the translation of the 352 Division Telephone Diary of Omaha Beach and its battles along the Bayeux Coastal Defence Sector, a fascinating twenty-four-hour command post view of the invasion battle.

The Führer wanted answers. How could the Allies break in so quickly? The Chiefs of Staff of both OB West and Army Group B were requested to explain what alarm procedures were in place on June 6, because 'the English have again, as in the *Nettuno* [Anzio] operation reported that German soldiers had to be hauled out of their beds in their underclothes'.[1] Excuses were needed for some reports. Many of the accounts are postwar interrogations conducted by the victors, 'lessons learned' in US Army parlance. Senior German officers, humiliated in defeat liked to offer a sanitized interpretation of events, to preserve their view of history, or infer that responsibility for shortcomings lay elsewhere.

Occupied mainland France was at relative peace for four years before the invasion, providing a rest and recuperation area for many units. German readiness in this context was less problematical than credibly believing what reconnaissance was telling them. No German aerial photographs were taken of Allied disembarkation ports after May 24. Hauptmann Eberspächer flew his low-level reconnaissance flight from KG 52 over the invasion fleet while it was underway, dispatching a report by 0500, which appears to have been ignored.[2] Blaming bad weather was another excuse for not detecting the approaching allied armada, but German meteorological reports did not report unfavorable weather, simply that conditions around the Pas de Calais were worse than Normandy. When the first live rounds were fired as paratroopers dropped on the eve of D-Day, German coastal units were still conducting night exercises with blank ammunition. Not one contemporary German document dared admit that psychological surprise was complete.

The Wehrmacht was land-centric, unable to visualize the size and breadth of such an invasion fleet. In 1940 it had made a similar mistake, failing to detect the scale of the naval evacuations at Dunkirk. Floating harbors and swimming tanks lay outside conventional army staff planning parameters. Landings at Anzio on the Italian Mediterranean coast had been checked earlier that year. Units fortifying the Atlantic Wall knew that conditions would be much more boisterous on the stormy Channel.

There is much in these documents after the Ultra/Enigma code-breaking revelations in 1974 that senior German commanders could not reasonably be expected to know. Allied deception measures suggesting that the invasion would be at the Pas de Calais, the nearest point to the Continent, was convincing. The true litmus test to apply to these documents is the General Staff Lage West situation map prepared for Adolf Hitler on July 3. Almost a month into the invasion it was showing sixteen of fifty-six Allied infantry divisions committed to the Normandy bridgehead and just five of sixteen assessed tank divisions. In reality Eisenhower had only thirty-seven divisions in total to deploy for operations on the European mainland. It was difficult for professional senior officers, some still basking in the reflected glory of successful Blitzkrieg campaigns, to admit they had been duped.

Isby's selection of documents showing the impact of the invasion at the 'boots on the ground' operational and tactical level, reveal the innate ability of the German army to regenerate after setbacks. This ability to quickly recover from local defeats was to

---

[1] *Kriegstagebuch Heeresgruppe B.* 15.30 9/6/44.
[2] *Die Welt* nr 219. Quoted Kershaw *D-Day* p. 226.

surprise the Allies time after time in Russia, the Mediterranean, and later in northwest Europe. The so called 'veteran' 352nd Division that checked the landings at Omaha was in fact a reconstituted 321st Division shattered on the Russian front in 1943, reinforced with seventeen- to eighteen-year-old recruits called up the previous November alongside Stalingrad survivors and large numbers of Russian 'Hiwi' auxiliaries. They pinned two American regimental combat teams at the water's edge until midday on June 6.

The Allied parachute landings broke up the coherence of the staff and planning responses to deploy reserves along the invasion front. The documents show they were committed too soon or in the wrong direction. They were often bicycle borne or mounted on obsolete civilian wood-burning trucks, unable to relocate in the teeth of Allied air attacks. The scattered nature of the landings bedeviled a coherent response, the 23rd Panzer Division ended up on the wrong side of the Orne River, distracted away by parachute landings from the amphibious landings. They lost vital hours detouring through a bombed-out Caen because glider troops had captured the key Orne river bridges.

David Isby's edited selection of these documents is a must for any serious study of the German perspective of D-Day.

Robert Kershaw
November 2015

Editor's Introduction

This volume seeks to show, from the viewpoint of the German Army, one of the most decisive operations of the Second World War – the Allied invasion of Normandy on D-Day, 6 June 1944, and the events leading up to it. These views were represented in a range of military studies written for the US Army by senior German Army officers after the war, and these documents have provided the source material for this volume.

The documents have been used as source material in all subsequent writing on Normandy, especially that in the English language. Taken together, they represent the most detailed German account of the fighting. As has often been pointed out, however, they all have to be used with caution. The earlier reports were compiled when the authors were prisoners of war, the later ones when they were paid employees of the US Army. Most of them—especially the earlier reports—were written largely without reference to war diaries, wartime maps (although the US Army provided the authors with reference maps) or official papers. Moreover, although they were written by participants (many of whom never wrote their memoirs or other accounts in any language) while their memories were still fresh, their immediacy is not matched by attention to detail (for example, dates and places are sometimes wrong or inconsistent) or by their impartiality.

In some cases, the threat of prosecution for war crimes was hanging over, if not the authors themselves, then at least their subjects. Blumentritt's admiration of his boss, Field Marshal von Rundstedt, was doubtless genuine. But it is not difficult to see his account as a message of special pleading that von Rundstedt should not be subjected to prosecution for war crimes (in fact he was not, on grounds of ill-health). Von Rundstedt's knowledge (and explicit approval) of a broad spectrum of atrocities simply did not get included. Nor was this atypical of these documents. A more charitable interpretation would be that, in operational accounts, the authors felt that issues such as complicity with members of the Nazi regime, who ordered atrocities against the French Resistance or Canadian prisoners and the shooting of vast numbers of German soldiers after drumhead courts martial, were simply off-limits.

In even the more reliable of these documents, the authors find it easier to talk about their successes than their setbacks, and to point fingers to establish blame rather than look in a mirror. No one has a good word to say about any of the ten "Ost" battalions recruited chiefly from former Soviet prisoners of war that were in the German order of battle in Normandy. Yet before D-Day someone obviously had enough faith in them to put vast stretches of the invasion coast in their hands. Looking at the record, these units often fought as well as the Germans could expect.

The authors do not expend much ink on introspection and self-revelation. General Feuchtinger, of the 21st Panzer Division, was well known for taking off—without leave—from his command and for failures of nerve (which led to his relief and court martial). General Geyr, of Panzer Gruppe West, was apparently—and understandably—shell-shocked after his headquarters was destroyed by Allied bombing. But the reader will not learn these facts from them. However, this shortcoming is partially offset by our inclusion of comments from other authors who reviewed the completed documents.

The Germans' tactical prowess and adaptability, which the authors of these documents so often show, is certainly well documented. Even if the operational principle of unity of command is largely conspicuous by its absence, the papers demonstrate the importance of reconstitution to the tenacious German defense. Even the much-scorned "Ost" battalions and static division units show tremendous resilience. The 352nd Division was attacked every day from D-Day on, and by the end of June only 180 of the 15,000 personnel available on D-Day were still with the Division. Yet, reading the accounts of this Division, we discover that it always pulls together some reserve and reforms its defense. The Allies' attack proceeded with limited speed and shock. This was due to the terrain, their own limited forces, and the overall incremental operational planning. As a result, the pressure was never kept on the German defenses long enough to keep their highly effective reconstitution and their shoestring logistic resupply from taking place until the breakout at the end of the Normandy fighting.

Not only German tactical prowess, but also the failure of German strategy, logistics, and intelligence in Normandy is evident from these documents: the divisions within the German command structure and the lack of concentration of both authority and effort are all apparent in the first chapter. The complex, overlapping German chain of command helped to prevent rapid, decisive action. More to the point, the absence of a workable strategy is apparent. It has all been reduced to operations at best and more often simply tactics: defeat the invasion and improvise from there.

As for logistics, the documents show the reader that Normandy was, like Gettysburg, basically a "meeting engagement." The beachhead may have been established through hard fighting, but it was maintained because the Allies could bring up troops and matériel faster across the Channel than the Germans could bring up reserves. In the end, the German logistics system would no longer be able to bring up forces or sustain those already in combat, but these documents show the reader that the German artillery was out of ammunition, in many cases, by the end of D-Day.

German intelligence not only failed to identify the time or scope of the invasion, but was unable to take advantage of successes such as the capture of a US corps operations order on D-Day+1. Only tactical intelligence—such as signal intercepts—remained to guide the authors of these documents.

The significance of Allied airpower, both in the interdiction mission and over the battlefield, is repeated time and again in these documents. In part, it provides a palatable rationale for the German defeat, allowing the authors to point at the absent Luftwaffe. Yet there is also evidence of how tactically adept divisions could minimize the effects of airpower, how camouflage prevented the loss of artillery to air attacks, and how effective march tactics reduced losses. These accounts show that the effects of air attack on combat units are certainly greater than the number of casualties inflicted. Napoleon famously said the moral is to the physical as three is to one. These sources suggest that, for the impact of air attacks on troops, the ratio may be even higher.

As a narrative, this volume has a *Rashomon*-like quality, with the same events being described by multiple writers while—even more frustratingly—events of greater significance are ignored. The reader actually has a choice of how to proceed, either chronologically or following a particular author. The quality of the writing and the translation varies greatly. Those authors who had a good command of English, such as Geyr (formerly an attaché in London) and von der Heydte (who had an academic background) apparently did some or all of their translation themselves. There is little attempt at consistency in matters such as grammar and capitalization or in the use of German or English-language terms and abbreviations (although we have gone some way to address these shortcomings).

These documents certainly do not tell the complete German side of D-Day. The range of postwar German-language books, memoirs, battle studies, and unit histories certainly have looked at D-Day with the benefit of all the resources that these documents' authors lacked. German Army records—many available on microfilm at the US National Archives—and the personal papers of many of the commanders (including some of the current authors) today give the potential for a more complete picture. But the documents included in this volume remain a valid part of that picture, for all their limitations.

Unless otherwise identified, the editorial notes in square brackets are from the original (c. 1946) US Army editors.

David C. Isby
Washington, DC, 2000

Glossary

(a)	American
AA	antiaircraft
Abn	airborne
Abt	abteilung (battalion/unit)
AC	army corps
Adm	Admiral
AK	Armee Korps (army corps)
Am	American
Arty	artillery
Aus	ausbildung (training)
Bodenständ	static
Brigf	Brigadeführer (Waffen-SS rank equivalent to US Brigadier-General or British Brigadier)
CofS	Chief of Staff
CP or c.p.	command post
Div	division
(e)	English
Feld	Field
Feldersatz	Field replacement
FH	Feldhaubitze (field [light] howitzer)
FH 18	Feldhaubitze 18 (standard German 105mm divisional artillery piece)
FHq	Führerhauptquartier (Hitler's headquarters)
FHW	Fremde Heere West (Foreign Armies West; military intelligence)
Flak	anti-aircraft artillery
FS	Fallschirmjäger (airborne; Luftwffe troops, nominally airdrop-capable)
FSR	field service regulations
Genfldm	General Field Marshal, equivalent to US General of the Army or British Field Marshal
Gen	General, usually of a branch (e.g. Panzertruppen), equivalent to Lieutenant-General

Gen Fl	General der Fliegertruppen (Luftwaffe General)
Genobst	Generaloberst (Colonel-General, equivalent to US or British General)
Gp	Gruppe
Gren	Grenadier (infantry)
Hauptmann	Captain
Heeres	Army
Heeres Artillerie	Army-level artillery
HGr	Heeresgruppe (army group)
ID	infantry division
iG	im Generalstabdienst (General Staff officer)
Kfgr	Kampfgruppe (battle group)
Kp	Kompanie (company)
Konteradminral	Rear-Admiral
KTB	Kriegstagebuch (War Diary)
KWK	Kampfwagen Kanone (armored vehicle cannon)
LAK	Lehramt Kurse (instructional course)
LL	Luftlanding (airlanding; army light infantry, air-transportable)
LW	Luftwaffe
M-boat	minesweeper
Maj	Major
Marder	German turretless tank destroyer, armed with a 76.2mm Soviet-made gun
MLR	main line of resistance
mtz	motorized
Nachricht	signals
Nachshubs	supply
ObdH	Oberbefhelshaber der Heeres (Commander-in-Chief of the Army)
ObdW	Oberbefhelshaber der Wehrmacht (Commander-in-Chief of the Armed Forces)
Oberf	Oberführer (Waffen SS rank between Colonel and Brigadier)
Oblt	Oberstleutnant (equivalent to Lieutenant-Colonel)
Obst	Oberst (equivalent to Colonel)
Obstgf	Obersturmbanngruppenführer (Waffen SS rank equivalent to Lieutenant-Colonel)
OB West	Oberbefehlshaber West (Commander-in-Chief West),
OKH	Oberkommnado des Heere (Army High Command)
OKL	Oberkommando der Luftwaffe (Air Force High Command)
OKM	Oberkommando der Marine (Naval High Command)
OKW	Oberkommando der Wehrmacht (Armed Forces High Command)

Oqu	Oberquartermeister (Assistant Chief of Staff for Supply)
Ost	East (Ost battalions were recruited mainly from former Soviet PoWs)
OT	Organization Todt (labor organization)
Oyster	German nickname for Allied light artillery-spotting aircraft
Pak	antitank gun
Panzerfaust	'Tank fist'; single-shot man-portable antitank weapon
Panzerjäger	tank destroyer
Panzerschreck	'Tank terror'; reloadable man-portable antitank weapon
Pionier	combat engineer
Pz	Panzer (armor)
Pz IV	Mark IV medium tank armed with 75mm gun
Pz V	Mark V Panther medium tank armed with long 75mm gun
Pz VI	Mark VI Tiger heavy tank armed with 88mm gun
PzG	Panzergrenadier (mechanized infantry)
Qu	Quartermeister (supply; broader than US Quartermaster)
RAD	Reichs Arbeitdienst (German labor service)
R-boat	Räumboot (motor minesweeper)
RF-SS	Reichsführer-SS (i.e. Heinrich Himmler)
SIGINT	signals intelligence
S-Boat	schnellboot (motor torpedo-boat; called E-Boat by the Allies)
Stanf	Standartenführer (Waffen SS rank equivalent to Colonel)
Stellung	fortress, static
Sturm	storm, assault.
V-1	German surface-to-surface land attack cruise missile
Volksdeutschen	People of German descent or ethnicity living in eastern or southern Europe
v. R.	of reserves
Werf	Werfer (multiple rocket launcher "Nebelwerfer")
WFA	Wehrmachtführungsamt (Armed Forces Command Office of OKW)
WFS	Wehrmachtführungstab (Armed Forces Command Staff of OKW)
Ia	Operations Staff Officer/Section (equivalent to US G-3)
Ib	Supply Staff Officer/Section (equivalent to US G-4)
Ic	Intelligence Staff Officer/Section (equivalent to US G-2)
13th Co	Thirteenth (artillery) company of a German infantry regiment
14th Co	Fourteenth (antitank) company of a German infantry regiment

PART ONE

Preparation:
Commands, and Commanders

The writings in this chapter are the views from the top, of how the high and operational levels of the German military saw the preparations for the coming invasion. Together, they do little to support the common postwar view that the only failings that mattered in the German High Command were at the very top—Hitler and his immediate circle, including men such as Jodl and Keitel—despite this being a convenient view for the majority of the writers, who would like to portray themselves as a highly professional military machine that served apolitically (or even anti-Nazi) but with Prussian efficiency.

In fact there is little Prussian efficiency in evidence here. The divisions among the leadership make those of the Allies seem mild in comparison. The divisions already existing within the German command appear in bold relief in these postwar accounts, the authors having every incentive to associate themselves with the views of those who were neither disgraced nor discredited in the postwar world.

There was no answer to the strategic problem presented to them. There was no way in which forces could be withdrawn from the East in the face of a Soviet Army growing in offensive power and keeping the pressure on throughout the winter and the muddy Spring of 1944 as the Germans weakened, nor was it possible to use the increasing resources earmarked for defense against the strategic bomber offensive (half of Germany's artillery tubes would end up "at home pointing skywards").

If there was going to be any solution to the strategic problem, the first step in these scenarios—the Germans might have imagined scenarios if they could not fabricate a strategy—was the defeat of the invasion in the West. Once this had been accomplished, then all things might be possible. This led to the divisions over the placement of the reserve forces and over the concern—the result of Allied deception efforts—to meet multiple invasions. Much less could be done about the weakness in areas such as intelligence and logistics that would inevitably doom any arrangement the Germans might make for their Panzer divisions.

D.C.I.

Report of the Chief of Staff

by General der Infanterie Günther Blumentritt

I. OB West Situation Prior to Invasion

During the period 6 June–24 July 1944, I was the Chief of Staff, OB West. OB West, under OKW, was responsible for the areas of Holland, Belgium, and France only with regard to coastal defense. Directly subordinate to OB West were Army Group B (Fifteenth Army, Seventh Army, and troops in Holland) and Army Group G (First Army, Pyrenees security forces, and Nineteenth Army). Third Air Force and Navy Group West were subordinate only for the tactical defense of the coast. The Militärbefehlshabers (military commanders) of France and Belgium–northern France were under OB West only for defense against invasion. However, the Militärbefehlshaber of Holland was not subordinate.

The chain of command was very complicated and muddled; there was no absolute responsibility as was given to Field Marshal Montgomery or General Eisenhower. The C-in-C West was responsible only for the defense of the West Front against invasion. Only the elements of the Heer (Army Group B and Army Group G, with their subordinate units) were directly under OB West. Third Air Force, Navy Group West, and the two Militärbefehlshabers were independent, being under OKL, OKM, and OKW, respectively. All of these commands not under the Heer had a direct channel to their superior command and without having to contact OB West. The C-in-C West could give direct orders to these non-Heer commands only on matters pertaining to the coastal defense.

The Waffen SS, subordinate to the various commands for tactical purposes only, were in direct contact with RF-SS Himmler, over the head of the Heer. The Militärbefehlshabers had their own security troops, responsible to them only. The C-in-C West could only *request* the service of these troops. For the Heeres troops, there was no court martial jurisdiction above Army level. The Navy, Luftwaffe, SS, and Militärbefehlshabers had their own military courts, with independent jurisdiction. OB West had no courts and no jurisdiction.

Moreover, OB West had only limited authority, and this only in strategic and tactical matters pertaining to the defense of the area against invasion. The C-in-C West was actually only the senior strategic head, not a commander-in-chief—*primus inter pares* in strategic matters. As a result, responsibility for the area and for all strategic and tactical measures was made considerably difficult. The commanders-in-chief of the Navy,

Luftwaffe, and SS (Dönitz, Göring, Himmler) were close to Hitler and their wishes received more attention than those of the C-in-C West, who had no such representation in OKW.

A dictator does not favor putting too much power in the hands of one man. *"Divide et impera!"* Let this example be a warning of how *not* to organize the high-level commands. Formerly the German principle was "The man in whom I put my trust will have power over all in order to accomplish his mission, but he will also be absolutely independent and will have full responsibility. If he is not equal to the task, then another shall take his place." It was otherwise in Germany in 1939–45 . . .

Headquarters

OB West	St Germain (northwest of Paris)
Army Group B	Castle at La Roche-Guyon (on the Seine river, northwest of Paris)
Army Group G	North (?) of Toulouse
Navy Gp West	Paris
Third Air Force	Paris
Militärbefehlshaber for France	Paris
Militärbefehlshaber for Belgium–Northern France	Brussels

The first three commands had forward command posts which were temporarily occupied as the situation demanded.

In OKW strategic reserve were Panzer Lehr Division and the 12th SS Panzer (Hitlerjugend) Division, west of Paris approximately in the area northeast of Le Mans, and the 1st SS Panzer (Leibstandarte) Division, in the vicinity of Brussels. OB West had no strategic reserves. (The possibilities in the event of invasion had been considered. The fronts not under attack were to free certain previously designated divisions for OB West use. OB West, after obtaining permission from OKW, would then be able to commit these divisions in the invasion area. These preparations were made in detail on all fronts.) Army Group B and Army Group G had their own divisions or units in reserve.

The rear positions in Holland were the Grebbe Line and the Yssel Position. In all of Belgium and France there was no prepared rear position. Once the Allies had broken through the coastal defenses, there would be nothing to stop them until they reached the West Wall on the German frontier.

On the map (only on paper) there was a line Abbeville–Amiens–Compiègne–Soissons–Reims–Chalons-sur-Marne–St Didier–Chaumont–Langres–Gray–Dole–Swiss border, following the Somme, Aisne, Marne, and suitable high ground. However, this position was never constructed; there was no labor or material available and no time. Even if the position had been constructed, there were no troops available to occupy it. For political and psychological reasons, OKW permitted only a "secret" reconnaissance of the position, but no actual construction. We were to hold the coast

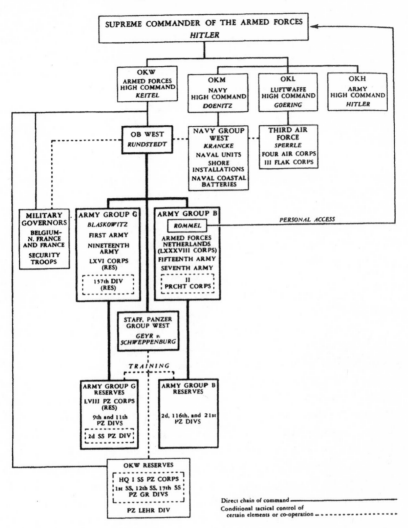

and not to think of "rear" positions. (The same principle applied on the Eastern Front.) Only after the invasion was this position to be hastily constructed by Gen Fl Kitzinger. At that time, of course, construction was still less possible.

The West Wall, built before 1939, was close to the Western frontier of Germany and ran south of Aachen–Belgium–Luxembourg border–along the Saar to Saarbrücken–south of Pirnasens–Bienwald–Rhine river–along the east bank of the Oberrhein to the east of Basel. The West Wall was built primarily for political reasons. It was not nearly as strong as propaganda abroad purported. Since the fortifications were erected before 1939, they were unable to withstand aerial bombs of 1944; their concrete works were too weak. The West Wall was only a chain of bunkers and lacked the depth that every defense must have. Once through the weak, thin line, the enemy would find no fortified defense in depth. After 1940, the West Wall was neglected and no longer improved upon. Permanent weapons were removed and sent to the fronts. Wire entanglements were taken up and used elsewhere. Thus, in 1944, the West Wall was not a strong position; above all, it lacked sufficient occupying troops for its defense.

The last rear defense line was the Rhine. When the Allies crossed this river there would be no further obstacles and the war would be virtually over. Only the Upper Rhine (West Wall) between Rastatt and east of Basel had weak fortifications. The Middle and Lower Rhine were not fortified. In addition, the Middle Rhine is so narrow that between Bingen and Andernach it does not represent a strong barrier. Moreover, there were no permanent security troops. Actually the only "rear position" was the West Wall.

The unusual command channels in the service of supply made strategic leadership more difficult. Supply of the entire area was under the direction of the Oberquartiermeister West in Paris (Gen Finch, previously Gen Eckstein). This officer was subordinate to OB West, the Militärbefehlshaber for France, and the Generalquartiermeister of OKH (Gen Wagner, later Gen Toppe). Thus, he was under three separate commands and received orders from three different men! The supply situation, during the invasion from the high-level standpoint of OB West, was as follows:

a. There was not enough motorized transport to meet the needs of the action in Normandy. OB West had no motorized columns of its own and therefore was forced to borrow these from the armies in the West. These columns were composed of purchased French and Belgian trucks of all types and ages. The drivers were French civilians, insofar as they would drive voluntarily. The transport columns of the Seventh Army were in no way sufficient. Only the Panzer-type divisions had organic transport columns; the infantry divisions had none.

Since the French and Belgian railroads had been disrupted by Allied air attacks and the French Resistance movement, they could be used very little. On many days, only seven to ten trains could be moved during a 24-hour period. These trains also had to carry supplies of coal and food to the population of Paris and southern France in addition to troops and tracked vehicles. This railroad net, crippled by air attacks on the Seine and Loire bridges and on important railroad yards, could therefore transport only a small percentage of the supplies. Thus, the few motor transport columns were even more burdened. The crippled rail net forced us to unload troops and supplies far behind the front and resulted in an extraordinarily long supply line. As the Allied air force destroyed many moving convoys, the available transportation dwindled more and more.

b. The supply of fuel was so critical that our few planes were unable to fly because of the shortage of gasoline. The fuel requirements for Panzer-type divisions, for the Luftwaffe, and for the Navy (U-boats) were so great that, even with the available motor transport, gasoline supply was insufficient. (Fuel requirements for the Eastern Front, the Balkans, and Italy were also very great.)

c. There was no shortage of small-arms ammunition, but artillery ammunition, particularly for light and medium field howitzers (Model 1918), was very critical. The great number of foreign weapons with varied types of ammunition increased the difficulties of ammunition supply.

d. Medical and veterinary services in general were adequate.

e. Spare parts for the much too many types of tanks and motorized vehicles were often unavailable. Tank and vehicle repair often took weeks because the required spare parts were not in stock.

The OB West right boundary was the German–Dutch border to the mouth of the Ems river on the North Sea. Adjacent on the right was the North Sea Naval Command at Wilhelmshaven. The left boundary of OB West was the Franco–Italian border at Menton (Mediterranean). The adjacent command on the left was OB Southwest in Italy (Genfldm Kesselring).

The mission of OB West was as follows: "OB West is to prevent any hostile landing in its area. The MLR is the high tide line on the coast. Should the enemy land at any place, they are to be immediately thrown back into the sea."

Essentially this was the text of the order given by the Führer (OKW). The order would have been of value only if OB West were permitted freedom of action to carry it out in detail. OB West should have been able to order the disposition of divisions and should have reserved full freedom to bring up, without approval, all divisions suitable to the existing situation. However, this was not the case, and every detail was ordered or approved by the Führer (in East Prussia!). Thus, command leadership of the type in which we had been schooled was made impossible.

We had been educated to work according to general operational instructions issued by responsible high command, which gave the commander a free hand. From 1942 until the Spring of 1944, OB West had requested similar general instruction several times, the last time in late June 1944 when the Führer was in the West for 24 hours. (The Führer's headquarters were northeast of Soissons, on the Soissons–Laon road.) These instructions were not issued. In accordance with our training, these instructions could have been approximately as follows:

"The mission of OB West is to prevent a hostile landing on the coast of its area. Should the enemy, contrary to expectations, succeed in landing, they are to be thrown back immediately with all free and available forces. In the event of an enemy breakthrough deep into the OB West area, they are to be defeated by a fluid field operation under the direction of OB West, even if southern France has to be given up. If this operation does not achieve results, then OKH will issue further instructions according to the situation. In the closest circle of the OB West staff, a planned retreat to the West Wall in order to conserve forces should be contemplated. This plan is to be kept secret and is not to go beyond OB West. In any event, the final decision rests with OKW."

Thus, our best strategist, Genfldm von Rundstedt, would have been free to conduct operations in the manner taught by Moltke, Schlieffen, and Hindenburg—boldly and independently.

I shall evaluate the divisions in the West only from the high-level viewpoint of OB West. We had a total of about 60 divisions of all types and all degrees of efficiency.

a. The bulk of the SS Panzer divisions and Heeres divisions were the best. A few SS and Heeres Panzer divisions had not yet completed their reorganization and were inadequately equipped with tanks. The 21st Panzer Division (Feuchtinger) was an expedient, having been assembled and organized with obsolete French armored vehicles. The personnel were better. The Panzer Lehr Division (Bayerlein) and 2nd Panzer Division (von Lüttwitz) were probably the best equipped. Both divisions were combat-experienced and energetically and well led. The command leadership of most of the SS divisions was less satisfactory. By 1944, all divisions had been employed both in the East and in the West. They had been reorganized several times and were not the divisions of 1939–40. Because of the fuel shortage, tank drivers were not sufficiently experienced and therefore were not good enough to drive in rough terrain and were responsible for the large number of tanks deadlined.

b. The Fallschirm divisions were next in the evaluation. These divisions did their best under the proved, experienced leadership of Gen Meindl (II FS Corps). (These divisions, however, had no parachutes!) The Panzer and Fallschirm divisions were preferential units with the best personnel, the best equipment, and the longest rest periods.

c. In third place came those infantry divisions which were not employed in the coastal fortifications. However, these divisions were for the most part newly reorganized, only hastily trained, and weakened by combat in the East. These were horse-drawn divisions. Their personnel and equipment were much less suitable for a large-scale war of matériel than the Panzer and Fallschirm divisions.

d. In last place were the coastal divisions. Most of these divisions had only two organic infantry regiments, weak artillery, and very limited mobility. For a long time they had been occupying a rigid defense of a broad front and were unaccustomed to mobile warfare in open terrain. Most of the officers and men had been wounded and were in limited assignment status. Their weapons were no match against a modern, well-equipped enemy. One division was composed only of men with stomach ailments.

e. The Luftwaffe Feld divisions varied in quality; some were good, some were inferior. The men and equipment were good, but the personnel did not have adequate training in ground combat.

In 1944, there were approximately 25 waves of divisions—meaning 25 types of divisions which varied in organization, artillery, and composition. Before committing any division it was necessary to know to which wave the division belonged. On this subject there was a large, red book marked "Secret." It does not follow that the first wave was the best and wave 25 the worst. In 1943–44, OB West had to release the best infantry divisions to the Italian Front. The morale of these heterogeneous troops, considering the serious situation in general in 1944, ranged from very good to satisfactory. There were no moral difficulties; the troops did their best as far as their varied composition, equipment, and leadership permitted. Further details can best be given by the respective division and regimental commanders.

In summarizing Genfldm von Rundstedt's situation, the following facts should be borne in mind. The German officer had always been trained to stand above politics. Politics had never been the concern of soldiers. Soldiers were always only the instrument of politics and had no other task than to discharge their duty to the Fatherland, the people, and the head of state. Genfldm von Rundstedt adhered to this old, traditional Prussian-German principle. Naturally, political questions were often discussed in private. War cannot be waged without politics. It is not possible to work only with the blood and sacrifices of the armed forces. However, this occurred from 1939–45. Politics were calm and silent. Thereby were we engaged not only in a two-front war as a country in the middle of Europe, but faulty politics brought about a war on all fronts. In the long run, the Wehrmacht on its own could not withstand a many-front war, in spite of its sacrifices. In 1942–43, the Western command hoped for an agreement with the Western Powers. During 1943, this hope disappeared for the following reasons:

a.   The responsible politicians did nothing and made no really generous attempt.

b.   The publication of the Moscow and Teheran agreements demonstrated that the German people were to be totally defeated. All important political speeches abroad contained the same sentiments. Consequently, in 1943, hope for a peaceful settlement with the Western Powers faded, and the stark necessity of fighting for the very existence of the nation became obvious.

II. Estimates of Invasion

After 1943, it was clear that invasion was coming. It was not evident before because we did not know the political intentions. In 1942–43, OKW was informed of the strategic situation many times, in official reports, in private letters, and verbally. Genfldm von Rundstedt gave the last large-scale estimate of the situation to Hitler, the Führer, in October 1943. An attempt was made to present the general situation in the West to OKW in the most descriptive and impressive manner in the form of a strategic-tactical expository thesis. This had little effect; probably OKW had no way out after politics had failed.

Anyone who traces the German fronts of 1944 on a map of Europe can see at a glance that there was no "defense" from a military standpoint. The fronts were occupied at the most by security forces and, on long fronts, by observation posts. "He who defends all defends nothing." The fronts were northern Norway–Norway–Denmark–North Sea– English Channel–Bay of Biscay–French Mediterranean coast–the Italian "boot"– Adriatic–Dalmatian coast–Greece–Rumania–Black Sea–a long Eastern Front to Leningrad–Finland–Arctic Sea. Any layman knows that "Fortress Europe" could not be defended in a military sense by one people and one already weakened Wehrmacht. The

Allies were on exterior lines. Their war potential grew while that of Germany decreased. After Stalingrad (1943), the Allies were on the offensive; we were on the strategic defensive. The Allies were free to decide whether to attack and when and where to attack. They could make feints anywhere in Europe. Their absolute air and sea superiority permitted them to make rapid, concealed movements, especially on the sea and in the West and South. From all sides, their airbases moved ever closer to Fortress Europe.

OKW expected invasion on a different front each month. Invasion was expected first in Norway, then in Denmark and the North Sea, in the OB West area, in Spain and Portugal, in Genoa and upper Italy, in the Adriatic, and in Greece and Turkey. Expectations changed continually. Moreover, there was uncertainty as to when and where the Russians would begin their offensive. We were on the strategic defensive, with all its well-known disadvantages of uncertainty. The Allies would have been successful at any point they chose to attack.

A "defense"—narrow and deep defensive sectors, strategic and tactical reserves, positions in depth, etc. (as in World War I)—was not possible on such extended fronts. In addition, there came the strict order to hold rigidly and not to give ground. That was not "strategy!" Allied air superiority, increasing after 1943, destroyed more and more of Germany's industry, cities, and railroads. Therefore, rapid movement of forces on interior lines was very difficult and almost impossible. We were bound to arrive too late every time. However, not only the impossibly long fronts, but also the numerous small islands off the coastline (often occupied only by one platoon or company) were to be held. There was no way in which OKW could be convinced of the impossibility of the situation.

The command of OB West constituted only a small sector of Fortress Europe. It was an important sector, however, since the invasion would probably be launched from England to hit the most vulnerable position—the nearest to Germany. That invasion would come was obvious after Fall 1943; that it would not take place in the winter was also clear. Therefore, invasion was expected between May and September 1944. It was assumed that there were two army groups in England with about 60 divisions and eight airborne divisions. The Americans were in western England, the British in eastern England; the boundary was Southampton. The commanders were known. Where would they come?

Genfldm von Rundstedt and his staff expected the invasion primarily in the Fifteenth Army sector, somewhere between Calais and the mouth of the Seine, at Le Havre. This was the most vulnerable area for the shortest thrust through northern France and Belgium into Germany and the Ruhr. Here the Channel was narrow, and the difficulties of air support and supply from England would be considerably lightened. Strategically, the southern fronts of OB West would be cut off from the Reich when Anglo-American tanks, after a successful landing, suddenly appeared on the completely surprised and unsecured German frontier. The Allies did not have to fear a German flank attack from the south, from the vicinity of Paris toward the north. We had to stand fast in the south, and we could bring up only a few divisions, with great difficulty and in piecemeal fashion, because we had no available strategic reserves. The Allied air force could have prevented such an operation. Simultaneously, the V-weapons could have been eliminated with one stroke. There were no more reserves behind the coasts of Belgium and northern France.

The Atlantic Wall was propagandists' bluff; it was not as strong as was believed abroad. Outwardly, it was very strong on the coast of Holland and in the Fifteenth Army sector on the Channel. However, the batteries of these mighty concrete works were silent when they were blanketed by pattern bombing and heavy naval artillery. The guns had only limited traverse; they were unable to fire to the rear, on the land front. The ventilation (escape for gases caused by firing) did not function. The "Wall" was a line, a chain of individual works without depth. If the enemy penetrated to a depth of one kilometer, they would be in free terrain. The installed guns were captured French, Belgian, Dutch, Polish, Russian, and Yugoslavian matériel of all types and calibers with a variety of ammunition. Many of these guns had only a limited number of rounds available. Under heavy bombardment from the air and strong artillery fire from the sea, blanketed by smoke and attacked by airborne troops from the rear, the "Wall" could never have stopped an invasion. It was apparent that these concrete monsters were greatly overrated. We had to assume that these facts had been made known by the many foreign laborers.

The possibility of a large-scale landing on the wide, jutting peninsulas of Normandy and Brittany was considered, but the route to Germany was longer from these areas. Consequently there was the possibility of a landing in the Bay of Biscay (First Army), where 500 kilometers of coastline were covered by only three divisions, of which two were composed of recruits. The defense points were only field fortifications. In conjunction with a landing in the Bay of Biscay, we anticipated a landing in the Nineteenth Army sector on the Mediterranean with a junction of the two forces at Toulouse.

On several occasions, OKW considered landings in Spain and Portugal and ordered preparations for countermeasures. OB West never believed in this possibility; political and military reasons made it very unlikely. Because of the terrain, railroads, and roads, Spain is not suitable for military operations. The Spaniard fights well on his own soil. The Pyrenees would have to be crossed. All these conditions spoke against a landing in Spain.

However, the Nineteenth Army and its fortifications were weak. The French Resistance movement in our rear caused excessive casualties and considerable confusion. A landing in this sector would have been simple. We also considered the possibility of a diversionary attack on the Mediterranean coast, with the objective of containing our reserves. Then, the main attack on the Channel would be carried out. However, these considerations did not have as much weight as the estimate that the decision would come in the Fifteenth Army sector between Calais and the mouth of the Seine.

The first indication that Normandy was threatened came in April 1944, from OKW. The sources of the information were not known. Only then were reinforcements (91st LL Division) sent to Normandy. However, we did not know whether the invasion would take place only in Normandy or whether another would follow later in the Fifteenth Army sector. We knew that a large-scale exercise had been staged in England and that travel by diplomats and all leave had been cancelled. However, we did not know that the invasion was intended to be launched a few days before 6 June 1944 for the following reasons:

a. Our aerial reconnaissance did not get through and was able to bring back only scattered, individual reports.

b. On the sea, our E-boats and destroyers were too few to fulfill their mission.

c. We had only five or six agents in England, at the most. Consequently we were "blind," and did not know what was going on more than a few miles beyond our coast.

We picked up many of the secret communications between England and the French Resistance, but we did not know their meaning. Every possible eventuality was discussed in diplomatic circles in Paris and Vichy. The fact was established that, from April 1944 on, Normandy was at least threatened. Naturally, however, the exact location, between the Orne and the Vire, was not known.

Since everything was ordered by OKW, initiative did not exist. Positions had to be held, everyone in his place; there were no operational possibilities. If Genfldm von Rundstedt had been allowed a free hand, he would have given up southern France, evacuated all of these troops (First and Nineteenth Armies, etc.), and formed a Panzer army consisting of the Panzer Lehr Division, the 12th, 2nd, and 1st SS Panzer Divisions, and the 11th Panzer Division. The entire army of five Panzer and eight infantry divisions would have been concentrated in the vicinity of Paris. He then would have launched a counteroffensive against the Allied open flanks when they approached Paris. This would have been a war of free movement in northern France north of the Loire, in accordance with the situation and German doctrines. However, this suggestion would never have been approved. Von Rundstedt would also have requested stronger air forces from the Reich. The idea of a "central army" near Paris played an important role in von Rundstedt's thoughts, since movement and free operations were our only strength. According to the existing situation, this strategic reserve army could counterattack either between Orléans and Paris or north of Paris, wherever the Allies presented an open wing or exposed flank.

The ratio of air strength between the Luftwaffe and the Allies on 6 June 1944 was 1:25. The Allies had not only air superiority, but complete mastery of the air, with all the obvious consequences for us. In the entire OB West area, the Navy had only twelve destroyers. I do not recall the number of E-boats. There was only a limited supply of naval mines. The Resistance movement in southern France was so strong that troop movements were delayed, communications were destroyed, and considerable casualties were sustained as a result of ambushes.

III. Invasion; Operations in Normandy

On 5 June 1944, a map exercise, in which several commanders participated, was conducted in the Seventh Army sector. About 2200 on 5 June 1944, we intercepted a coded message from England to the French Underground. We did not know its meaning, but thought it suspicious. This message was passed on to Army Group B. Fifteenth Army had also intercepted the message and had ordered Alert II (the highest stage of alert) for the sake of security. Seventh Army had not yet ordered any alert. Some of the troops were working on positions and obstacles during the night. Shortly before midnight, an uncoded message was sent from England to France. This message revealed that something was in the wind. Seventh Army had interrupted its map exercise, and the commanders were en route to their troops. Genfldm Rommel, on leave in Germany, was notified by telephone. He arrived in La Roche-Guyon on the evening of 6 June 1944. (No damage resulted from this absence, as all measures had been prepared in detail and the entire fighting was in the Seventh Army sector. Army Group could not do much in the first 24 hours without reserves.) The plans and orders of OB West were rigidly dictated by the Führer and OKW; freedom of action on the part of OB West, Army Group B, and Seventh Army was impossible.

The actual invasion, the landing between the Orne and the Vire, took place in the early morning of 6 June 1944. Beforehand, from about midnight, Allied airborne troops had been committed near Carentan and Lisieux. The first reports of enemy paratroops were received by OB West at about 0030 on 6 June 1944. Between 0030 and 0500 there were more reports of airborne landings, some of which were false. At about 0300, the C-in-C West ordered Alert II and himself assumed responsibility for ordering the Panzer Lehr Division and the 12th SS Panzer Division to prepare for movement. The request to OKW to release these divisions was rejected. About 0500, two Kampfgruppen from these divisions were advanced toward Lisieux and Falaise, on the responsibility of OB West. A second request to OKW to release these divisions was also rejected. During the morning and early afternoon of 6 June 1944, further urgent requests were made and rejected. At 1600, the last request was approved. These two divisions were ordered to advance and to throw back the enemy. For this mission, they were subordinated to Army Group B, and, because of an air threat, began to move in the evening of 6 June 1944.

On about the fourth day of the invasion (9 or 10 June 1944), the Allies succeeded in joining the inner wings of their two bridgeheads, near Arromanches. At that time, OB West, Army Group B, and Seventh Army were certain that a counterattack with the forces available would be hopeless. However, counterattacks were ordered repeatedly by OKW, and, against our better judgment, we also ordered repeated counterattacks. Success was not achieved.

During these days, we captured an important attack plan of an American corps. This plan contained detailed information on the phases of operations for the landing, an accurate estimate of our divisions, the political situation, the lines to be reached, the time period for each phase, and so forth. Naturally, this document was valuable and gave us the entire overall plan of operations for the first few weeks. Practically, however, this loss did not harm the Allies because we lacked the forces, the means, and the time to upset the plans of which we had become aware.

The Panzer Lehr Division and the 12th SS Panzer Division, under I SS Panzer Corps, became engaged about 9 June 1944 [?]. They were to thrust through to the sea, but the enemy mastery of the air and the extremely unpleasant naval heavy artillery fire prevented this intention. The attack never reached its objective.

In the middle of June 1944 [about 16 or 17 June 1944], after urgent requests by Genfldm von Rundstedt, the Führer arrived at his headquarters northeast of Soissons for a 24-hour conference. Genfldm von Rundstedt, Genfldm Rommel, Genlt Dr Speidel, and I were present at this conference. Previously the two Feldmarschalls had reported the gravity of the situation by teletype and had made a renewed request for general instructions. The situation was again explained. Our intention was to conduct a voluntary and planned withdrawal of the [LXXXIV Infantry] Corps front behind the Orne in two or three night movements. By this withdrawal, all Panzer divisions were to have been disengaged in order to prepare, further south near Flers and Mortain, for a large-scale counterattack to the north, against the inner wings of the British and American armies. The Führer made no comment on this plan; neither was any decision made. However, general instructions for the overall strategic conduct of the war in the West were again requested and were promised.

During the conference, a report arrived from the front stating that advance elements of American armor were pushing from east to west and had crossed the Coutances–Valognes–Cherbourg highway. Thus, Cherbourg and the area immediately to the south—that is, the northern half of the peninsula—were cut off. On 16 June 1944, OKW, bypassing OB West and Army Group B, gave a direct order to Seventh Army to operate in such a manner as to maintain sufficient forces in the north for the defense of Cherbourg and still have enough forces to withdraw to the south in order to prevent a southern advance of the enemy. Since the German forces were already severly battered, this order was impossible to carry out. The forces were torn apart; one part was pushed north to Cherbourg, and the other to the south. Both were supposed to build up another front. The Führer wanted to throw the strongest force possible into Fortress Cherbourg. We, on the contrary, wanted the strongest force to be in the south. To us, Cherbourg was not so important as the need for a southern front to prevent the enemy from breaking through into France. (Fortresses were a "fixed idea" with the Führer. His propensity for a rigid defense and a "hold at any price" policy blinded him to any genuine strategy and tactics—freedom of action, attack, defense, and yielding ground on a flexible basis.) OKW's direct order to Seventh Army was not mentioned at Soissons.

Preparations Against the Invasion

by Generalmajor Rudolf, Freiherr von Gersdorff

There remains no doubt but that the Anglo-American invasion brought about the decisive turn of the tide on the European continent, from both a military and a political point of view. It is therefore a matter of great importance to all historical research pertaining to the grounds which caused the German defense to become a failure—in the invasion—to find out the real reasons why the decision was wrought by the invasion, and why Germany lost this war.

a. *Did the invasion embody a complete surprise for the German Command when it came, with reference to the time and location of its occurrence?*
In the first place, the planned landing operation in France of the Allies was on so large a scale—and of such decisive importance—that the preparations for it could certainly not be kept secret. These preparations were being executed with such intensity—so systematically, and on such a large scale—that the German propaganda machine of that time, which was terming these preparations as mere "bluff," was believed by no German commander who had any sense of responsibility at all. Everyone realized that, sooner or later, the invasion would have to become a reality.

With regard to the moment at which the invasion would be carried out, we realized that the Allies would not overhasten, but that every detail of the preparations would be brought to completion first. On the other hand, we also realized that the political situation of the world—a rivalry against Russia, the headache caused by the revival of the German submarine weapon, and the effect which the V-bombs had upon the morale of the British people—pressed the Allies to bring about a decision as soon as circumstances permitted. After a thorough analysis of these facts and preconditions, we came to the conclusion that the invasion would occur as soon as our agents reported that the Allies had brought their preparations to an end—aside from weather and tide conditions of course. These reports arrived and were to the effect that the invasion would presumably start in the Spring of 1944, so that, if the weather permitted, we could probably figure on it then. As every day that the invasion was still a matter of the future meant a day gained for us to strengthen our fortification works, it was a matter of paramount importance for the German High Command to win time. Field Marshal Rommel thought that an effective defense against the eventual invasion had been brought into existence by the building of the coastal barricades and fortifications. The necessity of reorganizing the planned Allied tactics was reported by our agents, who assumed that the invasion had been postponed for some months, for the Allies were still training on the English coast. This was also ascertained by our air recomnaisance. In the event that this postponement should become reality, then the fortification works which had been built in record time and with great endeavor—and which otherwise were termed inadequate by the German soldiers—would at least be in a state where they could serve their purpose effectively.

Reports from our agents in the British Isles, as well as information acquired from members of the French Resistance movement, revealed the date of the invasion quite accurately. We did not have to fear the surprise element of the invasion therefore.

As to the probable point at which the Allies would land, we figured that, if they succeeded in landing in the Seine Bay and on the Cotentin peninsula, they would have to land at a moment which was a total surprise to us, otherwise it would be impossible here—although General Field Marshal Rommel did not reckon a landing here an impossibility. The German Command, however, reckoned that the Allies would carry out test landings before the actual grand-scale invasion would be started. These would probably occur:

1. Between the Somme and the Seine;
2. On either side of Boulogne.

The coastal conditions, operational possibilities, and a speedy push towards Paris, as well as towards the V-1 bases in the Pas de Calais, explain our assumption. On the other hand, the German Command reckoned that several landing operations might be carried our, either at once or at moments with brief intervals between them. It was considered that operations would perhaps be carried out for the sole purpose of fooling the German Command with regard to the knowledge the Allies had about the strategic importance of the different points. The fact that the German Command realized this possibility proved to be at this Command's disadvantage during the course of the invasion, for the invasion of 6 June proved to be the one and only operation. In addition to this, from information acquired from Ic references, we believed almost certainly that the Allies were capable of staging another operation of the same dimensions as the invasion of 6 June, and that they had not committed all of their troops in this first operation as they did not have the necessary ships at the time. We believed that their air force was also capable of supporting a second operation of the size of the invasion of 6 June, and that a second operation was probably pending.

The German Command took these assumptions into consideration, and was therefore reluctant in giving up terrain to the enemy. The enemy forces attacking the coast were kept back as much as possible in delaying tactics. These tactics proved fatal and were actually the first step towards the impending phase of the war where all tactics were "too late." This final phase of the war was characterized by German countermeas-ures which were unfavorably affected by these preliminary misconceptions.

Other reasons why the invasion was a surprise in as far as its location was concerned was the attitude of the Naval Command authorities. They saw to it that an invasion on the Seine bend would be as good as impossible, and that if the enemy wanted to succeed he would first have to gain the possession of a harbor which was in usable condition. This was a matter of paramount importance in the first place, because the construction of the Atlantic Wall—the barricades and coastal fortifications in it, as well as the distribution of our forces in this zone and the condition on the actual invasion front—was inconvenienced by the tactics employed by the enemy, namely, concentrating at certain points, particularly against harbor areas. As an example, I might mention here that on either side of Boulogne about ten very heavy naval batteries as well as a great number of coastal batteries had been installed, while on the entire stretch of the remaining invasion front only one very heavy coastal battery in cement was to be found.

From a general point of view, we came to the conclusion that the invasion would certainly not be carried out as a surprise where the time was concerned, but that the Allies had nevertheless succeeded in making a sound choice where the location of it was concerned, and that the Allies had also succeeded in fooling the German Command in this manner and had consequently plucked rich fruits.

b. *The organization of the German strategic reserves: was it good or was it bad?*
Field Marshal Rommel and the C-in-C in the West were of a different opinion on this question before the invasion was brought to reality. The Commander-in-Chief in the West thought that the reserves should be assembled away from the coast so that it would be possible to bring them to any point where they might eventually be needed in about the same span of time. General Rommel wanted the reserves close up to the coast, so that it would be possible to organize them in groups behind the sectors where strongpoints would develop. He wanted the reserves to be sent into the fighting immediately after the first Allied soldier had set foot on the Continent in order to insure that any eventual enemy bridgehead would immediately be destroyed. He repeatedly expressed his opinion that the enemy attempt to start an invasion should be checked every time and immediately, no matter what the circumstances would be. If the enemy should succeed in setting up only a small bridgehead, it would be a matter of great difficulty to get him off again, for the enemy air force was superior and also at sea. "We were inferior," according to Rommel.

The organization of the German reserves, as was actually carried out, was more or less in accordance with a compromise ruling between the two above-stated opinions on 6 June 1944. A few armored divisions—the 2nd, 21st, and 116th—stood in the near-vicinity of the coast, though not as near as Rommel had wanted them to be. The other divisions—the Panzer Lehr and the SS Panzer Divisions—stood so far from the coast that it would be impossible for them to intervene in the eventual fighting there for the first few hours after being alerted. Two armored divisions which were in process of reconstitution, the 9th and the 10th, stood in southern France. They had been stationed here because it was reckoned that a subsidiary landing operation might be carried out in northern Italy.

The 2nd SS Panzer Division was engaged in southern France, where it had to keep down the French Resistance movement.

The compromise solution described above resulted in a scattering of the units throughout France and the coastal area of the European continent, which was in sharp contrast with the old German leadership maxim which states, "Where all is covered— actually nothing is covered!" I was in favor of Rommel's point of view, for the defense of a coastline requires entirely different measures than the defense of an area. In a battle on the coast, it is possible to shift forces just behind the main line of resistance, and this is impossible on a land front. From the point of view of the enemy air force, there exists a great difference between troop movements from inland to the coast and troop movements along the coastline. In coastal defense the sea must be exploited as the most important helper, and as the enemy sets foot on the soil it must be understood that this moment is his weakest moment. This is, however, only possible if forces deep inland are not brought to bear. All the available troops must be brought within very close range of the coast, as well as all weapons and heavy guns, where they can concentrate on the enemy while in process of landing, which will enable us to destroy the enemy forces as they land.

It remains a question as to whether Field Marshal Rommel would have allotted his forces to the right position if his suggestion had been listened to. In any event, if the reserves had been organized into a compact band along the coast, they would have been able to fight more effectively, and the distance to the point of danger would not have been so great. The organization and assembly of the reserves were carried out also with regard to a possible enemy airborne landing on a large scale. It is beyond doubt that the German Command was influenced excessively by exaggerated possibilities. It was taken for granted that the Allies, in a very short period of time (20 minutes!), would drop whole divisions on the Continent. Our command was also of the opinion that the enemy could drop an entire army from the air into the interior, and thus be able to set up a front here. This intellectual grasp, based on reports from our agents and newspaper announce- ments, was also of influence in the distribution and assignment of our forces to their respective positions and zones. In this regard, Rommel was also of the opinion that the enemy forces landing on the beach would have to be reckoned with as the greatest danger, and that forces should be concentrated on them during the landing itself. Our attitude toward the enemy airborne troops would, according to Rommel, have to be of a defensive nature for the time being, for these would only become a menace when the enemy had succeeded in setting up bridgeheads on the coast. In any case, his opinion was that enemy forces would land in the near-vicinity of the coast, and he had therefore ordered the construction of a land front from three to five kilometers from the coast.

Field Marshal Rommel wanted a secured fortress zone set up which could be defended both from the rear and the front, along the coast, and inside this zone all the forces, including the reserves, were to be assembled and prepared for commitment. In my opinion, his opinion was not altogether listened to, for the German Command feared the Allied air force and figured that a heavy concentration in this manner—including the supplies such as ammunition and provisions—would be an easy target for this air force.

c. *The Allied superiority in the air: did it have a decisive influence in the invasion fighting?*
Considering the fact that the surprise element in the landing operation of the invasion—and the unfortunate organization and location of the German Army at the time of the invasion, as has been affirmed above—had an unfavorable effect on the German countermeasures, the Allied superiority in the air (which was an overwhelming superiority) also had a decisive effect on the outcome of the invasion battles.

This decisive role is not so much to be seen in the support of the Allied landing units, but rather in the fact that all movements of the German forces, and their supply troops, were made almost impossible during the day by the Allied air force. The German Command could therefore reorganize its troops and allot them to their positions only during the few hours of darkness; in the Summer, these were no more than seven or eight. Considering the fact that the Allied forces were completely motorized and we only partly, they had a large advantage over us. Furthermore, the Allies had the whole 24 hours of the day in which to move forces about—in short, they were not as handicapped as we were tactically and strategically. It was like pitting a racehorse against a motor car.

We are now considering the decisive matter of the final phase of the Second World War. Earlier, a continuation of the war by Germany could have been considered only if we had at least been able to neutralize the air situation. Despite the fact that the German Command never succeeded in, and never could have reckoned with success towards, this aim if it had thought out soundly and if the production situation with regard to machines and fuel, as well as the situation with reference to the strength of our forces, had been given due regard, the German Command defied the possible consequences of these overall considerations, and never really did see our disadvantage and that it would lead to our fall.

The Wehrmacht Commanding Staff (OKW) was still commanding along the same lines as in the period between 1939–41. All calculations with regard to troop movements were made without consideration of the air situation, as though there were no such thing as an air situation. The result was that disagreement arose between the Wehrmacht Commanding Staff (OKW) and the field commanders—who experienced all ills in person—which finally led to a total misunderstanding between the two parties, and finally to an almost ridiculous state of affairs during the last phase of the war, where orders were issued which could not possibly be carried out.

The resultant drawbacks increased to the point of becoming intolerable, considering that Hitler held the reins tightly (all the way from East Prussia to Normandy, let it be remembered), and any type of speedy independent decision on the commanders' part was rendered extremely difficult. This meant that any delays intervening had a sort of snowball effect, inasmuch as in the long run every order was already out of date at the time it was issued! And as, in my view, the air situation on the West front was one of the main reasons for this constant dawdling behind of the leadership, it follows that an overwhelmingly decisive role must be attributed to the Allied air forces! Not that this remark is meant in any way to deprecate the significant role of the Allied ground forces; it is only meant to clarify the otherwise inexplicable failure of the tried and well-tested tenets of the traditional German tactical leadership and the quality of the German formations. What had taken place in France was now merely repeating itself, with the only difference that now the tide had turned and that now the operations were on a larger scale. The clarifications given above of the influence upon the German soldiers and their commands are necessary to gain a clear picture of the invasion struggle in France, which proved to be the ultimate decision of this war.

To be sure, we must not forget that, from a general point of view, the Wehrmacht Command, ever since the taking over of the active military command by Hitler himself, had sunk to such a degree as was never experienced before throughout the annals of German history. The intentional ignoring of all tried German leadership principles—of the tactics of its mission, of an accurate calculation with regard to location and time, and of a sober estimate of the fighting ability of the troops—as well as the chaotic absence of an overall, well-organized supreme military command, became more and more to our disadvantage. It is no wonder, nor is it a coincidence, that since the day Hitler took over the Supreme Command in 1942—of the Army, in every theater of war in the world— not one significant German operation was led to success aside from the capture of Sebastopol, which cost us a very heavy toll in men.

Ideas and Views of Genfldm Rommel, Commander of Army Group B, on Defense and Operations in the West in 1944

by Generalleutnant Hans Speidel

I. Preface

The following is an account of the ideas and views held by Genfldm Rommel, Commander of Army Group B, before the beginning of the invasion, on the conduct of battle in the West, which the Marshal discussed with his Chief of Staff. These memoirs were written from memory. No records of any description were available. (My own records had to be destroyed at the time of the arrest, which took place by order of Himmler on 7 September 1944.) These memoirs need to be supplemented by, and coordinated with, available war data and records of the men concerned.

Exact data are needed for treatment of the battle in Normandy from the beginning of the invasion on 6 June 1944 on. In passing judgment, it is important to consider the interference of Hitler and of OKW in the strategic and tactical command down to the smallest elements, which increasingly made any clear-cut conduct of battle practically impossible.

The ideas and preparations of Genfldm Rommel for an independent end to the war in the West and, connected with that, for a change in the Nazi despotism, will be treated in a later study.

II. The Mission as Basis

Unyielding defense of the entire coastal front. No freedom of operation.

My Own Experiences

a. On reporting at Obersalzberg before leaving for the West on 1 April 1944, I requested an operational directive for the command in the West. Hitler and Genobst Jodl rejected issuance of such directives as "superfluous," saying that OB West and Army Group B had the binding mission of defense of the coast. In the event of a local landing, troops which might have landed during "the battle on the beach" were to be thrown back into the sea by an immediate counterattack. No mention was made of the Italian experiences, at Salerno and Nettuno. After all, if danger of invasion threatened, bringing up of sufficient complete Panzer units could be counted on, and the new jet-propelled fighter planes, "Turbojäger" (a thousand was mentioned as a

37

starting figure), naval units, especially submarines, and "the devastating use of the V-weapon."

b. In a concluding personal pronouncement, Genobst Jodl stressed again the necessity of preventing the enemy from making any landing, or of annihilating immediately any elements which might have landed. Freedom of operation in the West was forbidden.

c. Defense of the coast at any cost was, therefore, the combat mission. Propagandist ideas were the decisive influence in Hitler's decision on this as at Stalingrad, on the Don fronts, and in the Crimea, Sicily and Italy.

d. Frederick the Great once said: "Defense lines take up more ground than one has troops to occupy . . . Little minds want to defend everything, sensible people see only the main thing, parry the big blows and tolerate a slight misfortune in order to avoid a greater one. He who will defend everything defends nothing." The earlier famous German superiority in operation was given up in favor of a spiritless propagandist conduct of battle.

III. Estimate of the Western Situation Before the Invasion

Genfldm Rommel definitely expected the invasion, with land, sea, and air superiority of the enemy.

The usual risks taken in any large-scale landings were almost negligible for the Allies:

a. There was no German fleet of any consequence to be eliminated. The Allied navy was undisputed master of the sea.

b. The German Luftwaffe was practically put out of action and thus an important danger-factor for an invasion was eliminated. The Allied air force not only dominated the sky before the invasion, but also contributed decisively to the success of the landing by landing airborne troops without interference from the German air force.

c. A "cordon position," such as the rectilinear Atlantic Wall was after occupation and improvement, could never be regarded as an adequate defense position. It was an outpost position.

d. The Allied landing units were far superior in number and equipment, and especially in mobility (see below).

Historical war experiences also were used as a basis for determining the full difference in situation:

a. Napoleon, in the Egyptian campaign in 1798, had to reckon with a superior enemy fleet, which later destroyed his near Aboukir.

b. In 1854 the Allies, on approaching the Crimea, expected the strong Russian fleet, which, to their great surprise, however, was not sent into action.

c. Before their landing in Korea Bay in 1904, the Japanese eliminated the Russian fleet (surprise attack on the harbor of Port Arthur).

d. In the American Civil War, the superiority of the Northern fleet was so great that the naval-war situation of the Southern states can almost be compared to that of the Germans on the Channel and Atlantic coasts.

In view of the latest experiences in Italy, Genfldm Rommel saw clearly that, in the event of a large-scale landing operation, the enemy would pass the classical crisis quickly and surely within the first three days, unless the strength ratio in air, ground, and seapower changed fundamentally.

IV. Enemy Situation about Mid-May 1944

Army Group B counted on commitment, in case of an invasion, of four motorized or armored armies of American and British forces, the main body of the air force, and the fleets of both powers. The US and British land forces were estimated at first at 60–65 divisions—armored, mechanized and motorized.

Genfldm Rommel saw as probable invasion areas the mouths of the Somme, Bresle, and Arques with the harbors of Abbeville, Le Treport, and Dieppe, the mouth of the Seine with Le Havre, the Calvados coast, and the Cotentin peninsula with Cherbourg. He looked upon quick acquisition of an adequate harbor as absolutely essential. (He could not suspect the invention and readying of an "artificial harbor," such as was used effectively off the Calvados coast and adequately filled the needs of the Allies.) Of course, the favorable condition for this was the complete superiority of the Allied air force. Genfldm Rommel counted less on a landing on the Channel front (Cap Gris Nez), since the enemy, in spite of the physical proximity, would not butt against the strongest spot; nor did he expect a landing in Brittany, in spite of favorable harbor conditions, because of the limited strategic possibilities.

Genfldm Rommel judged the further intentions of the US and British command to be as follows. After a successful landing—whether it was north or south of the Seine, cutting off Brittany—the enemy would try to reach the Paris area as first objective, in order to rally his forces there and set out for Germany. Attainment of the Paris basin seemed to Genfldm Rommel as decisive for the Allies on strategic, political, and psychological grounds.

Enemy operations perhaps from the Channel coast in the direction of the Ruhrgebiet and from the Mediterranean coast along both sides of the Rhône to unhinge the Atlantic front were seen as possible secondary operations.

V. The German Situation

In the Army Group B area there were only six Panzer divisions being reorganized or rehabilitated: the 2nd, 21st, and 116th Panzer Divisions, the Panzer Lehr Division, the 1st SS Panzer Division "Leibstandarte," and the 12th SS Panzer Division "Hitlerjugend." In France south of the Loire, the 9th and 11th Panzer Divisions and the 2nd and 17th SS Panzer Divisions were in process of reorganization under LVIII Panzer Corps. The cadres with combat experience were weak, and matériel was still lacking, in the main.

On the Atlantic front, 2,000 kilometers in round numbers, 23 [?] "static" infantry divisions were committed. They consisted of personnel from old-age classes, frequently without combat experience. Their training by outdated leaders of all grades was not on the level of the task ahead. Materially they were quite inadequately equipped, similar to the type of infantry division at the end of World War I! Almost immobile and poorly horse-drawn, they could never be a match for a motorized, maneuverable foe if the fighting should become a war of movement. These shortcomings were repeatedly reported to OKW by Army Group, and once orally to Hitler by Genfldm Rommel with the correspondingly challenging inference. (I listened over the telephone.)

The Atlantic Wall was a rectilinear coastal fortification of varying strength. The construction was farther advanced at the places which OKW suspected would be landing areas and points of main effort (along the Channel, the mouths of the Somme and Seine, the northern tip of the Cotentin peninsula and the British Channel Islands group, and at Brest and Lorient). On the later landing front there stood, I think, only five "fortress batteries," one of them a solidly mounted 125-mm naval battery.

The Navy, on its side, had characterized the stretch of coast between the Orne and the Vire as not in danger, because of its geological formation (reefs). Probably for this reason, no large-scale mining of the Normandy coast was carried out. Organization Todt had equipped this stretch of Calvados only with field-type positions spaced at one to three kilometers.

After the first overall inspection of the Atlantic Wall in the Winter of 1943/44, Genfldm Rommel was bitterly disappointed over the state of construction and tried to make up for what had been neglected by the work of the troops committed. He gave fundamental instructions for the construction of "foreshore obstacles" which he had thought out—iron beams built out into the sea, with wire entanglements and mines— for a resistance zone of field-type construction, and for construction of air-landing obstacles. The "fortress construction" suffered from a shortage of material, but most of all from jurisdiction difficulties, the result of a confused chain of command (see below).

The Navy was in a perhaps tragic dilemma during the whole war between what it wanted to do and what it could do. It could and dared, because of its strength and its possibilities, be only an auxiliary arm; but Hitler, in his inability to judge the naval war situation, made extravagant demands and assigned absurd missions. He seems to have met never opposition, but rather agreement, on the part of the leading men, especially after the dismissal of Adm Raeder. This meant a regrettable lack of insight into the problems of grand strategy. The Navy led an existence of its own and its command showed little understanding for a unified command, while subordinate stations showed practical comradeship. The Commander Navy Group West had as naval forces only minesweepers and outpost craft of an old type, a few destroyers, a torpedo-boat flotilla, and some speedboat flotillas. Forty U-boats were to go to sea in case of an invasion; only 10–15 did go out later, and they could not achieve any significant results in the face of the enemy superiority on the sea and in the air.

Naval reconnaissance failed completely for the same reasons. Navy Group had been mistaken about the range inland of the enemy naval artillery. It was given as 15 kilometers for a steep coast and 20 for a flat coast. In reality it was over 30 kilometers. The use of numerous naval stations in the coastal fortifications did not correspond to the missions of the weak Navy; in view of the Western chain of command, it could not fail to lead to a dualism of the administrative staffs of OKW, OB West, and OT.

The Air Force, its commitment, and its possibilities for effect were the most burning problem, as in the Reich itself. It was impossible to get clear information about its missions and strength from the High Command of the Air Force in East Prussia. The US and British air forces were masters in the air and crippled all German air activity, especially reconnaissance. Satisfactory aerial photographs could no longer be obtained of the British homeland, especially coverage of the harbors and the Atlantic near the front. Air combat forces for defense against the almost incessant hostile air penetration were not available, not even when concentrated as if for a main effort. The technically superior enemy fighter-bombers neutralized practically all traffic during the day and took their toll. Heavy bomber formations destroyed rail and highway junctions, and also buildings, so thoroughly that the supply problem in case of invasion would be fatal. The destruction of railways west of the line Brussels–Paris–Orléans was making regulated railway supply impossible as early as mid-May 1944. Lack of loading space and gasoline prevented a shifting to highway supply. Lack of fuel later paralyzed all movement. The Seine bridges below Paris and the Loire bridges below Orléans were destroyed from the air before 6 June 1944, and subsurface bridges had not been built, in spite of repeated requests.

On the other hand, the enemy began his invasion operations by comitting more than 11,000 planes over the beachhead alone (according to Allied reports), while we had barely 300 ready to take off in the whole Western Theater; but the promised 1,000 pursuit and bomber formations did not appear. In addition, there was the enemy's strategic air force, which increased its attacks on homeland and occupied areas. Genfldm Rommel emphasized this air situation in his oral and written reports to Hitler again and again, and drew comparisons with his African experiences. Once he asserted to OKW: "In five years of war it should have become clear even to the highest command of the Wehrmacht that the Air Force, acting with the Army, will decide battles, yes, will decide the war." But all pleas, admonitions, and warnings died away unheard; reproaches and empty promises followed.

VI. Organization of Major Commands
and Genfldm Rommel's Recommendation

The organization of major commands in the West corresponded neither to the timeless laws of warfare nor to the demands of the hour or of reason. Hitler thought he could carry through also in waging war the revolutionary principle he practiced everywhere of division of power and playing forces against each other to his own advantage. This led not only to a confused chain of command, but to a command chaos.

Army Group B (Genfldm Rommel) in the Low Countries–mouth-of-the-Loire area and Army Group G (Genobst Blaskowitz) in the mouth-of-the-Loire–Spanish border–Mediterranean–Alps area were subordinated to OB West, Genfldm von Rundstedt. Navy Group West (Adm Krancke) and Third Air Force (Genfldm Sperrle) were subordinated directly to the Directorate of Naval Operations, OKW, or the Reichsmarschall, and only "assigned" to OB West.

Genfldm Rommel had also received a special "Führer mission" to check on the state of defenses on the whole Western front from Denmark to the Alps, including the Bay of Biscay, the Pyrenees, and the Mediterranean, and to coordinate the defense measures. For this it was his duty to report directly to Hitler or to OKW; OB West would be informed.

The military commanders of France and of Belgium–northern France were subordinated to OB West for military matters and to OKW for matters of administration and exploitation of the country for carrying on the war. But since Spring of 1942 the higher leaders of the SS and of the police with the SD had exercised the executive power in France and Belgium; they took their orders from Himmler. Operating politically were the SD and the fictitious German embassy in Paris, which received its instructions from Ribbentrop. A further duty of the higher SS and police leaders was the supervision of the Wehrmacht by the BD.

Organization Todt also worked independently, "on orders from the Führer," according to instructions from the Reichsminister for Armament and Ammunition, and from OKW. Here, too, OB West could only instruct and not command. Among the consequences were the meaningless structures on the British Channel Islands with the strategically purposeless and unprofitable use of valuable personnel and matériel. Army Group B could institute absolutely nothing independently in its defense sector, but had to plod the hopeless path of channels. OT was overorganized, so that "l'art pour l'art" was practiced and pressing military demands were neglected.

Citing the experiences in the Mediterranean area and the examples of the Allies in World Wars I and II—for the invasion operations all three branches of the armed forces of Great Britain and the United States were subordinated to the American commander Gen Eisenhower—Genfldm Rommel proposed that all three Wehrmacht branches and OT be subordinated to him for the one decisive defense mission in his command area. The proposal was sharply rejected by Hitler after repeated counter-questions. Hitler wanted fluctuation in the chain of command, and did not want too much power concentrated in one hand—least of all in Rommel's.

VII. The Problem of Strategic Reserves

In answer to an inquiry about the conduct of battle in the West, Hitler and OKW had again confirmed definitely the order that the fighting was to be done at the Atlantic Wall ,and preparations for an operation perhaps in the interior of France were not worthy of discussion. "The defense lies on the coast, which is to be held. Local penetrations, therefore landings, are to be paralyzed by automatic counterattack."

Disposition of the few reserves—one Panzer corps and six still unready Panzer divisions—had to be based, therefore, on the combat mission assigned, defense of the coast, "a tout prix." Here, at first, divergent conceptions of the field marshals came to light. Genfldm von Rundstedt originally contemplated concentration of these units in the Paris area. Genfldm Rommel wanted to have the six Panzer divisions brought up close to the probable invasion points in view of the thin coastal defenses. Without mobile Panzer reserves, landings of fairly great local significance could not be eliminated. One or two Panzer divisions, as contemplated, were not enough as a "fire department," considering the air situation and the deficient facilities for moving troops.

Genfldm Rommel considered five Panzer divisions, at the very least, necessary for performance of the combat mission. These Panzer divisions should help in their areas with the improvement of the resistance zone, which had been neglected up to this time, and construction of antiair landing obstacles, and should prepare for all combat possibilities, such as counterattacks, active defense against air landings, displacement to other fronts (especially over the Seine sector), and also for fighting while withdrawing. Genfldm Rommel was afraid that, if these Panzer divisions were concentrated in the Paris area—too far away in view of the enemy air superiority—they might arrive everywhere too late. In a conference he said: "Elements which are not in contact with the enemy at the moment of invasion will never get into action, because of the enormous air superiority of the enemy . . . If we do not succeed in carrying out our combat mission of warding off the Allies or of hurling them from the mainland in the first 48 hours, the invasion has succeeded and the war is lost for lack of strategic reserves and lack of Luftwaffe in the West."

His own and others' experiences in this war had taught Genfldm Rommel that the only divisions really ready for immediate use were those subordinated and in the area. In the case of all so-called OKW reserves, the decision to commit usually came too late, and then frequently the units were sacrificed to Hitler's dilettantism in leadership. Military requirements correspond with military-political interest in having reliable Panzer units in hand for coming events.

Genfldm Rommel proposed, in addition, having ready an adequate strategic reserve, that is, Panzer and motorized units, under a unified command in the Paris area and east of there. Hitler had consented to this when the Chief of Staff of Army Group B reported on 1 April 1944.

After the ideas of both sides had been sketched in detail, Genfldm von Rundstedt approved the concepts and proposal of Genfldm Rommel. The Panzer divisions were concentrated, as they became available close to the front, behind the threatened stretches of coast (north and south of the Seine). For the Paris area, an urgent request was made for an adequate armored reserve group—at least six to eight Panzer divisions and a motorized infantry division—for strategic use; in spite of the promise of OKW, this never came.

The Inspector General of Armored Forces, Genobst Guderian, raised no objections to the disposition and planned use of the Panzer divisions at the time of his visit to the command post of Army Group, and he was going to try to influence OKW in favor of bringing up immediately an adequate operational group of Panzer divisions.

VIII. Studies in Strategy

In spite of having been expressly forbidden by Hitler to concern himself with thoughts of strategy in the West, Genfldm Rommel did not stop at linear defense of the coast but weighed, in strategic studies, other possibilities which corresponded to his estimate of the situation, that is, the probable intent of the enemy to gain the Paris area in order to strike into the Reich from there.

In these studies Genfldm Rommel was interested in clarifying possibilities and preparing to get the initiative again by fluid operation. Three important cases of the many variants considered will be mentioned here.

a. **Case 1:** Based on Hitler's order for unyielding defense of the coast: An adequate armored strategic reserve is assumed to be in the vicinity of Paris. Successful enemy landing:

1. Between Seine and Loire: fall back to the Seine line, which is held. Attack south of the Seine to destroy the enemy troops which have landed.
2. Between Seine and Somme: preparation of positions in the rear in the line Amiens–Vernon and on the Oise. Move forward for counterattack between the rivers. This must lead, however, to a battle of attrition.
3. North of the Somme: small likelihood. Construction of a strong zone of resistance. Any Panzer operation very difficult because of the terrain. Nevertheless, preparations thought out for a thrust from south to north.

b. **Case 2:** Enemy landings south of the Loire and on the Mediterranean: abandonment of southern France. Defense of the Loire line. Assembly of an operational group of two to three armies, with as many Panzer units as possible between the bend of the Loire and the Jura for fluid operation.

c. **Case 3:** Enemy landings south of the Seine and on the Mediterranean: abandonment of southern France. Defense of the line Seine–Yonne–Burgundy–Canal. Assembly of the operational group in the Troyes–Dijon–Langres–St Dizier area.

The cases were carried through in different variants, with Panzer units at times coupled with adequate air forces.

Besides, for special reasons, all possibilities were weighed and conclusions were reached, on a large scale, as to how an evacuation of the whole West and a strategic withdrawal behind the West Wall must be carried out; first, in battle, second, after an armistice (strategic possibilities, technical necessities, time and troop requirements, etc.).

Sgd: Dr Hans Speidel

Commentary on Genlt Speidel's
Treatise on the Battle of Normandy

Genlt Speidel is to be considered one of the pillars of knowledge in the field of history of the Battle of Normandy. His sagacity as an individual and as a soldier gives this report the stamp of value. However well thought out these memoirs are, though, the report can still not go uncontested in many points.

Marshal Foch used to ask the question: "De quoi s'agit-il?" Applied to the Speidel description of the Normandy battle, the answer is: it is a question only of the historical events and their explanation, and of the human side only to the extent required in the writing of history.

It is a fact that:

a.   The Wehrmacht Operational Staff (WFS) did forbid fluid operation in the West. This was, after all, not made known to commanders of armies. Therefore, "pure" Panzer corps were not needed in the West.

b.   The Atlantic Wall was an outpost position. Therefore the whole defense theory of Hitler, Jodl, Rommel was unjustified. Since Hannibal, decisive battles had not been fought in outpost positions. With their theory, Hitler, ignorant of military matters; Rommel, the pure tactician; and Jodl, who was untouched by the holy spark as far as strategy was concerned, stamped themselves as indistinguishable from the trench-war soldiers of 1918.

The following Rommel theories are fundamentally unjustified and have proved false:

a.   Panzer divisions cannot be moved when the enemy has air supremacy. Under skilled leadership, the 12th SS Panzer Division and the 2nd Panzer Division reached their operational area without serious losses. The Panzer Lehr Division had its considerable losses only because of Rundstedt's express command to move forward by day, an order foreign to air and armored warfare.

b.   A main landing on the Channel coast is still to be expected. This is a model example of clinging tenaciously to a preconceived opinion.

c.   Without mobile Panzer divisions, landings of fairly great local significance cannot be eliminated. "Pure" Panzer divisions cannot fight with their mass and shock effect at all within range of great enemy battle fleets, least of all in flooded and mined terrain. Anyone who fought in Sicily and Salerno will confirm that. Besides, for the sake of logic, it must be stated that it is comparatively easier to bring up Panzer divisions from a location far to the rear than to move aside mobile Panzer reserves near the front. If the latter is possible, the first must be, too.

The following errors in Genlt Speidel's work are pointed out for later correction:

a.   All ten Panzer divisions in the West on 6 June 1944, except the Leibstandarte, were long past the stage of reorganization or rehabilitation. In matériel they were almost entirely up to full strength; in the matter of training, ready to be committed. The statement that the six Panzer divisions in the Army Group B area were "unready" is erroneous. Since the pause between the 1940 and 1941 campaigns, no German troops in a rather large unit were able to be trained more thoroughly, for longer, and in accordance with more modern principles.

b. Genobst Guderian indubitably shared the Geyr view. Rundstedt remained practically neutral. Hitler himself wavered when Guderian tried to win him over. His answer was "I must be able to rely on Fldm Rommel. Go to him and speak with him yourself." This was of no avail and neither was the Guderian-Geyr idea of holding the Panzer divisions, divided into two groups, ready as strategic reserves at a location far to the rear.

Gen Speidel's judgment of the Navy, Luftwaffe, and organization of major commands is exact and dignifiedly mild. The last was, in good German, organized confusion and conflict.

Historically, the following remains to be said:

a. In soldierly qualities and in strength of will, Fldm Rommel was probably the strongest personality among the leaders in the West. His faultless soldiery is to be honored. Out of the mass of generals whom propaganda purposely and systematically held in anonymity, the Third Reich elevated him on the shield as its own. History will not absolve him from responsibility for having been the strongest motive force behind an inept use of the entirely battle-fit German Panzer Command. By turning part of it into mobile coastal pillboxes and having another part follow hesitatingly, because of a suspected later enemy landing on the Channel coast or for other reasons, he wasted its concentrated force. He had been warned sufficiently—emphatically by the unusually farsighted Gen von Falkenhausen, among others.

b. In a time when the German leaders, because of compulsion, resignation, or opportunism, had given up the battle of wits against the Hitler dilettantism, he courageously supported his views in higher quarters as no other did in the West before or after him. This does the man honor.

The distinguished and faithful loyalty of his old Chief of Staff, Gen Speidel, can change nothing in the light and shadows about this strong-willed descendant of the Alemannen, and he does not want to change anything—at least wittingly.

For the dispassionate study of the history of the war, the judgment of the former enemy will be of real significance.

Sgd: Leo Frhr Geyr von Schweppenburg

Von Rundstedt and Rommel

by General der Infanterie Günther Blumentritt

Naturally, Von Rundstedt and Rommel belonged to two different generations; they were so dissimilar in origin, education, and outlook that they seemed members of different worlds.

Von Rundstedt: For 50 years an old-Prussian soldier, a member of an old-Prussian military family, a former Prussian cadet, 68 years old, he lived in his memories of 1914–18 and before. Besides, he was excessively modest, was too reserved, led a simple life, had no particular indulgences (with the exception of smoking and drinking), and was indifferent to money or possessions. He was taciturn, not fond of writing or telephoning, and used to fulminate against the state as then constituted, frequently even in the presence of strangers—Italian officers, for instance. He had a marvelous memory, a deep knowledge of human nature, a head for strategy, and a photographic memory for 1:1,000,000 maps. He had a strikingly good grasp of the French and English languages and had picked up enough Italian after a few weeks in the country to understand the language, without ever deigning to learn it properly. He was fond of uttering bitingly sarcastic historical and political judgments and had an intuitive presentiment of things to come. He was affable, even to inferiors, and a pronounced Francophile in all things, insofar as his military duties permitted him to be. He was completely immune to the influence of propaganda and to remarks about himself. He was extravagantly polite to women and French citizens, but also to all insignificant people.

His defects: It is true that he acted in the interests of persons intimate with him, but not passionately, not arbitrarily. If nothing could be done for Mr A, then the report or the written request was set aside so far as he was concerned. In such a case he might still do something, but he did not fight for the person, did not suggest alternative solutions.

I know my Field Marshal quite thoroughly! He does not know fear; his personal safety and comfort are matters of indifference to him. He still lives the customs of a bygone day: absolute and forthright execution of orders, and acceptance of decisions, such as was found so often in the old-Prussian style. It is bred into the officer and into the official!

Since the Field Marshal was no longer quite so agile as formerly, he traveled to the fronts only if he had to do so. He did not like to leave his staff, even for a few days. Nor did he like my occasional trips out to an army; he always wanted me to be at his side. You know that even our private rooms were adjacent to each other? He was beyond doubt a lover of the static.

I was so intimate with the Field Marshal as a human being that my judgment may be biased. But I see him as described, and, having given my loyalty to a man, I do not take it back.

Rommel: Speidel can judge Rommel much better than can I. I see him thus: youthful, active, agile, aggressive, and hot-tempered. Accustomed to an "independent" position, he was not inclined to submit to others. He had no strategic ability, but he was a good tactician and he recognized clearly the technical possibilities of modern warfare. He was an admirer of new technical engineering refinements and clever new gadgets. Courageous and personally ready for action, he was a natural front-line commander (Führer von Vorausbteilungen!). He was not without ambition. In 1943 and 1944 he was conscious of having the confidence of the Führer, and he referred to the fact very often! He was the "Führer's Marshal." His pride had been hurt on account of his having been deserted in Africa by OKW. Once, during an all-night drive from Brest to Paris, he talked to me for several hours about his defeat. On this occasion he expressed his discontent and bitterness. He left the Führer out of the discussion, but he strongly censured OKW for the African débâcle.

In the spring of 1944, he hoped to re-win great fame in the West. "Der Rundstedt"—that was his South German expression—was esteemed by him, but Rommel executed his orders only if they harmonized with his own ideas. He could, if he wished, always fall back on Hitler, and used to say frequently: "The Führer gave quite explicit orders to me." This statement was meant as pressure upon the C-in-C West. He never said so to Genfldm von Rundstedt himself, but he let him know it through me or my Ia!

Rommel liked to be mentioned in propaganda, whereas von Rundstedt, with his time-honored conceptions, took any marked allusion to his person almost as an insult. Propaganda was alien to von Rundstedt and he thought it "dirty" and "obtrusive." The Field Marshal was never known to have said one caustic word about Rommel. Sometimes he called him, good-humoredly, the "Marshal Laddie," and he told me more than once to let Rommel enjoy his propaganda. It may be that Rommel criticized von Rundstedt somewhat freely from time to time. However, Genfldm von Rundstedt never did vice-versa. He was like an old, noble-minded father, who does not understand his lively, different-natured son, but who allows him to sow his wild oats without paternal interference. Von Rundstedt used to say quite frequently: "When the invasion comes, he will certainly become more at peace in his mind." Moreover, the two Field Marshals met very often, had tea together, entertained each other, and so on.

The quiet, the negative pole, was von Rundstedt; the active and positive one was Rommel. I have described several times the contrast in their thinking as regards operations, but I have heard only once a violent utterance by von Rundstedt (with regard to the 2nd Panzer Division, near Amiens). Moreover, von Rundstedt did not force his will upon Genfldm Rommel in this respect. But this whole question is not of such decisive importance, because, in the last analysis, neither von Rundstedt nor Rommel had freedom of action. The Führer gave detailed orders for each division, and he had to be asked beforehand with regard to every single one.

I do not know anything about the bitter conversation which he had with you at Le Vesinet on 7 August 1944. I visited Rommel there twice. He said to me, "Such imbecility, this attempt on the Führer's life." I know that on one occasion he spoke with von Rundstedt alone in the bunker at St Germain in June. But I do not know what they talked about, for von Rundstedt did not say anything to me afterwards.

After discussions, whether with the Führer or with others, it was difficult to find out later what had been said. If I myself had not been present, I gleaned fragmentary details only occasionally and then generally after supper in the evening. The Field Marshal was not one who came with a slip of paper and enumerated the results of an entire conference, even one concerning purely tactical matters. The accompanying officer had to do that. Coming from the Führer, he always expressed himself very sharply, said that the officers of the higher command were all idiots, but, even so, one did not learn much more concerning the matter. He did not like to talk at all, and wrote and telephoned only when he had to. He never telephoned the Führer, and the Führer never telephoned him. On the other hand, I know that Rommel, von Kluge, and others spoke frequently on the phone with Hitler. In 1941, in the East, von Kluge had frequent telephone conversations with Hitler lasting up to three-quarters of an hour!

Von Rundstedt was "taboo." Schmundt* told me that once when von Rundstedt was, as an exception, ordered to the Führerhauptquartier [Hitler's headquarters in the field], Hitler was pacing up and down a quarter of an hour before von Rundstedt's arrival, putting on and pulling off his gloves, and as soon as von Rundstedt arrived he left everything just as it was and went to meet the car of the Field Marshal. Hitler had never done these things when any other marshal arrived. I always think it is just the same as with reserved, wilful children whom you want to assure of your love. The "higher-ups" did not dare reproach the Marshal!

The American psychologist in Nuremberg, Dr Goldensohn, gave the following judgment about von Rundstedt: "The Marshal—you need only look into his eyes." Dr Goldensohn was surprised at the rapidity and ease with which the Field Marshal went through the psychotechnical tests, lasting three-quarters of an hour. He solved them very easily indeed! He had brains!

He was liked very much in French circles; and many foreign visitors, such as Bulgarians, Hungarians, Spaniards, Turks, Italians, and Finns wanted to see him, just for five minutes! He was the perfect cavalier; he addressed visitors mostly in French,

---

* Gen Inf Rudolf Schmundt, simultaneously Chief Adjutant to Hitler and Chief of the Army Personnel Office, fatally injured in the 20 July 1944 attempt on Hitler's life.

pronouncing only three or four courteous sentences, and saying goodbye to them after ten minutes! Outside, everyone exclaimed: "He has a heart." "That is a Marshal!" and so on. These were the judgments I heard.

Genfldm von Rundstedt is no Talleyrand, no Von Seeckt!* He is completely uncomplicated, great but quite simple, an old-Prussian soldier of the nineteenth century. Perhaps it may interest you to know that he has spoken unfavorably of Bismarck, who seems not to be his favorite. He has expressed himself in no uncertain terms about the great chancellor! However, he respects von Moltke. He esteems Wilhelm I highly, Wilhelm II not at all. Again, he respects Severing,† former minister of the Republic. He has criticized Frederick the Great, without failing to recognize his inherent greatness. I might almost say he is a Prussian who, like Wilhelm I at the beginning, would have been most happy if Prussia had remained alone, just as before 1866.

His health is good (heart, etc.). The doctors told me once that he belongs to the "vasomotor" group. Arteriosclerosis has a limiting effect on his activity, but not a very grave one. Nicotine does not do him any good.

He is a remarkable man, representing the past century, but having almost a visionary's gift of sensing the great developments. Besides, he has always looked only toward the West, and he also knows the East from two world wars. The Marshal belongs to that rare class of an older epoch when silence and obedience were bred into the man. So I do not know what Rommel meant by "the ground having been cut out from under him." But, I can imagine that von Rundstedt perhaps listened to ideas of Rommel and perhaps consented generally to them, but then did not fight for them.

"Hier steh ich—ich kann nicht anders" is not his way.‡

---

* Hans von Seeckt, successively Chief of the General Staff in World War I, of the Third Brandenberg Army Corps, and of armies on the Russian, Balkan, and Turkish fronts. He crushed the Russians at Gorlice and conquered Serbia. As military dictator, 1919–20, he suppressed the Kapp revolt. He formed and led the Reichswehr until 1926. He was deputy of the people's party in the Reichstag (1930–32).

† Wilhelm Karl Severing, Social Democrat deputy in the Reichstag (1907–11). He was elected to the Weimar assembly in1919, and served (1920–32) almost continuously as Prussian Minister of the Interior.

‡ "Here I stand. I can do no other. God help me. Amen."—Martin Luther, end of his speech at the Diet of Worms, 18 April 1521. Inscribed on his monument at Worms.

Seventh Army, June 1942–6 June 1944: Report of the Chief of Staff

by Generalleutnant Max Pemsel

I. The Poor State of the Western Defenses

The location and strength of the Allied air, ground, and sea attacks which began on 6 June 1944 came as a complete surprise to OKW. Therefore, from the very beginning, the success of the invasion was taken as a foregone conclusion. Three weeks prior to the attack, OKW had pointed out that, on the basis of very reliable information, the invasion would take place in Normandy. In spite of this information, necessary conclusions were not drawn before or immediately after the invasion, and the Allies secured strategic surprise.

To understand the poor state of preparations, it is necessary to know the causes. The most significant part of the order which opened the campaign against France in 1940 stated: "It is of the utmost importance to occupy all large ports along the Atlantic coast as quickly as possible, so that from these we can carry on intensified submarine warfare against England." It was quite natural that, once in possession of these harbors, OKW should put OT (Organization Todt) with its equipment and forces, plus Heeres construction troops, at the disposal of the German Navy for the improvement of submarine bases at Brest, Lorient, St Nazaire and the Gironde estuary. The preference given the Navy for the improvement of U-boat bases continued even after the Spring of 1943, when Allied defensive weapons paralyzed German submarine warfare. The Navy still hoped for a revival of a successful U-boat campaign, with the aid of improved submarine equipment. OT was not inclined to transfer any of its personnel and equipment to conform to the demands of the local commanders. Favorable building conditions in the large Atlantic harbors, plus the size of the fortresses themselves, made it possible to report to OKW that immense quantities of cement were being utilized. The enormous quantities of cement used in the construction of submarine pens and the completed defenses on the Atlantic coast in contrast to the unfinished defenses on the actual invasion front are mute but eloquent testimony to this policy.

Since the Russian campaign did not progress as OKW had planned, and the grave danger of a second- or several-front war threatened, OKW decided during the Fall of 1941 to accelerate improvements on the "Atlantic Wall."

In improving the fortresses of the most important harbors (Dunkerque, Calais, Boulogne, Le Havre, Cherbourg, St Malo, Brest, Lorient, St Nazaire, and the Gironde estuary) and the strongpoints of the entire coast, the MLR was fixed on the beach. In

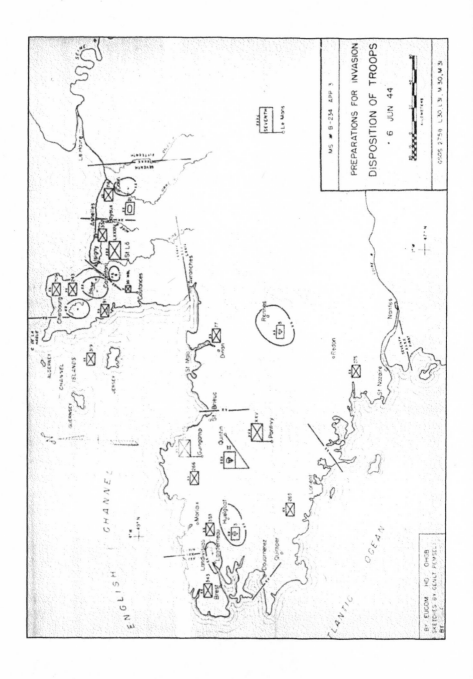

compliance with Hitler's personal desire, the British Channel Islands were to be built into "the strongest sea fortresses in the world." The 319th Infantry Division, with technical units from the Heer (Army), Navy, and Air Force, was shipped to the Islands during the Summer of 1941, thereby eliminating it from active participation in the war. With this decisive order, OKW established the bulk of the defense in the West in a rigid line, which extended from Holland across the Spanish frontier to the French–Italian border on the Mediterranean (a distance of more than 4,000 kilometers).

Would it not have been better to make fortresses of the large harbors and merely to keep watch over the intervening coastland? The bulk of the available forces could then have been held centralized in France as a strategic reserve and committed according to the requirements of the situation.

It was quite natural to make full use of the sea as a great obstacle in front of the shore defenses, and therefore to lay the defenses directly along the coast. If we were very strong in this line and still had a sufficient reserve available, we could hope to prevent an invading enemy from gaining a foothold on the Continent. The greater the capability of the enemy to effect a surprise landing with large, well-equipped forces, the less likelihood there was of being able to prevent his gaining a foothold. This was particularly true since the sea favored swift approaches and the shifting of troops from one beach to another. It became even more evident as the defenders got weaker in their 4,000-kilometer line and sufficient reserves did not become available at the right moment.

The basis for the order to build up a "rigid" Atlantic Wall was a sober evaluation of Germany's potential strength, the military and political situation in the Fall of 1941, and probable future developments. The order was compatible with the following assumptions:

a. That Russia could be decisively defeated by 1943 at the latest, and military strength subsequently transferred to the West.
b. That America could be kept out of the war.
c. That U-boat warfare could be brought to its zenith and maintained at that level.
d. That the efficiency of the Luftwaffe could be brought to the level attained prior to, and at the beginning of, the war.

However, even as orders were being issued to OB West in December 1941, catastrophe threatened the German armies in the East. The swift arrival of the severe Russian winter, for which the armies were only partially prepared, made an early victorious end of the war in the East more then doubtful.

At the time orders were given for the improvement of the Atlantic Wall, the following were directly under OB West:

a. Fifteenth Army (extending from the Dutch–Belgian frontier to the Bay of St Malo, including the British Channel Islands).
b. Seventh Army (on the left, with its center of gravity on the Atlantic in the submarine bases).

In accordance with natural topography, Fifteenth Army had its center of gravity along the Channel narrows, especially in the vicinity of the Somme estuary; and, by orders, on the Channel Islands. Fortification of Normandy, and particularly of the coastal region between the Orne and Vire rivers, was given a low priority by Fifteenth Army because the Navy considered the area unfit for assault landings.

In February 1942, something happened which caused us to stop and think. In a surprise raid, British forces in small wooden landing craft succeeded in penetrating St Nazaire and demolishing facilities. The German defense was poorly organized and had not stood the test.

As a result, the fortifications mentioned above were improved in strength and thickness, to an extent determined by the nature of the coast, the degree of danger, and the size of available forces. Major ports were to be built into fortified areas having all-around defense, with first priority to the sides facing the sea. If construction work on these harbors was already sufficiently advanced, they were to be declared "fortresses" and defended to the last. Between the fortresses the defense was to be based on a system of single strongpoints, mutually supporting strongpoints, and resistance pockets.

OKW ordered a defensive strength of three divisions as the basis for the improvement of Cherbourg. The defense belt around the fortress on the land side was to extend far enough south to prevent the enemy from viewing the port installations. Selecting positions on the rolling terrain of the Cotentin peninsula, which was covered with trees and hedges, was very difficult and never entirely satisfactory. During the invasion, while the battle for the fortress was going on, only a fraction of the troops provided for the defense was present.

In both the overall conduct of the war and the building of the Atlantic Wall, the lack of a strong central organization in OKW was a grave disadvantage. The interests of the Heer, Navy, Air Force, and OT could not be subordinated to the general defense because OB West had control only over the Heer. Other services which had greater prestige and more influence with Hitler frequently turned the scales in important decisions, with results not always for the good of the whole.

As an example of this situation, all naval and air force units assigned to coastal defense were subordinated to the local Heeres coastal-sector commander. For the naval coast artillery, however, there was the restriction that any fire mission against an enemy on the sea was to be directed by the naval commanders, even though naval command posts were often a great distance from the local Heeres commander. Only after the enemy had succeeded in landing was fire control to be transferred to the Heer. The Heer, however, insisted upon complete fire control from the beginning of the landing operation. Volumes had been written on this problem. As might have been foreseen, the problem solved itself on the day of the invasion when the local commanders took control of all artillery fire. (The Heer argued in vain against the shore line emplacement of the naval coast artillery.)

In 1942, the bulk of the Wehrmacht was engaged on the Russian front in an effort to bring that campaign to a close. Consequently, only a few poorly equipped divisions were stationed in France. In spite of increasing pressure from the Russians [for the opening of a second front—Ed.], we counted on the fact that the Allies had not completed sufficient preparations to launch an invasion.

II. Organization for Defense

During June 1942, the staff of First Army assumed command of the Atlantic front from the Loire (exclusive) to the Spanish frontier. The Normandy sector, including the British Channel Islands, was transferred from Fifteenth Army to Seventh Army, so that the latter's sector extended from the Dives estuary, northeast of Caen, to the Loire estuary (inclusive). The staff of Seventh Army was transferred from Bordeaux to Le Mans.

The Commander of Seventh Army was Genobst Dollman, a distinguished officer, with the ability to comprehend rapidly any situation confronting him. As former Inspector of Artillery, he was a noted expert. He especially advocated field training and was also most interested—and a specialist—in field fortifications. In spite of his age, he remained physically vigorous. During the French campaign in 1940, he became famous for his brilliant Rhine crossing. He had no experience in the East.

When Seventh Army took over the Normandy sector, it also assumed command of LXXXIV Infantry Corps (St Malo), which had as boundaries the Dives estuary on the right and the Bay of St Malo (inclusive), on the left.

Owing to repeated changes made in Corps planning, construction projects fell behind schedule. Things improved after April 1943 when Genlt von Zangen [promoted to Gen Inf on 1 June 1943—Ed.] assumed command of the Corps.

How radically different were the evaluations of the Seventh and Fifteenth Army areas may be seen by a comparison of the allotments of concrete for fortification construction. While LXXXIV Infantry Corps, in Normandy, was assigned 20,000 metric tons of concrete, the allotment to the left wing corps of Fifteenth Army, LXXXI Infantry Corps, located on both sides of the Seine estuary, came to four times as much for the same period of time. The result was that available labor forces in the LXXXIV Infantry Corps area could not be fully utilized for fortification construction. Upon the protest of Seventh Army, the amount of cement issued to Seventh Army and LXXXIV Infantry Corps was finally increased during the Fall of 1943.

Seventh Army evaluated its sector as a location for large-scale enemy landings which could be expected after the Spring of 1943. Normandy and Brittany were ideal for large-scale enemy landings because of their peninsular form.

a. In Normandy, the coastal sector between the Orne and Vire rivers was declared unsuitable for landing operations by both the Navy and Fifteenth Army. The east side of the Cotentin peninsula, with its relatively calm waters, was especially subject to danger. On the north side of the peninsula, small landings were possible in individual bays. The west side was scarcely considered in danger, because of the difficult channel and the fortified Channel Islands.

b. Because of its steep shores and cliffs, the north coast of Brittany—with the exception of a few bays (particularly St Brieuc and the area north of Brest)—was less suitable

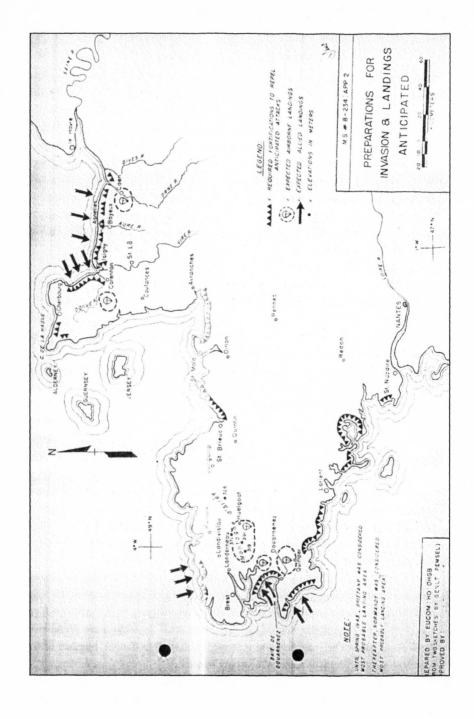

LEGEND

▲▲▲ = REQUIRED FORTIFICATIONS TO REPEL
         ANTICIPATED ATTACKS

⊙ = EXPECTED AIRBORNE LANDINGS

↑ = EXPECTED ALLIED LANDINGS

• = ELEVATIONS IN METERS

M.S. # B-234: APP 2

PREPARATIONS FOR
INVASION & LANDINGS
ANTICIPATED

NOTE:

UNTIL SPRING 1943, BRITTANY WAS CONSIDERED
MOST PROBABLE LANDING AREA

THEREAFTER, NORMANDY WAS CONSIDERED
MOST PROBABLE LANDING AREA

EPARED BY EUCOM HD OHGB
ROM TWO SKETCHES BY GENLT PEMSEL)
PPROVED BY :

for large-scale landing operations. The south coast was in danger of landings in the areas between the fortresses of Brest, Lorient, and St Nazaire (especially the Bay of Douarnenez).

c. Simultaneous large-scale attacks against Normandy and Brittany seemed improbable. A second attack would be possible only after the first landing had progressed favorably. Small-scale landings were expected in Normandy on the east coast of the Cotentin peninsula, aiming at the swiftest possible approach (from the south) to the important harbor and airdrome at Cherbourg. In case of a large-scale landing operation along a wide front, the terrain between the Orne and Vire had to be taken into consideration as a possible assault objective, in spite of its unfavorable coastal and water conditions.

d. In Brittany, a large-scale landing was primarily expected at the extreme western end of the peninsula, in order to capture Brest. This landing would probably be coordinated with pincer movements in the bays north and south of Brest (Bay of Douarnenez).

e. The following locations were considered to be in especial danger from airborne landings:

1. Normandy: area around Caen, and that northwest of and surrounding Carentan.

2. Brittany: Montagne d'Arée, particularly the western part.

Airborne operations were possible, however, almost anywhere in Normandy and Brittany. Seventh Army always expected that the first enemy airborne attack would be coordinated with the sea attack, and that airborne forces might be landed as far as 20 kilometers inland.

There were two different views held in reference to flooding endangered air landing areas:

a. The rivers should be dammed, the sea let in, and airborne landings at certain places made impossible.

b. The landing areas should not be flooded, since by so doing the enemy airborne troops would be protected from counterattack.

The Seventh Army's decision to employ these defense measures on a large scale, in order to upset the Allies' landing plan, was made rather late—in the Spring of 1944. Vast areas were then flooded in Normandy, including the Dives valley east of Caen, the area east of Isigny, and the Douve valley northwest of Carentan.

Throughout 1942 and up to the Spring of 1943 (a time when German submarine warfare was still very effective), fortification construction was concentrated in Brittany, since primarily we had to expect an attack against the submarine pens.

The armed forces were distributed accordingly. During the Spring of 1943, eight to ten divisions were located in Brittany (center of gravity around Brest); there were only three to four divisions in Normandy (center of gravity on the east coast of the Cotentin peninsula).

Supply of construction materials worked similarly. Since OT and the Arbeitsdienst (Labor Service) were committed in the fortress areas, the construction of strongpoints and resistance pockets progressed only in accordance with the number of available troops. Thus, the distribution of forces also explains the more rapid progress of all types of construction in Brittany as compared to Normandy.

The Dieppe raid in August 1942, with its fateful outcome, took place in the Fifteenth Army area. The raid was carried out to obtain practical knowledge for the invasion, and it probably also had a political background. It surprised us that, precisely at that time, the strongly fortified town of Dieppe had been selected as a target for this attack, and that the enemy tank and air forces had hardly gone into action. Even before our counterattack had become effective, the British forces—as we had foreseen—evacuated the Continent, leaving behind a considerable amount of equipment. Dieppe was played up by the German propagandists as a great success, while the Allied press had its own reasons for keeping silent. Thus, in German public opinion and through self-deception in OKW, there arose an utterly fallacious conception of the defensive strength of the Atlantic Wall.

In 1942, Germany resumed the offensive in the East, but after initial successes the attacks slowed down in the Caucasus and on the Volga. Russia could not be conquered. In Africa, after the landing of US forces, the situation became hopeless. The turning point of the war, the causes of which lay much farther back, now became plainly visible. A many-front war with its world-wide circle extending from Africa to the Dodecanese, from the Caucasus to Murmansk and via Norway, Denmark, and France down to Spain, could no longer be won by Germany.

The situation was made worse by the fact that OKW would not subscribe to an elastic defense, but clung to a cordon defense, without being willing under any circumstances to yield so much as a foot of soil. Wherever the Allies launched a sledgehammer blow, the Axis Powers' defense ring was bound to crumble.

Beginning in the Spring of 1943, we had to consider the possibility of a great invasion of France. How much the mere threat of invasion influenced events on other fronts is illustrated by the fact that, from the Winter of 1942–43, a varying strength of 10 to 15 divisions was maintained within the Seventh Army area, although troops were much needed elsewhere.

Nevertheless, even these forces were much too inadequate to defend a line more then 1,200 kilometers long. The divisions which came to Seventh Army from the South or East were for the most part battle-weary and without equipment. In addition, the supply and replacement systems functioned so irregularly that the fighting power of these divisions fluctuated a great deal. As soon as a division was refreshed to some extent, it was transferred to another front. It was only natural that divisions scheduled for the East or South trained primarily for those theaters of war, and consequently the coastal fortifications were neglected. The constant shifting of troops, with the necessary orientations and terrain studies, always meant a material weakening of the front concerned.

Upon request, Bodenständige (static) divisions—which were less mobile than normal divisions, but were particularly interested in 'their' sector—were set up for coastal defense. Only a few of the units of these divisions had any transport whatsoever, and their artillery was only partially mobile. The average age of the men was approximately 35 years, and, as a result of the repeated combing out of replacements for the Eastern front, there was eventually not a man left fit for duty in the East. Eight percent Volksdeutsche [racial Germans from foreign countries]—many of whom did not understand the German language—were assigned to the Bodenständige divisions.

The only really full-strength combat division retained by Seventh Army continuously (the 319th Infantry Division) was in the British Channel Islands. Since an enemy attack against these islands (inhabited by British subjects) was extremely unlikely, Seventh Army repeatedly recommended the exchange, or material reduction, of this division. However, orders from OKW specified that nothing was to be changed in the occupation of these islands. On orders from OKW, protested against by Seventh Army, several German battalions were sent to the East during the Summer of 1943, in exchange for which, in the course of time, Seventh Army received 21 Russian battalions. On D-Day, more than a fourth of Seventh Army's battalions consisted of undependable Russians.

Seventh Army's artillery pieces came from nine different countries and had varying calibers and types of ammunition. Some of the pieces had only half the normal issue of ammunition available, with no hope of getting the full amount. The Army had only one Panzer battalion, whose equipment consisted of old French ordnance. This equipment was worthless, and for this reason the battalion was sent to the Channel Islands. The number of antitank guns and self-propelled assault guns was completely insufficient.

Fuel was more and more strictly rationed. Thus, regimental commanders were able to use their cars only once a week. Otherwise they were dependent upon the use of horses or bicycles in the more distant areas. We had to improvise continually, and this made the situation truly difficult.

III. Normandy Considered Allied Assault Area

Allied air superiority increased steadily throughout 1943. Owing to improved Allied methods, submarine warfare began to collapse. Because of this, Seventh Army considered Brittany second to Normandy as the major Allied assault objective. Therefore, Army's center of gravity had to be shifted in its entirety to Normandy. Nevertheless, OKW continued to require as strong forces as possible in western Brittany, in the vicinity of Brest.

In July 1943, at a Seventh Army lecture before a large group of representatives of the Heer, Navy, Air Force, OT, and RAD (Reich Labor Service), the weaknesses of the defense and their consequences were discussed. Representatives from OKW were invited, but did not attend. It was established that an invasion could be prevented only if:

a. The construction of fortifications, especially in Normandy, was expedited in every possible way.

b. Actually strong combat divisions were assigned.

c.   Enough strong, mobile strategic reserves to launch a counterattack were promptly assigned.

d.   Correspondingly strong Luftwaffe support was assured.

Aside from larger total cement allotments given the Army and the promise to adjust "b," "c," and "d," above, in sufficient time before an invasion (which OKW apparently did not expect until 1944), nothing was actually done.

We continued to be hopeful—placing our faith particularly in the new weapons and inventions with which the Allies themselves had been able to counter the danger of the deadly U-boat. From the beginning of the Summer of 1943, there was intense reconnaissance activity in Normandy, by special staffs of OKW and OKL, especially in the Cotentin peninsula. These staffs were searching for installation locations for the new V-weapons, of which marvelous tales were being told.

From the very beginning, Seventh Army was opposed to the selection of Normandy as a launching site for these V-weapons, because the Normandy defenses were not sufficiently strong to protect the new weapons. Furthermore, the Allies were given one more reason for selecting Normandy as their invasion objective. In the Fifteenth Army sector the situation was different, because, there, greater combat strength and stronger fortifications offered sufficient protection for the new weapons.

Owing to the fact that OKW, in principle, gave priority over all other construction work to the new V-weapon project, Seventh Army experienced the greatest difficulty in obtaining the labor forces and equipment required for its own defense installations. It was all the more tragic that, because of the technical defects of the new weapons and air attacks against their launching sites, the deadline for the order to commence fire had been so delayed that not one V-weapon could be fired prior to the invasion.

As a result of the shifting of Seventh Army's center of gravity from Brittany to Normandy, and the necessary transfer of fuel dumps, ammunition dumps, and other installations, transportation requirements increased materially. There was only one double-track railroad leading into Normandy, and that had to carry all the freight. Consequently, supply servicing of all construction projects was inadequate, and the amount of fuel available for motor transportation was negligible.

Seventh Army established the following priorities for the construction of defense installations in Normandy:

a.   British Channel Islands (by orders from OKW).

b.   Fortress Cherbourg.

c.   East coast of the Cotentin peninsula (beginning from the north) and the Orne estuary north of Caen.

d.   Coast between the Orne and the Vire.

e.   West coast of the Cotentin peninsula south of Cap de la Hague, and installations north of Carentan.

At the start of the invasion, construction for "a," "b," and "c," above, was nearly completed; "d," for the most part, was under construction; and construction on "e" had not yet begun. The majority of the strongpoints and resistance pockets were only field fortifications. Along the east coast of the Cotentin peninsula, strongpoints and resistance pockets were spaced approximately 800 meters apart, and between the Orne and Vire approximately 1,200 meters apart. Thus, along the coast there was an unbroken line of fire, as long as none of these fortifications was knocked out.

Since only a few OT forces were available, Seventh Army put part of the Angres Sturmpionier (Combat Engineer) School to work in Normandy and also employed the bulk of the Sturmpionier battalions stationed in Normandy and the Channel Islands. French civilians were employed later on also for the construction of a second position along the Aure (northwest of Bayeux). Their labor efficiency was good. There were repeated Seventh Army requests that the French population in the vicinity of the coast not be employed by the Organization Sauckel, but instead be placed at the disposal of the armies for fortification construction; but these were rejected.

In August 1943, Gen Inf Marcks took command of LXXXIV Infantry Corps in Normandy. Marcks was one of the most capable men of the German General Staff, possessor of keen intelligence and a broad general background. At one time the right-hand man of Gen von Schleicher [Minister-President ousted by Hitler and killed by the SS in 1934—Ed.], he was a political suspect and became very bitter when Hitler cancelled his promotion to army commander. However, he was primarily a soldier, and though handicapped by a very bad wound (necessitating the use of an artificial leg), he devoted all his skill to the preparation of troops and defenses for the invasion. His death in a fighter-bomber attack early in the invasion was an irreplaceable loss to Seventh Army and to the Heer.

The Fall of 1943 went by without a large-scale attack against the Continent, and then it was important to make full use of the Winter and Spring. Troop commitments, training, procurement of weapons and equipment, installation improvements, and procurement of extra supplies of ammunition, fuel, and rations had to be expedited in preparation of Normandy for the invasion.

In the event of invasion, Seventh Army had three different plans, all of which called for mobile forces. In any of the three eventualities, the coastal divisions and one division in the Cotentin peninsula were to remain in Normandy to protect the harbor of Cherbourg.

a. Normandy: In case of an attack against Normandy, preparations were made to bring up a division from each of the coastal sectors of St Malo and St Nazaire, one division located east of Brest (only with approval of OKW), and one reinforced regiment from each of the static divisions located in the coastal sectors of Morlaix and Lorient. In the Army plan, only two divisions were to remain in all of Brittany—a coastline of 800 kilometers, which included four fortresses. This would mean, of course, an extreme weakening of Brittany in favor of another attacked front. A number of divisions (up to seventeen) from other army areas, and from the zone of the interior, were to be brought up in case a Normandy attack materialized.

b. In addition, we prepared for eventuality "b"—Brittany, and "c"—outside the Army area. Transportation of units and equipment over the longer distances within the Army area, particularly the tracked vehicles (tanks, etc.), was to be by rail. Special separate routes for bringing up units and supplies into the Army area, resting places, detours around large towns, and defiles were established and properly marked; special traffic regulation groups, Auffang Kommandos [straggler collection parties], and combat commanders for important localities were appointed.

A great deal was done for the training of the troops. By many alerts, drills of all kinds, map problems, terrain discussions, etc., the soldiers were prepared for their probable mission. After 1943, exercises in defense against airborne forces were also held. Under the influence of airborne specialists, these exercises led to an exaggerated conception of airborne troops.

Numerous bicycles and French vehicles with French drivers were assigned to the units to make them mobile. The untrustworthiness of the French drivers during air raids was well-known, but, in spite of repeated requests, no German drivers could be obtained.

Two static divisions—the 346th Infantry Division (St Malo) and the 275th Infantry Division (St Nazaire)—were temporarily removed from the front for maneuvers with a larger force, and made mobile with the help of resources obtained from the countryside.

IV. Genfldm Rommel

Toward the end of 1943, Genfldm Rommel, on orders from Hitler, inspected the defenses in the West from Denmark to Brittany, coming last to Seventh Army. At that time Rommel had no other assignment. In the disagreement between Genfldms Rommel and Kesselring on the conduct of the Italian campaign, Kesselring, with his proposal to defend the Appennines, won against Rommel, who wanted to withdraw to the Alps. Rommel, wishing to regain his lost prestige, put his ideas into effect in every conceivable way.

It is probably true that Rommel came to the West with the idea and definite intention of withstanding an enemy invasion. His successor, Genfldm von Kluge, when he took over Rommel's command, probably thought he could be the saviour in time of distress. Both Generalfeldmarschalls died tragic deaths, preceded by the frustration of their military and political missions. It was astounding how certain Rommel was (toward the end of the year 1943) that the invasion would take place in the Fifteenth Army area. The most telling argument for this premise was that this was the shortest route into Germany's nerve center, the Ruhr.

From his extensive experience with landing operations in Africa and Italy, Rommel had formulated the opinion that an enemy, once landed and prospected by covering fire from naval artillery and from the air, was extremely difficult to throw back into the sea. It was therefore a proposition of making the coastal defenses so strong in manpower and equipment that the enemy could never gain a foothold on the shore. Reserves which were not located close to the coast could only be used belatedly and with heavy loss because of the supporting fire from enemy naval artillery and air forces.

He concluded that as many defense troops as possible should be committed in the beach fortifications, and that all reserves should be located directly on the coast and incorporated into the defense. The artillery of divisions in reserve and Panzer battalions of Panzer divisions in reserve should be moved close enough to the front that they could dominate the coast with fire from their cantonment areas. By bringing up the troops from the reserve areas, the fortress garrisons would be reinforced and more labor made available.

Rommel's ideas concerning the large-scale emplacing of obstacles along the coast were something new. By making a barrier of partially mined tree trunks, concrete blocks, etc., which were submerged at high tide and above water at low tide, the landing of enemy craft was to be made difficult, if not impossible. A major commitment of airborne troops was to be prevented by the emplacement of obstacles in endangered areas. Rommel expressed the above views during his first visit, and subsequently put them into effect in his own energetic way.

Rommel had the right ideas, but they were feasible only in a smaller sector which could be defended accordingly. From an operational and strategic point of view, especially with Germany's situation at the turn of 1943–44, the basis for a defense of the West, as carried out by Rommel, was no longer present.

At that time, Germany no longer had the forces and matériel available to utilize a cordon defense in a 4,000-kilometer front. An enemy well equipped on land, on sea, and in the air, and able to attack with far superior forces at any chosen point along this front, could not be prevented from gaining a foothold on land and establishing a solid beachhead. And if the enemy should succeed in doing this, then—according to Rommel's views—the invasion was successful and the entire Atlantic Wall built for nothing.

Rommel expected the invasion to take place in the Fifteenth Army sector, and he did everything possible to reinforce the defenses already existing there. On the basis of the grouping of forces in Fifteenth Army, it was expected that a large-scale attack in that area could be repulsed, particularly if there were sufficient time to organize the defense. A major enemy assault against Seventh, First, or Nineteenth Armies would have quite a different outcome.

The same thing must have been apparent to the enemy, who was swiftly and surely oriented by his smoothly-working intelligence service about everything going on in France. Therefore, the stronger the defense of Fifteenth Army, the less chance there was of an attack in that sector.

In estimating the possibility of an enemy invasion in Fifteenth Army area, Rommel agreed with OKW, and partially also with the C-in-C West, Genfldm von Rundstedt. Von Rundstedt looked skeptically upon the success of an Allied invasion; believing that the enemy's superiority in manpower and matériel was so great that a landing itself could not be prevented, he considered the problem to be that of smashing the enemy beachhead the first day.

In their views on the assembly areas of the strategic reserves of Panzer divisions, Rommel and the Panzer specialist in the West, Gen Panzer Frhr Geyr von Schweppenburg (Panzer Grooup West), differed radically. While Rommel insisted on having all Panzer divisions as close as possible to the coast, Geyr urged the necessity of building up a strong strategic reserve of the best Panzer divisions, to be held ready in the forests of the large area surrounding Paris north of the Loire. Geyr wanted to commit the Panzer divisions, together with the Luftwaffe being held in reserve, in one single concentrated assault against the enemy when he emerged from the beachhead. Geyr expounded his views in large-scale map problems in Paris.

The most advisable course would probably have been a compromise between the two ideas based on the following principles:

a. The following were considered the major objectives in the two army areas: in Fifteenth Army area, the region on both sides of the Somme; and in Seventh Army area, the Normandy region from Caen to Cherbourg.

b. The stronger the defense in Fifteenth Army area, the less likely it became that the enemy would attack there. Consequently, it became more urgent to transfer the center of resistance to Seventh Army area before the invasion.

c. An enemy landing could not be prevented, especially since Rommel's new methods were not as effective as had been assumed, owing to the great pressure of the water in the Channel.

d. Troops from all less mobile divisions had to be sent into the coastal defenses, in order to inflict the greatest possible casualties during landing.

e. The beachhead had to be attacked at the time of its greatest weakness—at the latest, by the third day.

f. Individual Panzer divisions had to be held in readiness near the coast, though not within enemy naval artillery range. With the great superiority of enemy airpower, it was feared that Panzer forces advancing from great distances would be delayed or else would arrive at the front badly mauled.

g. A strong strategic reserve of Panzer and mobile infantry divisions had to be moved into the wide area surrounding Paris, so that they could attack in force in the vicinity of the Somme and Caen within three days at the latest.

h. The other fronts—Channel, Brittany, Atlantic, and Mediterranean—had to be consciously neglected, and, in the event of a major attack, a delaying action had to be relied on to defend the fortresses.

Prior to the invasion, there was a total of 50 infantry and ten Panzer-type divisions available in the West. Of these, three to five Panzer-type divisions and 10 to 12 infantry divisions were to become strategic reserves in the Paris areas, two to three Panzer-type divisions tactical reserves for Fifteenth Army, and three to four Panzer-type divisions tactical reserves for Seventh Army. By shifting the concentration of the Panzer divisions, the enemy was kept in the dark about our plans and intentions.

For future planning, OKW ordered that in case of a major attack on Seventh Army in Brittany or on First or Nineteenth Armies, the fortresses were to be defended to the last, while the remaining forces were to withdraw in a delaying action to the line running southwest from the Seine, above Paris, to Switzerland. If a major attack were made against Seventh Army in Normandy or against Fifteenth Army, defensive-offensive tactics were to be adopted. In case of a defeat in Normandy, the defeated troops would withdraw behind the upper Seine. For the defense of the Channel coast and the line running southwest from the Seine to Switzerland, enough forces were still available.

Actually everything remained unchanged. We thus made it as easy as possible for the enemy to evaluate our situation.

At the beginning of January 1944, Seventh Army had to release the 346th Infantry Division to Fifteenth Army. This division had just been withdrawn from the St Malo sector, to be made mobile, and was now placed east of the Seine. In all allotments of matériel for the defense, Seventh Army was far behind Fifteenth Army.

One essential point urged the holding of several Panzer divisions near the two Armies. In order to spare the equipment and conserve fuel, it was ordered that armored vehicles—that is, the actual combat force of the Panzer divisions—be transported by train from the Paris region to the front, while the other elements moved by road. Thus, the separation of divisional units would occur from the very beginning, and serious consequences would ensue if enemy air attacks should make rail transport impossible. The dependence of OB West upon the conservation measures of the Generalquartier- meister of OKH, who restricted the use of fuel to a minimum, resulted in fateful disadvantages.

It was of vital importance for the overall conduct of battle in northern France to have free movement of reserves along the shortest routes between Seventh and Fifteenth Armies (across the Seine below Paris). By using French labor, as many Seine bridges as possible were to be restored to a serviceable condition. (These bridges were to be heavily protected by flak.) The French population could be much more easily recruited for work projects in their own country than through the Organization Sauckel, outside the country. The Seine barrier played a fateful role during the course of the invasion.

In order to relieve forces for strategic reserve, OB West submitted a proposal to OKW to man the fortresses with adequate complements and simply keep watch over the intervening terrain. OB West also desired to reduce drastically the personnel and matériel of the Channel Islands. This proposal was rejected by OKW, since it deviated from the cordon defense theory of not yielding a foot of soil voluntarily.

There was widespread opinion, particularly in OKW, that the enemy might attempt diversionary landings simultaneously with, or previous to, the main effort.

At the beginning of March 1944, Genfldm Rommel assumed complete command of Seventh and Fifteenth Armies. Although Rommel was subordinated to OB West, he retained freedom of action with his Armies. Because of the contradictory views held by Rommel and von Rundstedt, this situation was bound to lead to all kinds of friction. OKW, however, probably quite consciously gave Rommel a free hand because its views on the conduct of the defense coincided with those of Rommel.

Genobst Dollman, commanding Seventh Army, deplored being subordinated to Rommel, for many years his own subordinate. However, through Rommel, he hoped to gain certain advantages for Seventh Army, provided Rommel could be moved from his stubborn point of view. As a representative of the compromise solution—a strong front with strong assigned armored reserves stationed relatively near the coast and stronger strategic reserves retained centrally by higher headquarters—Dollman hoped to achieve a strengthening of Seventh Army. This, however, occurred only to a limited extent.

When Rommel assumed command of Army Group B, at the beginning of March 1944, his ideas had already been put into effect.

V. Troop Dispositions

In Normandy, along the 400-kilometer front of LXXXIV Infantry Corps, there were the following:

a. On the coastal front:

1. 716th Infantry Division, from the Dives to the Carentan Canal;
2. 709th Infantry Division, from the Carentan Canal to the Bay of St Malo (inclusive);
3. One Russian battalion guarding the 100-kilometer front from Cap de la Hague to the Bay of St Malo; and
4. Reinforced 319th Infantry Division on the British Channel Islands.

b. In reserve:

1. 352nd Infantry Division, around St Lô;
2. 243rd Infantry Division, in the Cotentin peninsula (center);
3. 30th Infantry Brigade (Mobile), north of Avranches; and
4. 77th Infantry Division, which had been located around Caen, was—by an OKW order—to be inserted in the St Malo sector to replace the 346th Infantry Division (transferred to Fifteenth Army).

In response to Seventh Army's pressure for additional troops, the following reinforcements were received during the Spring:

1. 21st Panzer Division, in the area around Caen (after temporary assignments elsewhere);
2. 91st LL Division, in the area northwest of Carensen; and
3. 6th FS Regiment (from the 2nd FS Division, which was being reorganized in Germany), in the area around Carentan; although the 21st Panzer Division was in Army reserve, it could be committed only after approval by Army Group B. The 91st LL Division, at first transferred on orders of OKW to Nantes on the Loire estuary, was returned to Normandy only after protest by Seventh Army.

At the end of March 1944, the 352nd Infantry Division, with two regiments, took over the left half of the 716th Infantry Division sector, up to Asnelles (inclusive), one reinforced regiment remaining in Corps reserve.

One battalion of the 243rd Infantry Division later took over the sector on the northwest coast of the Cotentin peninsula from west of Cherbourg on; the Division remained in reserve in its former area.

The combat efficiency of these divisions at the beginning of June 1944 was as follows:

a. 716th and 709th Infantry Divisions: static; the two of approximately the same quality; two regiments of three battalions each; well acquainted with their sectors for years; well trained for defense; not much combat experience.

b.   319th Infantry Division: high quality division, with three regiments of three battalions each, reinforced with one Maschinengewehr (MG) battalion, one French Panzer battalion, and naval and air force units; average age 26–27 years; well suited for attack and defense; little combat experience.

c. 21st Panzer Division: recently reorganized with German weapons; good enlisted personnel who had completed training.

d. 352nd Infantry Division: recently reorganized with three regiments of two battalions each, and one fusilier battalion; bulk of personnel young men with training nearly completed.

e. 243rd Infantry Division: recently reorganized, same as 352nd Infantry Division; fusilier battalion hastily rendered mobile by equipment with bicycles; bulk of enlisted personnel young men unschooled in combined arms.

f.   91st LL Division: newly organized with three regiments of two battalions each; weapons and equipment not yet complete; bulk of enlisted personnel young men; training completed only to platoon level; not yet suitable for assault.

g. 30th Infantry Brigade (Mobile): name unjustified; recruit training unit with four Fahrradbewegliches (bicycle infantry) battalions and brigade staff (total strength approximately 1,200); remaining battalions located in Holland and Belgium.

h.   6th FS Regiment: an especially good regiment in training and leadership.

Of Seventh Army's 21 Russian battalions, only four remained with LXXXIV Infantry Corps, and only two of these were committed on the coastal front. One battalion, which was especially noted for its trustworthiness, was committed on the left wing of 716th Infantry Division, at the request of this division. The other Russian battalion was committed on the west coast of the Cotentin peninsula.

The LXXXIV Infantry Corps sector was reduced and LXXIV Infantry Corps (Brittany) took over the inner bay of St Malo. In Brittany there were the following units on the 800-kilometer front:

a. Under LXXIV Infantry Corps (Gen Inf Straube):

   1. 77 Infantry Division in the St Malo sector; and

   2. 266 Infantry Division in the St Brieuc–Morlaix sector.

b. Under XXV Infantry Corps (Gen Art Fehrmbacher):

1. 343rd Infantry Division, at Brest;

2. 265th Infantry Division, in Quimper–Lorient sector; and

3. 275th Infantry Division, in Vennes–St Nazaire sector.

c. In reserve:

1. 353rd Infantry Division, in area near Brest; and

2. 3rd FS Division, to the east of Brest.

After the departure of the 21st Panzer Division from the area surrounding Rennes, the 5th FS Division was transferred to this area and the 3rd FS Division and 5th FS Division were assigned to II FS Corps (Gen FS Meindl) for training.

Ever since Rommel's arrival, the troops had worked very diligently in carrying out the construction of new beach obstacles and emplacing poles throughout the areas considered to be in danger of airborne invasion. In a very short time a great deal was completed, but hardly any time was left for the badly needed troop training.

Several grandiose command post exercises in communications had been carried out in Normandy since April 1944, to stimulate the existence of new army and corps staffs and individual divisions. Thus, west of St Lô, the enemy was bluffed into believing in the existence of a new division, by the moving up of the "advance party." Three weeks after the invasion, the enemy still thought that the division in question might be located in the area.

For the unification of command, the word "Küstengefechtsgebiet" (coastal combat area) was introduced. In the zone dominated by enemy naval artillery (to a depth of 30–50 kilometers) the combat troops had command authority.

In opposition to Rommel's defense principles, Seventh Army held back strong reserves because:

a. Not enough troops were available to set up a solid cordon defense; and

b. The Cotentin peninsula with its three fronts and its fortress (Cherbourg) required strong reserves for any emergencies. Strong airborne landings at the neck of the peninsula, to cut off the peninsula towards the south, were especially dangerous. Since the Spring of 1944, naval officials, on the basis of more recent examinations of coastal conditions, figured on the possibility of a landing in the northern sector of the peninsula's west coast. Genfldm Rommel ordered the commitment of strong units of the 21st Panzer Division (three-fourths) for the direct defense of the coast, but otherwise approved the defense measures of Seventh Army.

VI. The Heer Alone to Counter the Invasion

Meanwhile, long before, the Allied air invasion had started. Since Fall 1943, an ever-increasing number of bombing missions had been carried out against traffic centers and rail lines in the communications zone, and against airdromes, V-weapon emplacements, bridges, factories, and so forth. Our air force had scarcely put in an appearance. Repair of railroad installations fell further and further behind, causing a great hold-up of trains.

The construction of many defense works along the coast had to be halted because of shortage of materials. Attacks by the Allied air force were aimed at the entire front, without any perceptible point of main effort. A concentration of these bombing raids against traffic points was to be found centered on the traffic ring of Paris.

A very serious omen was that our own airfields, close to the front, had to be transferred into the interior, out of direct reach of enemy air activity.

To the Heer's repeated expressions of apprehension at the ever more visible weakening of our airpower, assurance came from the Luftwaffe that, in case of an invasion, it would be considerably reinforced on the second or third day at the latest, after the invasion.

Our own aerial reconnaissance, above the Channel, individual harbors, and the British Isles, was unable to penetrate the Allied blockade. During the Spring of 1944, Seventh Army received only two good aerial photographs of British southern ports, which showed large concentrations of landing craft.

For a long time the Allies had dominated the sea, with a combination of air and sea supremacy. German U-boats were no longer on the sea. They could not operate in the Channel, because of water conditions, and no midget submarines were ready. A few speedboats, minesweepers, and artillery-tank landing craft were the only naval vessels commanded by the Admirals in charge in Seventh Army sector. The few naval craft could move along only with the greatest difficulty under protection of the French coast. No real reconnaissance could be expected on the high seas and particularly along the British Channel coast. The Navy thought that it could warn of the approach of an enemy invasion fleet, in time, with the aid of its position-finding equipment. However, the Allies at certain times jammed the equipment, which on D-Day, as had been feared, failed to work.

We had only a dwindling number of intelligence agents in the British Isles. Their work was made extremely difficult through the blocking of long stretches of the British coastal regions. Reports concerning troop movements and ship concentrations were received very late and often contradicted one another. News arriving through neutral countries was very considerable, but usually contributed more to the concealment than to the clarification of Allied intentions.

The French Resistance movement in Seventh Army area was negligible. The population of Normandy—for the most part well-to-do farmers—were behaving peacefully. Only in Brittany was there an increase in sabotage and scattered raids during the Spring of 1944. In the same region were dropped most of the Allied supplies for the Resistance. In general, the central headquarters for the Resistance movement first urged full activity on D-Day. From intercepted radio messages in the first days of June 1944, we gathered that an invasion was imminent.

No conclusions of any kind concerning the possible location of the enemy invasion could be deduced from the active or passive conduct of the French Resistance movement. In central France, however, the Resistance movement could claim greater success. It succeeded in so tying down strong units of the 2nd SS Panzer Division that they arrived at the front late and scattered.

From the beginning to the middle of May 1944, the following representatives of OKW inspected the defense sectors in the West:

1. Fifteenth Army: Genobst Jodl, Chief of Staff, OKW.
2. Nineteenth Army: Gen Art Warlimont, Jodl's deputy; and
3. Seventh Army: Genmaj von Buttlar, Jodl's Ia. Genobst Jodl also traveled for a day through the Seventh Army area from Caen to Cherbourg. The assignments of the individual officers to the various armies throws light on their interests and upon the evaluation of the sectors for the coming invasion.

The month of May 1944 went by with periods of fine weather, but no invasion materialized. It was remarkable that the enemy air force did not attack the 21st Panzer Division while it was being transferred from the Rennes area to the area around Caen, nor the transport of the 91st LL Division in the Cotentin peninsula. Could it be that the enemy did not wish to give himself away? Did not the enemy, on the basis of German preparations, anticipate that his intention had been recognized?

The Allies could assure themselves soon enough, however, that the center of gravity of the defense, since the turn of the year 1943–44, remained in the Fifteenth Army area.

The armed forces worked with extreme devotion and ingenuity in reinforcing the defensive fronts, especially in emplacing and mining beach obstacles. These obstacles moved farther and farther out into the sea. Previously it had been anticipated that the enemy would land during or shortly before high tide. Now it appeared more likely that the first landing would take place in front of the obstacles, either during low tide or at the beginning of high tide.

For a landing in Normandy at daybreak or later, the days between 4 and 7 June 1944 were favorable, especially since the full moon period, which particularly favored airborne operations, came at this time. Seventh Army figured on this period as the most probable for the invasion, but it did not issue any alert orders since the troops were in constant readiness.

A repeatedly delayed map problem in defense against airborne forces by II FS Corps in Rennes, which various division and regimental commanders were to attend, was scheduled for 6 June 1944, at an hour such that the commanders could arrive at the beginning of the exercise, providing the night had passed calmly.

German public opinion expected the thwarting of the invasion as a matter of course. With all its resources, the propaganda machine had so bolstered the belief in the "impregnability of the Atlantic Wall" that this fallacy had in many cases invaded the highest military leadership. They longed for the invasion in order to fight the Allies who, ever since the downfall of the Luftwaffe and the U-boat, could not be reached in the British Isles.

There were few far-sighted military men—among them Genobst Dollman—who either thought that, in the interests of European politics, there would not be an invasion, or else believed that there would be an attack with a limited Allied objective, which would leave the way open to a political solution of the war.

Since the latter part of May 1944, the enemy air force had been attacking combat installations and position-finding equipment along the Channel coast, but without any apparent point of concentration. Enemy aerial reconnaissance flights increased and reached great proportions on the nights of 3/4 and 4/5 June 1944. The invasion seemed to be at hand. The commander of Seventh Army, Genobst Dollman, who was on an inspection trip, returned to his command post on 5 June 1944. Genfldm Rommel was at this time with OKW in Germany, for some unknown reason.

We were most apprehensive about the impending operation in the Seventh Army area. After the arrival of the 91st LL Division in the Cotentin peninsula, we felt relatively strong. There was a definite weakness in occupation forces and the fortresses on the coast between the Orne and Vire.

How would our over-age static divisions, which were inexperienced in combat, as well as our other divisions, which were for the most part unprepared and hampered by makeshifts of every sort, fight against an enemy equipped with the most modern weapons and equipment? The enemy's superiority over our forces was known; only the degree was uncertain. In the event, it surpassed our most pessimistic estimates.

OKW had given an orientation concerning the possibility of invasion in the Normandy sector of Seventh Army's area. Rommel, too, figured during the last days on this possibility, but did not draw the necessary conclusion that Seventh Army must be reinforced before the invasion.

The hope remained that in case of a large-scale attack in Normandy, OKW would do everything possible to bolster and reinforce the attacked front with all possible available forces on the ground and in the air. In all conferences, map problems, etc., the guiding principle had always been that the enemy, wherever he should first set foot on the Continent with strong forces, was to be thrown back into the sea by concentrating every possible means. To await possible enemy assaults on other fronts was considered misleading. Thus one could expect that the decisive battle would have to be fought on the attacked front within three to four days at the latest after the invasion.

Should we win this first battle we must expect a second landing on a weaker or weakened front. However, if the enemy were able to land without a decisive engagement during the first few days, there would not be a second landing.

The Allied invasion troops went aboard ship during the first days of June 1944, put out to sea and turned back on account of bad weather, but the German High Command knew nothing of this. This proved the fact that prior to the beginning of this invasion, two parts of the Wehrmacht had been defeated: the Navy and the Air Force. Germany entered this hardest battle of the war with only one part of the Wehrmacht: the Heer.

Preparations by Panzer Gruppe West Against Invasion (mid-1943–5 June 1944)

by General der Panzertruppen Leo, Freiherr Geyr von Schweppenburg

I. Background of German Military Policy

The invasion on the Western front was bound to bring about the decision of the war. Even Hitler was cognizant of this fact at the end of 1943. He drew his conclusions and put them down in orders, yet he did not ensure their execution.

During the second half of 1943, the bulk of Hitler's forces were heavily engaged in two major theaters of war. In Italy a seaborne invasion had been carried out successfully by the Allies. From these events, neither Hitler nor his Ccontinental-minded Wehrmachtführungsstab (Armed Forces Operations Staff) learned the lesson of the importance of seapower and the necessity for strategical economy. Gela, where the 1st Infantry Division (US) suffered a temporary setback,* and Salerno did not reveal to the German Command nor to some others that a Panzer division is no match for naval artillery.

To understand the measures taken to defend the Western Front against invasion, one must be familiar with the general trend of the German leadership before and after the outbreak of this war, and with the character of training and organization for the defense. German training in leadership since 1920 had been thorough and had followed the traditional lines set by Moltke and Schlieffen. This training was satisfactory for a Continental war of the old type, but obsolete and inadequate for a major intercontinental war of combined operations. The leading class in the Army knew little or nothing about the Navy and the Air Force. No decision was made to form a general staff for the combined services. This type of mental attitude was represented also among army leaders of other countries in Europe besides Germany. The attitude in the German Army was due not entirely to lack of insight, but primarily to opposition to the merger by the leading personality of the Luftwaffe and to the lack of decision on the part of the political leadership and OKW. The dangers of this situation were easier to recognize from abroad, living among the Anglo-Saxons, than from the self-complacent paradise of Western Europe and National Socialism. The observer for the German Army in

---

* During the Allied invasion of Sicily, the Germans, on 11 July 1943, launched several counterattacks against 1st Inf Div (US) in the Gela beachhead. These attacks were spearheaded by strong formations of Mark IV and Mark VI tanks which pierced the division front and reached a point only 200 yards from Gela. The advancing tanks were finally stopped by the concentrated fire of all available naval and ground artillery.

London, the author, had reported on these dangers again and again—the last time in 1937.

The Wehrmachtsakademie (Armed Forces College) was outstandingly good in 1938–39. As far as I know, except for occasional voluntary attendances, no generals of the Army and Air Force or admirals who were earmarked for higher command in case of war participated in the courses.

A Continental army, under the old-style leadership, could hit hard and swiftly, as long as its leaders, thoroughly patterned after the same model, were in absolute and undisputed control. This was the basis for the successes from 1939 to 1941. At the beginning of 1942, the centralized "lance corporal" command came into existence. Winston Churchill characterized the event with a remark in the House of Commons which hit the nail on the head: "The German Command has passed from the expert hands of the General Staff to those of a lance corporal."

The last Hitler had seen of actual warfare was the purely defensive fighting in the trenches of 1918. His chief advisor, Jodl, was in the same position and, moreover, rooted in an arm—the artillery—which in the First World War was only mediocre in comparison to the artillery of the French, as well as to that of the Austrians. Furthermore, the artillery developed the unfortunate characteristic of the Bourbons—neither to learn nor to forget—and was in many respects more backward than the infantry. Until D-Day, it had not realized fully the superiority of air observation, the importance of smoke, and the necessity for antiaircraft defense. The artillery's dreams of caliber and concentration of fire had continued undisturbed. Hitler and Jodl were alike in their ignorance of the psychology of foreign nations and in the developments outside of Western Europe. Believing firmly that Western Europe was the Mecca and the source of military science and experience, they were convinced that other countries had been asleep for 25 years.

The strength of the German Army and General Staff lay in the fundamental principle of creating subordinate commanders from army down to platoon and thoroughly instilling in them the spirit of taking independent and responsible action within the limits of their respective missions. The education of the former Austro-Hungarian Army had been different; as if infected with a pernicious mental sickness, this army perished because of its fatal policy of awaiting orders and obeying them under any circumstances.

Another basic principle of German leadership was unity of command. It will be demonstrated that, as a result of the centralization of command in the Wehrmachtführungsstab, no dashing or strong or sweeping decision could be made, although such independent action was particularly essential to the Panzer forces. Authority to make strategic decisions passed from seasoned soldiers, well experienced in the special conditions of their respective theaters of war, to a self-complacent and pretentious dilettante, and was effected by a combination of influences. In comparison with this system, the former Vienna Court and War Council was a rather respectable and reasonable command unit.

II. The Anti-Invasion Defense

In the second half of 1943, the Western front comprised three-fifths of a circle extending from Holland to the French-Italian border. This presumably fortified arc was called the "Atlantic Wall." Its value was strongly emphasized by the German propaganda; from a military viewpoint, it was valuable only to the highest commander and to complete laymen.

In the Summer of 1945, Gen Panzer West had reported to the Generalinspektion der Panzertruppen (General Inspectorate of Panzer Troops) that the Atlantic Wall was worth exactly as much as the Panzer divisions behind it. The Atlantic Wall was occupied by poorly equipped infantry divisions composed of men from older age classes. For some time, Panzer divisions and individual tank battalions had been rehabilitated or re-formed in France and Belgium. As soon as they were fit for combat—and often earlier—they were transferred to the Eastern front or to Italy.

In the second half of 1943, the staff of Gen Panzer West was formed and attached to Army Group West. This staff, which formed the nucleus of the later Panzer Group West, had the mission of supervising the training of all Panzer units in the West and of advising Genfldm von Rundstedt on matters pertaining to Panzer forces.

Intelligence on enemy preparations and the insistence of the Russians for relief strengthened the probability of a large-scale Anglo-American landing. In this operation, it seemed certain that large airborne forces would play an important part. It was not clear, however, whether the preparations, training, and experience of the Anglo-Saxons had advanced to a state permitting strategic landings on a corps or army scale, or whether the enemy would still be restricted to tactical landings only. [The preceding sentence is not in the German original, but was included by Geyr in his own English translation.—Ed.] Until this time only small-scale exercises had been conducted in the defense against an airborne landing. The Panzer forces in the West considered that tanks were the most effective defense against hostile airborne operations, as well as the best support for German operations of a like nature. Therefore, the use of Panzer units in this respect was studied both theoretically and practically in the West.

The theoretical aspect of the training consisted of a large-scale wargame in Paris in September 1943 involving the commitment of eight enemy airborne divisions. The bulk of these divisions were represented on a strategical scale, not tactically. All the leading figures of the Panzer forces in the West were summoned to attend.

In a practical sense, individual Panzer divisions were engaged in maneuvers involving both day and night fighting against airborne troops. The Fallschirm (paratroop) school at Dreux furnished the cadre for these maneuvers. The objective was to "drill" these tactics.

The principle fault with the anti-invasion defense originated from opinions based on the commando raid at Dieppe. The ambition of a certain leading personality on the Western Front [Genobst Zeitzler—Ed.], as well as German propaganda, had recast the Anglo-Saxon experimental raid into a defensive success against a major landing attempt.

This idea was all the more irresponsible as it was completely evident from captured orders that there was a time limit for the operation. However, the self-complacent idea could not be dislodged from the minds of the Obersten Wehrmachtführung (Wehrmacht Supreme Command). Together with Rommel's misguided doctrine on coastal defense, this idea was fundamentally responsible for the grotesque defense situation, which was contrary to all experiences of strategy and recent war developments.

On paper, Genfldm von Rundstedt was the Supreme Commander in the West. In reality, he had no decisive influence with the Luftwaffe and the Navy during the preparation of the defense. Hitler or the Wehrmachtführungsstab interfered in both major and minor issues. Unity of command, which had been familiar and self-evident to the experienced old general from his early military career, was further jeopardized by the assignment of Genfldm Rommel at the end of 1943 to an ambiguously outlined special mission. Rommel was an able and experienced tactician, although entirely lacking in strategic conceptions. The personal animosity between Rommel and Jodl accentuated the difficulties. Consequently, Gen Panzer West considered it necessary in the late Fall of 1943 to request a decision from Genfldm von Rundstedt as to whether the Panzer divisions in the West were to be trained for mobile warfare or for coastal defense. The decision was made, as was desired, to train for mobile warfare.

With the assignment of Rommel in the West, a sharp controversy arose between the concepts of Genfldm Rommel and those of Gen Panzer Geyr von Schweppenburg. Genfldm Rommel represented the school of thought that a landing should be prevented at any cost. Once the Anglo-Saxons had established a foothold on the Continent, it would be impossible to drive them back into the sea. All available forces should be kept in readiness immediately behind the fortifications—which were in need of considerable reinforcement—in order to prevent altogether a major landing. The opinion of Gen Panzer West was that, in view of the formidable enemy air superiority and the number, caliber, and effectiveness of the naval guns of the combined Anglo-American battle fleets, a landing some place on 1,300 kilometers of coastline could not be prevented and would succeed in any case. The only solution would be to utilize the only German superiority—that of speedier and more flexible leadership which employed strategic mobile reserves. High-quality Panzer units should be held in reserve to crush an enemy penetration inland. Genobst Guderian, Hitler's advisor on Panzer tactics, agreed in full with the opinion of Gen Panzer Geyr von Schweppenburg, but this was of no avail. The practical result of the controversy was that one Panzer division after another was marched to the front and required to dig in 10 to 20 kilometers behind the coastline. Furthermore, this conflict was the main topic of conversation on the Western front. The state of affairs was anything but favorable to the prestige of leadership. Gen Panzer Geyr von Schweppenburg was so deeply convinced of the error of Rommel's policies that in May 1944 he requested permission from von Rundstedt to state personally his views to the Wehrmachtführungsstab at Berchtesgaden. Hitler ordered four divisions (1st SS Panzer, 12th SS Panzer, Panzer Lehr, and 17th SS Panzer Grenadier Divisions) to be held in OKW strategic reserve. On the first day of the invasion, this intention was abandoned, in spite of Genobst Guderian's protest.

III. Training. Administration,
and Strategic Exercises Prior to D-Day

The training in France was equally thorough for both the Panzer force leaders and the combat troops. For the latter, emphasis was placed on night fighting. During May 1944, compulsory night problems were held three nights a week. For training in the defense against air attack, one day a week was set aside as Fliegertag (Aviation Day). Special training was conducted in hedgerow fighting in Normandy and Brittany, utilizing demonstration battalions schooled in British methods of warfare. In individual training, superior marksmanship and sniper tactics had priority. It was well known that the standard of marksmanship was high in the British Army. The same standards had to be expected of the US Army. To increase the effectiveness of German marksmanship, existing regulations, unchanged for decades, were cancelled and replaced by the Kriegsnahe Schiessausbildung (Warlike Marksmanship Course). Since sniper tactics in the German Army were poor, the basis for this technique was established, later to be developed extensively throughout the Panzer Grenadier training units. Within the tank units, emphasis was placed on long-range combat and concentration of fire, in the spirit of the historical broadside of the British Navy. Believing that superior marksmanship was paramount in tank fighting, Guderian often came to France in person to satisfy himself in thorough detail of the performance of the tank teams.

Before the arrival of Rommel, still another interference had considerably impaired the quality of training. This was the large number of fatigue details which even the Panzer divisions had to furnish to dig positions and fortify strongpoints in the rear areas. Since most divisions had come from the Eastern front to be re-formed or were newly activated, the loss of valuable training time was most regrettable.

A weakness of the German Army was the lack of instinct and knowledge in practical intelligence work. In the unwritten tradition of the Heer, intelligence work had a slight odor of not being respectable—at any rate, not as important as the work of operational personnel who controlled the fighting. This criticism is aimed mainly at the senior generals, not the younger general staff officers. Intelligence, rapidly collected and evaluated, is the basis for success in Panzer warfare. To insure proper intelligence, the Commander of Panzer Group West directed and supervised the training of intelligence personnel—down to and including division level—in practical work, coordinating all branches of intelligence. Instruction emphasized the pressure of time, British and American military terminology and abbreviations, and the training of military interpreters. The courses culminated in an exercise demonstrating the 24-hour practical work of a Panzer division Ic in every detail—prisoners of war, civilians, captured orders, intercepted radio messages, and so forth. In all these thorough preparations, nothing was left to chance.

The supply system depended too much on railroads and on centralized supply depots. Until a few months prior to the invasion, the supplies of the Panzer forces, particularly spare parts and fuel, were centralized and frequently stored in localities such as major cities, which presented excellent bomb targets. The enemy intelligence service, assisted by the civilian population, seemed to locate all of these depots. It was impossible to set up a flexible supply system which took into consideration all the differences between the supply conditions of Panzer troops and those of the infantry. Panzer Group West, however, succeeded in having the Panzer fuel and ammunition dumps guarded by young, active troops of the Panzer forces rather than by older rear-echelon soldiers.

There was considerable idle discussion on the impending strategy of the enemy—talk which did not help to promote the defense. It was for this reason that Panzer Group West, on its own initiative and with a humble knowledge of the Anglo-Saxons, proposed a worthwhile large-scale strategic exercise, to be called "Invasion." We intended to give the "enemy" freedom of action in making its plans. The Allied air force, navy, and intelligence service were to be represented, as well as the viewpoints of the most responsible members of the British Cabinet. This exercise took place in Paris in the middle of February 1944, and was intended to bring out all the questions which were expected to influence the decisions of the enemy. The important role of political and economic viewpoints and the Anglo-Saxon mental characteristics were not excluded. Moreover, the potential divergencies of opinion among the Allies was to play a part in the exercise. The diplomatic expert of the ["Invasion"] directorate, the former minister in Oslo, was attached to the "Red" staff. Having been Chargé d'Affaires in Brussels and Paris, he was well acquainted with Western political relations. Moreover, he had been in close collaboration with the Commander Panzer Group West for a few years in Brussels. The roles of Commander-in-Chief, on both sides, were assigned to the most brilliant commanding generals. Incidentally, all these generals—including the directorate—were in political disfavor. The lecture delivered by the "Red" Chief of Staff, Gen Inf Marcks, was most excellent. While defending the Cotentin peninsula, Gen Inf Marcks was killed in action against the 101st Airborne Division (US). His fate was shared by a remarkable number of German generals in the early stages of the invasion. The conclusions drawn from this exercise pointed to the mouth of the Rhône, the Cotentin peninsula, and the Channel coast between Ostend and the Somme as the most endangered areas. Because of the large tonnage of the Allied fleet and the great number of available divisions, the possibility of an invasion near the mouth of the Loire could not be disregarded. We did not expect a breach of Spanish neutrality by the Allied ground forces.

It may be of special interest to note the pre-invasion opinion of Gen Inf Marcks on the defense of the Cotentin. (One must regard highly his brilliance and energy, for he had only one leg.) I motored up to see him at St Lô and learned the situation first-hand a few weeks before D-Day. He was not concerned about an Allied landing on the western coast of the Cotentin, but feared an assault on the eastern coast in the vicinity of Carentan.

One Seine bridge after another was systematically destroyed by the enemy. Since little bridging equipment was available, the mobility of the Panzer divisions became seriously limited. Gen Panzer Geyr von Schweppenburg, therefore, proposed the construction of underwater bridges, which could hardly be distinguished from the air and which had rendered excellent service on the Eastern front. Unfortunately, this proposition was turned down.

Upon special request of Panzer Group West, the Navy had calculated that the effective range of enemy naval artillery would be 10 kilometers inland where the coast was steep and 20 kilometers inland where the coast was level. This information proved wrong, for in the Caen–Bayeux sector naval artillery was effective up to 30 kilometers inland.

IV. Estimates of Allied Strategy

The estimate of the enemy's probable action was far from unanimous. Jodl and von Rundstedt's Chief of Staff [Blumentritt—Ed.] were in doubt whether the invasion would materialize at all; Allied preparations might have been only a bluff. Panzer Group West held a different opinion, arguing, from knowledge of British character, that there could be no question of bluff, since the King had bid his troops Godspeed and had thus engaged his own personality in the matter. The sectors in the area of the Rhône estuary, the Cotentin peninsula, and the Channel coast appeared to the responsible staffs to be the most probable invasion sites.

After an estimate of enemy strength, we determined that for Normandy there would be 30 enemy divisions, southern France 10 to 12 divisions, and the Channel coast—or wherever else the enemy chose to strike—the remaining 28 divisions. Estimates of Allied superiority in matériel were ten to one for tanks and fifteen to one for armored reconnaissance vehicles. A scale for measuring the enemy air superiority was non-existent. The number of airborne divisions to be expected was doubtful; estimates ranged from eight to ten at the most.

Von Rundstedt's operations staff harbored no illusions about the poor fighting quality of the infantry divisions, which were critically short of antitank weapons, artillery, and supply units. Since his staff fully realized that the defensive value of the Atlantic Wall was imaginary, they would certainly have agreed to an evacuation. However, owing to Hitler's mentality, this idea was out of the question. The combat efficiency of the Panzer divisions could be estimated at about 33 percent of what it had been on 1 September 1939. However, they were far superior to the units which saw action in the Ardennes, the latter being mere shadows of their former selves.

Jodl, Rommel, and the Commander of Fifteenth Army [Genobst Salmuth—Ed.] were certain that a second and presumably the main landing would follow on the Channel coast. Not until one week after D-Day was this conviction shaken.

Concerning the situation in the air, Panzer Group West was unable to agree with Third Air Force. It is poor tactics to engage an enemy piecemeal, and it is worse when the enemy is numerically superior from the beginning. The Luftwaffe believed that the Allies should be attacked during the landing with all available planes. Reinforcements were expected from the homeland. Panzer Group West had a different opinion and was certain that the enemy would provide the maximum air cover possible. Therefore, the Panzer Group requested the Luftwaffe not to commit its planes until the moment when strategic Panzer reserves began to counterattack. The mission of the Luftwaffe should have been to furnish, by the commitment of its own air reserves from the homeland, 48 hours of air cover and support for the counteroffensive of the Panzer reserves.

From the standpoint of cooperation of the services, the relations between the respective commanders of the Luftwaffe in the West and of the Panzer Group could not have been better. However, it was not for them, but probably for Göring—in absentia!—to decide these issues.

It was impossible to train the Panzer units in coordination with large air defense units. The latter were immobilized in static positions for the protection of endangered localities. Moreover, the Luftwaffe would give no fuel for this training. Even Flak units of Panzer divisions were required to take part in the territorial antiaircraft defense. It was easy to foresee that these units would not re-join their respective divisions in time for the invasion. This is exactly what happened.

A notice in the London *Times*, which apparently had slipped by the censor, gave us a general clue as to the date of the invasion. The article was found on the second page under agricultural news, which generally no one reads, and touched upon compensation of English landowners by American troop commanders. From this article it could be concluded that the invasion was not to be expected before the middle of April 1944 at the earliest.

V. The State of the German Command

The German Command lay in the hands of one man, who, even to people unfamiliar with medicine, had been a clear case for a psychiatrist since the beginning of 1942. He was at Berchtesgaden during the first four weeks of the invasion, and later in East Prussia, considerably farther to the rear than was the German Army High Command—to its disadvantage—during the Battle of the Marne in 1914. Things were different on the Anglo-American side.

The leading personality was assisted by a staff of which no influential officer, after five years of warfare, knew the war from any location other than an armchair. None of them had ever visited the headquarters of a single army in combat.

The C-in-C in the West was an elderly man. He was a soldier of thorough training with adequate experience in practical warfare, but without an understanding of a three-dimensional war involving the combined operations of the Heer, Navy, and Luftwaffe. He was a gentleman and had the personal confidence and respect of his subordinate commanders and his troops. His authority was limited and quite handicapped. His Chief of Staff was not a suitable complement, either as to capability or character. Von Manstein had been requested and would have been a more appropriate Chief of Staff for von Rundstedt. However, this request had been refused. It was impossible to obtain clear-cut decisions on the broader controversial issues. The ship was not steered; it drifted.

The army commanders, with the exception of the commander in Holland, were all thoroughly experienced soldiers.

A firm and well coordinated unity of command in the different branches of the armed forces was non-existent. It had been impossible to accomplish this unity.

The Invasion

by Generalfeldmarschall Wilhelm Keitel and Generaloberst Alfred Jodl

Note by Kenneth W. Hechler, Major, Infantry (Res)

This was not an oral interview, but rather constitutes the translated answers of Keitel and Jodl to a questionnaire on the invasion, the questions for which were forwarded by the ETO Historical Section. The questions were at a high enough level, and the answers allowed sufficient play for judgment, so that considerable weight can be given to the answers, despite the fact that neither Keitel or Jodl had access to German documents or maps at the time they prepared their answers.

I recall that Keitel and Jodl both signed the German text of their answers, and this text was then translated by Sergeant Kiralfy. I forwarded the English text to the Historical Section, but I do not know what happened to the German text.

It is unfortunate that I did not have sufficient time to go back and orally interview Jodl and Keitel at greater length regarding their observations on these important issues. At the time, I told General Jodl that we had so many issues to take up with him that I felt that it would be better for him to summarize his answers in brief form, and perhaps we could then expand on them after the members of the ETO Historical Section had had a chance to digest his preliminary reply. In this way, I hoped to skim off the cream of his observations during the entire European campaign, before he was yanked off to the War Crimes Trials in Nuremburg. It was obvious that Jodl was doing most of the work in preparing the answers. Keitel's major role seemed to be to question Jodl quite excitedly as to whether he had included any material which might be useful for War Crimes prosecution.

Q: Did the German General Staff feel that its forces would be able to stop the assault on the beaches, or did it figure that, once landings were made, mobile reserves could be moved to the assault areas soon enough to prevent a build-up of Allied forces and also drive the American and British forces into the sea? Did the Germans, assuming the Allies would have to have ports immediately, expect frontal assaults to be made on ports or on the beaches as they actually were? What were the estimates of the German General Staff as to the capabilities of the Allies as regards building up their forces and supplies over beaches once a beachhead was established? When were the Germans convinced that the Normandy assault was the main attack and not a diversion or just one of several attacks?

A: In OKW, before the invasion, we anticipated several landing points on the open coast, but they were in the vicinity of large harbors, that is to say, primarily on both sides of Dunkerque, Boulogne, Le Havre, or Cherbourg. We believed that, in a concentric land attack with support from the sea, one of these harbors would be captured for a port of debarkation. In view of the reported massing of invasion forces in southern England, we further were of the opinion that one group would jump off from the Dover–Folkestone area and the other from the Portsmouth–Weymouth area.

We did not anticipate direct frontal assaults on the ports from the sea; accordingly, we thought that debarkation on the open coast could only take place very slowly—much more slowly than actually happened—and that the rough water in particular would cause you serious delays.

We judged the timing and extent of the first major landing would be as follows: some three divisions would be disembarked at each of the two main landing points and their debarkation would require five or six days; besides these, two divisions of airborne troops would be set down at each of the two points. This calculation as to time justified our hope that we would be able to bring up superior forces on our side for a counterattack, even should the actual landing not be repulsed.

When the landing occurred in Normandy, we considered it as only one major assault, and expected a second in the German Fifteenth Army sector.

Q: Prior to the assault, what knowledge did the Germans have of the Allies' equipment or preparations for the establishment of artificial beach ports? Did the Germans have knowledge, perhaps through the Japanese and our amphibious operations in the Pacific, of our experience and experimentation with artificial ports? Did they underestimate our ability to build up the capacity of these beach ports?

A: We had observed, through aerial reconnaissance, the device which was used to form an artificial beach harbor. We believed its purpose was to form new quays in place of those destroyed in the port. We had no information from the Japanese as to the possibility of your producing artificial harbors. It came as a surprise to us.

Q: In view of later experience with the defenders of ports such as Brest, Cherbourg was surrendered after a relatively short fight. Why wasn't the siege prolonged? Was there a shortage of ammunition at Cherbourg?

A: The inadequate defense of Cherbourg was also a disappointment for the Supreme Command. We found a reason for it in the fact that a large part of the troops we contemplated to defend the fortress were employed in the fighting on the eastern coast of the peninsula, and that, contrary to the express orders of OKW, a great part of the troops brought into the peninsula after the invasion allowed themselves to be forced out toward the south or even suffered a breakthrough. So far as one can properly judge from so far away, the conduct of the Commandant of Cherbourg [Genlt von Schlieben—Ed.] did not come up to expectations and fell short of the example of Brest or St Malo.

Q: The Germans must have realized, before the fall of Antwerp, that this port would be of tremendous importance to the Allies. Why wasn't Antwerp defended more tenaciously and why, when the Allies approached the port, didn't the Germans destroy the port facilities as they did at Cherbourg, Brest, and other places?

A: The sudden loss of Antwerp caught OKW completely by surprise. We are unable to explain the reasons as we have not been acquainted with them. We refer you to Gen von Zangen, Commander of Fifteenth Army.

Q: Had the Germans made prior preparations for a siege-type defense of ports in France before the invasion, or was the tenacious hanging on of the German defenders the result of a post-D-Day realization of Allied supply difficulties or needs?

A: All the important ports were more or less strong as fortresses, and had complete all-around defenses. They were to be defended to the last in order to deny the enemy the opportunity to disembark quickly and on a large scale. This plan had still been maintained; therefore, when it became necessary in August 1944 to evacuate almost the entire coastline, we determined to leave certain coastal fortresses garrisoned in order to impede the supplying of the invading army for a long time. In addition, it was only in this way that we could benefit from the years of fortifying, the stationary artillery, the stocks of food, and the munitions of every kind.

Q: Why did the Germans allow the build-up over the beaches to proceed so relatively uninterrupted? Why didn't they bomb the artificial ports more than they did? What determined the German policy to lay mines via air at night in the Utah and Omaha areas rather than bomb beach and supply installations and ships?

A: The invasion came at a moment most disadvantageous for the Luftwaffe. The bomber units were being converted to the new airplane models Me 262 and Ar 234. Putting it generally, the relatively weak employment of bomber units, against the southern English port towns before the invasion as well as against the landing points after it began, is explained by the necessity of weakening severely the bomber arm even before the production of the new plane models for the strongest possible fighter arm.

The assault on the landing points, which was ordered as the main air effort, could be carried out by day only with fighter planes kept on call. The slight effect of these attacks is explained by the fact that it became more and more difficult for the fighter-bombers to penetrate the fighter screen extending from the beach, which was warned by the radar stations you installed in the very first stages of the landing. At night, all available bomber units in the West were employed. Although torpedoes and guided bombs were used, preference was given to the air-dropped mine. Through this and cooperation with E-boats, we promised ourselves the most comprehensive mine infestation possible of the sea in front of the landing points and artificial ports.

Q: What type of craft attacked the LSTs in the exercises off Portland on the night of 27/28 April 1944? Were the Germans aware that exercises were taking place, or did they suspect that the mounting of the operation had begun, or was it a case of a chance patrol discovering the unprotected Allied craft several miles off the coast?

A: I do not remember the circumstances now, but I am pretty certain that the clash of the practice units with German E-boats or torpedo boats was accidental.

Q: Was the light bombing of Plymouth, Torquay, Dartmouth, and other places just prior to D-Day aimed at concentrations or marshaling areas known to be there, or was it just chance that some of these were either hit or nearly hit?

A: In the southern English ports referred to, the assembly of shipping for a landing was observed by our aerial reconnaissance. On the other hand, bombers were employed to a slight degree when the weather permitted. See also the answer to Question 6 [i.e. that concerning the build-up over the beaches].

Q: To what extent did weather affect reconnaissance activities in the Channel by both planes and E-boats just before D-Day?

A: Channel reconnaissance, especially by air, of the southern English ports, was often obstructed by the weather.

Q: Were the Germans aware that the mounting was taking place in southern England in the two weeks prior to the invasion?

A: We were aware at the end of May 1944 of the movement of troops into southern England. From that time on, the troops of Army Group B (Rommel) were in a constant state of alert for any emergency.

Q: How near completion were the beach defenses along the Omaha and Utah areas? Was there a target date for the completion of these defenses, or were construction activities to continue indefinitely?

A: The complete construction of the coastal defenses was not yet finished and never would have been; therefore, no date for their completion had been set. It was ordered that, by the beginning of April 1944, the military installations must be put into a defensible state and the Organization Todt's construction offices, etc., be evacuated.

Since the Spring of 1944, no more permanent installations had been built, as the necessary sand and cement no longer could be brought up. Further improvement was limited to camouflaging the batteries and building small field fortifications, dugouts, and minefields and obstacles. Although construction of the Atlantic Wall was started as early as 1941, it had been constructed without any fixed uniform building plan by various branches of the service. Later, the construction work was carried on uniformly through the Inspector of the Engineers and Fortresses and with the aid of Organization Todt. The work was strongly influenced and personally supervised by the Führer himself.

The Invasion and the German Navy

by Grossadmiral Karl Dönitz and Konteradmiral Gerhard Wagner

Note by Kenneth W. Hechler, Major, Infantry (Res)

Admirals Dönitz and Wagner were both present at this oral interview, which was conducted with the assistance of Captain Herbert Sensenig, who acted as interpreter. Inasmuch as each group of sentences was interpreted into English, no German record was made at the time of the oral interview. Notes were taken by Sergeant Kiralfy, although this record does not pretend to be a word-for-word account of the responses of Admirals Dönitz and Wagner.

The response to Question 11 on the capitulation of Cherbourg was omitted from the report of the oral interview, inasmuch as Admiral Dönitz admitted that he was only speculating. Furthermore, the general nature of his speculations would, I felt, cast some doubt on the veracity of his other remarks, so I took the editorial liberty of omitting these speculations from my report.

Q: What was the disposition of various German surface and undersea craft prior to the invasion of the coast of Normandy on 6 June 1944?

A: At that time, our submarines were handicapped in Channel waters by lack of a device which would enable then to stay under water [for any great length of time—Ed.]. This device, known as a "schnorckel," was just being installed in June 1944, and was not completely installed until November 1944. Further, there was a current in the Channel, and at most places the waters were not deep enough to allow the submarines to evade depth charges once they were spotted. Nevertheless, at all the ports along the French and Dutch coasts, all means were concentrated to repel the invasion.

Q: Where did you figure that the invasion would take place?

A: I ruled out several places. The coast around Brest, and between Brest and Cherbourg, seemed unlikely because the coast was rough and steep, the current swift, the storms frequent, and the shoals many. It was conceivable that the attack might have come along the west coast of France near Bordeaux, along the south near Marseilles and Toulon, near Calais, or where it actually did come. If it were to come in Denmark, it could only come in the sheltered harbor at the extreme northeast tip, after entering the Skagerrak.

Q: Do you know what type of craft attacked the LSTs in the exercises off Portland on the night of 27/28 April 1944? Were you aware that exercises were taking place, or did you suspect that the mounting of the operation had begun, or was it a case of a chance patrol discovering the unprotected Allied craft several miles off the coast?

A: I recall the incident well. Those were E-boats which were based at Cherbourg and were under the command of Adm Theodor Krancke. I do not believe that more than twelve boats were involved in this attack. We did not suspect anything in particular, but naturally everyone was alert for a possible invasion, and we were attempting to slip closer to the English ports under the cover of darkness and thereby extend the range of our reconnaissance. Another reason for this was that the excellent air protection over the English concentration ports prevented our reconnaissance planes from getting adequate results. When we engaged American boats off the English coast, we did not know very much about their type, strength or intentions, since we could not recognize these things in the darkness. Appreciating that the enemy forces were too strong, we withdrew.

Q: What naval force could you actually move to the invasion area when it struck?

A: Twenty to thirty E-boats, six torpedo boats, twenty minesweepers, three or four destroyers, and four to five submarines in the Channel east of Cherbourg.

Q: How effective do you estimate these craft were in checking the invasion?

A: They could inflict only fleabites. Against the overwhelming power of your air force, there were insufficient German naval craft to stop the invasion.

Q: How did you plan to stop the invasion then?

A: The only thing we could hope for was to allow a landing and then throw the beachhead back into the sea. We all appreciated that this had to be done rather quickly after the landing, if at all, or the cumulative landings of your troops and supplies would be sufficient to establish a firm hold.

Q: After the invasion, did German naval units play an important part in keeping the flow of supplies from crossing the Channel?

A: Again we were handicapped by insufficient forces and the strength of your air power. The greatest disaster which hit us was early in July 1944, when American planes inflicted great destruction on our ships in Le Havre. This was largely due to lack of opposition from German antiaircraft guns. German planes had been in the habit of passing over to Le Havre while en route to England, and, for some reason, the antiaircraft commander at Le Havre mistook an American bombing raid for the Luftwaffe. Two torpedo-boats, twelve minesweepers, and twelve E-boats were destroyed that day by American planes.

However, there was one encouraging development early in July 1944, with the first use of one and two-man submarines (KKV) [Kleinkampfverbände—Ed.]. Had these been available at the time of the invasion, much greater damage might have been inflicted on the American and British ships.

Q: What knowledge did you have, prior to the assault, of the Allies' equipment or preparations for the establishment of artificial beach ports? Did you underestimate our ability to build up the capacity of these beach ports?

A: We did not believe that you had ports as big as the ones you used. We thought they were much smaller.

Q: Why weren't these artificial ports bombed more than they were? What determined the German policy to lay mines via air at night on the beaches, rather than to bomb beaches, supply installations, and ships?

A: Because of your air superiority, we could do little successful bombing by day. By night we could not see sufficiently to bomb the ports. It therefore was concluded that sowing mines probably would be the most expedient policy.

Q: Why were not the port facilities of Antwerp demolished, as they had been at Cherbourg and Brest?

A: That was, of course, a decisive mistake, but it was because the American columns came too fast.

Q: Why did Cherbourg capitulate so quickly?

A: I hear that the sailors at Cherbourg were angry at the Army's capitulation. [*Interviewer's note:* Adm Dönitz made some other speculations about the surrender of Cherbourg, but since they were only speculations which are not in agreement with the testimony of officers closer to the scene, they have been omitted.]

The Invasion

by General Walter Warlimont

Q: Did you anticipate that the invasion would take place where it actually did?

A: Hitler was the first one who decided for himself that this was the most probable spot for landing. On 2 May 1944, he ordered that antiaircraft and antitank weapons were to be reinforced all through Normandy and Brittany, counting mainly on an invasion in Normandy. Hitler's view was based on intelligence received as to troop movements in the British Isles. Two main troop concentrations had been noticed there: one in the southeast with mainly British troops, and one in the southwest, in Wales and on both sides of Wales, consisting mainly of US troops.

Q: Where did most of the other high-ranking officials believe that the invasion would take place?

A: Up to May 1944, when Hitler first spoke of it, we were all prepared for a landing in the Channel zone between the Seine and the Somme, by Abbeville and Le Havre. Therefore, throughout 1942–43, the coastal defenses were built up mainly in the Fifteenth Army zone.

Q: At what particular point?

A: I cannot say that we expected the landing at any particular point in Normandy. We expected it all along the coast with special reference to the small ports (which are mainly in the Bayeux area). We were not quite convinced that Hitler was right in expecting that attack, but he kept harping on it and demanded more and more reinforcements for that sector.

Q: Why did the generals predict that the invasion would strike at a different point than Hitler predicted? You both had access to the same sources of information, did you not?

A: We generals figured along the lines of our regular military education, but Hitler figured out of intuition as he always did. We figured on the Channel zone because (1) it is the shortest crossing from the British Isles, (2) once across the Channel, it is the shortest way to Germany and its industrial Ruhr, (3) it has at least one big harbor, Le Havre, better situated than Cherbourg and with better routes and lines of communication into the interior, and (4) your air force had better possibilities to support the attack closer to its bases.

Q: Upon what else besides intuition did Hitler base his conviction that we would invade Normandy?

A: Besides his observations from troop movements, Hitler based his theory on the idea that you would aim to build up a stable front, including one big harbor, and there was no better place on the whole coast than the Cotentin peninsula for this purpose.

Q: Did the regular army officers and High Command lean any more toward Hitler's view as the invasion date approached?

A: We recognized too that a landing in other parts of Europe further north was becoming more and more improbable as the British troops were grouped more and more to the south. The position of the US troops especially led Hitler to anticipate an attack launched against the west coast of Normandy.

Q: We, of course, did our best to deceive you into thinking that we would land in the Pas de Calais area, and, after the landing in Normandy, we still carried out elaborate deception plans in order to tie down your Fifteenth Army in this sector. What led you to feel that we would land in the Pas de Calais area?

A: The first air attacks were against fortifications of the Seine, and, since we had many standing fortifications in this sector, we took it as further evidence of your plans.

We attached great importance to the Resistance movements in the interior and tried to determine the place of landing by noting where most parachute baskets, etc., were dropped. As time went on, however, this became so widespread that it no longer gave us any help.

We also managed to get into some of your radio nets. Radio transmitters were dropped from planes to be used by your agents in France to inform you about our movements. We intercepted some of these and got into your radio nets and used them ourselves, and also used them to communicate with your stations. We had the impression that this action of ours had passed unnoticed by you. We found out that there were special catchwords with which you prepared your operations and by means of which you were going to inform the French Underground as to the day and hour of your attack.

Q: To what extent was it possible to complete the fortifications along the Normandy coast where the invasion was later made?

A: The fortification of Normandy was not at all complete. Such fortifications require a long time. In Picardy we had more workers from occupied countries and better communications, and no one had thought of Normandy much before. The Normandy fortifications were just the same as those of other parts of the French coast, with one big position every 20 to 30 kilometers.

Q: Was it a case of shortage of troops or shortage of materials for the fortifications?

A: Not many more troops could have been put in there, but we could have done much more in the way of fortifying. Materials, such as cement, were also rare, having to be divided among all the armed forces. Furthermore, railway transportation was getting worse all the time as a result of air attacks on the big junctions. So, we were well aware that the fortifications were by no means complete, but it was too late to complete them as we should have liked.

Q: What would you have liked to have done in the way of better fortifications on the Normandy coast?

A: We should have had more standing fortifications built by the troops and not by Organization Todt. As it was too late by this time, all we could do was to put more troops in Normandy and improve their equipment.

Q: What troops did you have available to repulse the invasion?

A: By about 2 May 1944, we had, so far as I can remember without diaries, maps, or operations books, one static division of old men [716th] (comprising two regiments around the mouth of the Orne), the 711th [Infantry—Ed.] Division, which was a static division, and the 352nd [Infantry—Ed.] Division in front of Bayeux, to cover a coastline of at least 60 or even 80 kilometers. There was a special force in Cherbourg.

We had three divisions (352nd, 716th and 711th) on the north coast of Normandy, another one (709th [Infantry—Ed.] Division) around Cherbourg, and the 243rd [Infantry Division—Ed.] on the west coast of Normandy. On 2 May 1944, Hitler put in the reinforcements of the antiaircraft and antitank weapons which were given to the units with a view in particular to their being better able to combat paratroops and airborne units.

On 4 May 1944, he ordered the 2nd FS Division, then on the Eastern Front, to be transferred to the West. One regiment of this division, 6th FS Regiment, which was already in Germany when the order was given, came at once to Normandy, somewhere near St Lô.

Hitler then ordered the 91st [LL—Ed.] Division, one of the very few divisions we had in Germany as an operative reserve, to be transferred to Normandy, also as a reserve. Most of this strength was on the base line of the Cotentin. So, actually only one parachute regiment and one division were sent in as we had no operative reserve to dispose of.

Rundstedt, as C-in-C West, tried to send reinforcements, but had no reserves either and could do nothing worth mentioning. All our troops were required to defend the various coastlines, and your attack in Italy was making great progress. One division of Fifteenth Army, the Luftwaffe Feld Division (number not known) even had to be sent to Italy.

Rommel, at the next echelon, had always fought for a more tactical defense of the coast. He wanted to put in reserves as close to the coastline as possible. This was possible, of course, once you knew where the enemy was going to strike. But when you did not know, and had a coastline of thousands of kilometers, it was too hazardous to risk. As soon as Hitler decided that Normandy was the likely spot, Rommel had his way and sent in his Panzer divisions, which were attached to him as Wehrmachtbefehlshaber [Military District Commander in Occupied Territory—Ed.] of Western Europe (Netherlands Headquarters). Army Group B extended right down to La Rochelle. Rommel had a reserve of Panzer divisions and, in accordance with his line of thinking, he now put in the 21st Panzer Division somewhere near

Caen, the 12th SS Panzer Division around Falaise, and the 2nd Panzer Division around St Lô (or a little east of it).

Rommel had one Panzer division left. He had two in Normandy, one quite close to the coast, and two just 40 to 50 kilometers behind it. He had one division behind Fifteenth Army. This took place about the middle of May 1944. Rommel took no infantry divisions from Fifteenth Army. Maybe this was due to uncertainty as to the division of spheres of Rommel and Rundstedt. I am not sure whether Rommel and Rundstedt were convinced Hitler was right. Rommel claimed it made no difference where the attack came as his defenses were now so good all along the coast.

There were four more armored divisions farther east which were reserved for the disposition of OKW. Two were in the neighborhood of Paris, the Panzer Lehr Division and the 2nd SS Panzer Division.

Q: Did you expect us to land only where there were ports and harbors, or did you know about our artificial ports? Why did you not bomb our artificial ports after you discovered how much we were using them to land supplies?

A: We always expected your attack with the aid of harbors, and if we had known more about your artificial ports, we should have done more to stop it. If you ask why the air force did not bomb more effectively the places where you landed, the answer is that our air force was unable to break through your defenses in order to find and hit the targets at all.

Q: Were you able to estimate the rate at which we could build up supplies and troops on the beaches after the initial landing?

A: We knew the capacity of the small (natural) harbors, but, not knowing about the artificial ports, we could not estimate your rate of supply. We were able later to gauge the rate at which you were landing troops, but confined ourselves to strength figures and the number of divisions as our reconnaissance did not give us much information on your troops and still less on your supply circumstances.

Q: Did you suspect that the invasion would take place on the date which it did?

A: The weather was right for an invasion and we had been alerted to the possibility for some weeks prior to 6 June 1944. Our chief intelligence source was the radio, and our intercepts revealed that the invasion would take place on the morning of 6 June 1944. This information was relayed to headquarters on the afternoon of 5 June 1944. Hitler knew it and Gen Jodl knew it, but the information was not made available to the troops in Normandy.

Q: Was this considered a great mistake by Hitler?

A: In Hitler's eyes, Gen Jodl, unlike other men, did not make military mistakes. Gen Jodl knew the state of alarm or alert under which the troops in northern France were operating and did not consider it necessary to give out another order. Furthermore, there had been a number of other false alarms prior to this one.

Q: Was your reconnaissance hampered any in the days immediately prior to the invasion?

A: Unfortunately, we had no regular air reconnaissance because of the superiority of your air power over the area. Air reconnaissance was made perhaps every fortnight, and even then was confined to photographs of possible points of embarkation. Sea reconnaissance also was rather difficult; it was difficult to keep boats in the open sea when the British Navy dominated the area.

Q: Do you recall any of Hitler's specific comments immediately prior to the invasion?

A: More and more in recent months, since Hitler had assumed his role of military expert, he would talk at great length and in broad terms at the semi-daily operational meetings. These meetings, attended by up to twenty high officers, would be held at 1300 and close to midnight. Hitler would speak honestly, but seldom directly to any individuals or individual. He would speak "out of the window." To answer your question, just before the invasion his line was that the impending invasion of France would be the decisive event of the coming year. Hitler said, "It will decide the issue, not only of the year, but of the whole war. If we succeed in throwing back the invasion, then such an attempt cannot and will not be repeated within a short time. It will then mean that our reserves will be set free for use in Italy and the East. Then we can stabilize the front in the East and perhaps return to the offensive in that sector. If we don't throw the invaders back, we can't win a static war in the long run because the matériel our enemies can bring in will exceed what we can send to that front. With no strategic reserves of any importance, it will be impossible to build up sufficient strength along such a line. Therefore, the invader must be thrown back on his first attempt."

PART TWO

Preparation: Organizing and Deploying the Units

If the previous chapter showed how the German High Command tried to deal with the impending invasion, this chapter shows how the war-fighters at corps, division, and regimental headquarters level addressed the same thing.

The Germans in muddy boots in this chapter do a much better job of things than the Germans in service dress in the previous chapter. In this chapter, they are asked to make the defense of Western Europe—which in mid-1943 was seen basically as a rest area for the Eastern front rather than the setting for the war's decisive battle—into something that was militarily feasible. Many of them came with experience in the East, where they had seen not only how devastating defeat could be, but that, if properly carried out, effective defensive tactics could defeat even skillfully delivered attacks from a numerically superior opponent.

They did a surprisingly good job of it, considering how little time and how few resources they had available. The surprising thing is that divisions, such as the 352nd, that made the fighting on Omaha Beach such a near-run thing had so little time for training. It was a newly-formed division, and its limited training time had been further diminished by the need to work on beach defenses. Yet, on D-Day and thereafter, it often showed a skill in defensive tactics that was superior to that of its main opponent, the US 29th Infantry Division, which had been training since called into service in mid-1940.

However effective the Germans proved on the defense, it remains that the divisions described here were inadequately trained by the standards of the Western Allies. Repeatedly, in the following chapters, the reader will see the inability of German units to mount coordinated multi-battalion counterattacks, especially when requiring coordination across divisional or corps boundaries. Omaha Beach would have been much more a near-run thing if the local German reserves had not been sent first one way then another.

While the previous chapter showed that the Germans had little idea of how to get out of its strategic dilemma in 1944—except that defeating any invasion in the West was a necessary first step—this chapter shows that they had a very good idea of how to improvise military formations out of limited resources in a short period of time. They would repeat this performance, time and time again, on the battlefield in Normandy.

When Allied firepower had destroyed the thinly stretched German forces in the path of an Allied offensive, there was a battlefield leader—usually an Eastern front veteran— who would rally the survivors, pull in reserves, launch a limited counterattack, and restore the stability of the defense. It is little wonder that, a generation after Normandy, the successors to both sides looked to German defensive tactics to provide guidance for those that were required on a battlefield that could be dominated by the ultimate source of concentrated firepower—the tactical nuclear weapon.

D.C.I.

Panzer-Type Divisions (Western Front)

by General der Panzertruppen Leo, Freiherr Geyr von Schweppenburg

I. Estimate of Panzer-Type Divisions, Western Front, 6 June1944

Panzer Gruppe West could give orders to the Waffen SS on training matters only. The activation or re-forming of Panzer-type divisions in the West was not the same for the Heer as it was for the Waffen SS. The Waffen SS had priority as a result of the aid and resources of Himmler or sometimes because of overriding the orders of Hitler. The principle advantage accruing to the Waffen SS was priority on replacements and matériel. On the other hand, the Waffen SS was short of officers and NCOs. Army officers did not wish to join the Waffen SS. The Heeres Personalamt, under Schmundt, Hitler's chief aide-de-camp, interposed by order to provide the 12th SS Panzer Division with the bare minimum of company grade officers necessary for training. The same method was sometimes applied to procure general staff officers.

The cadre of officers and NCOs was rather small and somewhat poor in quality. A few casualties or changes in the roster of an SS division might mean a great deterioration in fighting value. This value was largely based on the presence of a few "personalities." For instance, the performance of the 12th SS Panzer Division depended on Witt (killed during the invasion), Meyer (his successor) and a few battalion commanders.

The number of SS divisions and the activation of more greatly exceeded the number of corresponding personnel available. It became more and more evident that Hitler was not concerned with wearing down the Heeres Panzer divisions in the East. While these divisions were burned out fighting the Russians, the SS divisions were sent to France for reorganization.

The selection, by the Berchtesgaden staff, of divisions for a strategic reserve in France was characteristic: 1st SS Panzer Division (Liebstandarte), 12th SS Panzer Division (Hitlerjugend), Panzer Lehr Division, and 17th SS Panzer Grenadier Division (Götz von Berlichingen). I would have chosen from a military standpoint, on the basis of efficiency, the 2nd Panzer Division, 12th SS Panzer Division, 11th Panzer Division or 9th SS Panzer Division, and the Panzer Lehr Division.

The allotment of material was made by the Generalinspektion der Panzertruppen (General Inspectorate of Panzer Troops), strongly influenced by Hitler. The latter knew nothing about training and based his evaluation on "geist" (spirit). He believed this "geist" to be superior in the SS. In the Fall of 1943 and the Spring of 1944, there were a large number of battle-seasoned tank battalions in France which had come from the

Eastern front and were re-formed. These battalions waited several months for their matériel, whereas some of the SS Panzer divisions had already received their matériel, despite a lack of sufficient personnel and trained crews. However, it is only fair to say that in training as well as fighting, the SS divisions did their best to pull their full weight.

The SS officer corps was far more varied in origin, education and character than that of the Heer. One could find the ruthless mercenary, the "just a soldier" type, and the responsible officer side by side. For those who had come to dislike service in the Waffen SS, there was no "way back." Himmler, in a case with which I am familiar, left no doubt to a highly responsible and very able officer what would happen.

The conclusion of be drawn is that the staying and recovery power during and after weeks and months of fighting was bound to be superior in the Heeres divisions. The standard and thoroughness of the tactical education of subordinates was also superior in Heeres divisions. The following is a thorough estimate of the comparative combat efficiency of all Panzer-type formations between 1939 and 6 June 1944. The list has been compiled after interrogating my most experienced corps and division commanders. The average efficiency varies from 30 to 40 percent of the average division performance in 1939. This percentage does not apply to training methods, to which I would give greater credit because of modernization.

Order of Combat Efficiency

A. 2nd Panzer Division
9th SS Panzer Division
12th SS Panzer Division
Panzer Lehr Division
B. 11th Panzer Division
2nd SS Panzer Division
21st Panzer Division
C. 9th Panzer Division
17th SS Panzer Grenadier Division
116th Panzer Division (probably)
D. 10th SS Panzer Division
1st SS Panzer Division

(Estimate is of 6 June 1944, no matter what performance the divisions made later on.)

II. Remarks

2nd Panzer Division: The division commander was a good leader in the field, but less experienced in training. The division was well backed with personnel and matériel by the Generalinspektion. Genobst Guderian was in command of this division before the war.

9th SS Panzer Division: The performance of this division depended on the outstanding military personality of its commander, Oberf Bittrich, who was a first class trainer. The division was especially efficient against airborne operations (proved at Arnhem) and in teamwork.

12th SS (Hitlerjugend) Panzer Division: This commander was also good in training and possessed a will and a passion for advanced methods. The quality of conscripts was high, but that of the subordinate officers and NCOs was poor.

Panzer Lehr Division: The division was well provided for by the Generalinspektion. The commander was very modern in his thoughts and methods. There were deficiencies in infantry tactics and teamwork (combined arms).

11th Panzer Division: The commander was well experienced in mobile warfare. The division was thoroughly schooled in higher training methods. It had an adequate cadre of seasoned subordinate officers and was augmented by conscripts from 273rd Reserve Panzer Division.

2nd SS Panzer Division: The remnants of this division, which in 1944 was re-formed in France, still had sufficient veterans from the period when its first commander (Obstgrf Paul Hausser) had given the division very high standards. The division had the best tank battalion in the West.

21st Panzer Division: The division was reorganized after the African campaign with undesirable personnel from a large number of divisions. Even very thorough and experienced training could never overcome this basic fault. Part of its matériel was manufactured in French factories.

9th Panzer Division: There were too many changes in division commanders and principal staff officers and too much interference with training by employing the troops to build fortifications and so forth.

17th SS Panzer Grenadier Division: Its performance depended on two men, Brigf Ostendorf, its first commander, and Standf Fick, commander of the Panzer Grenadier regiment. The matériel was poor. The division, which was organized and trained in haste, was quite efficient but deteriorated rapidly after Ostendorf was wounded in Normandy.

10th SS Panzer Division: The division was unlucky in its assignment of division commanders.

1st SS Panzer Division: A type of "Praetorian Guard," the division was bled white in Russia and was unable to refill the gaps resulting from casualties and sending out cadres (the 12th SS Panzer Division was formed by a cadre from the 1st SS Panzer Division). Discipline was a sham; the NCOs were poor. The division did not have time for thorough training before the invasion.

Background: The 709th Infantry Division

by Generalleutnant Karl Wilhelm von Schlieben

Situation Prior to the Arrival of
Generalfeldmarschall Rommel on the Atlantic Coast

After two and a half years of uninterrupted assignment as commander of a Panzer grenadier regiment, a rifle brigade, and a Panzer division in Russia, I took over the 709th Infantry Division on the Cotentin peninsula in December 1943, just before Christmas. My wide experience in all sorts of mobile warfare was not of much use to me in my new mission, which was coastal defense.

The 709th Infantry Division was a division of the 15th Wave. It did not even have horses and was classified as a static division. The quality of its personnel had decreased through being drained by repeated transfers of men to the Russian front. Apart from steady individual detachments, the entire 1st Battalion of the 739th Grenadier Regiment, for instance, had been sent to the Russian front.

The age of the soldiers and the high percentage of men inexperienced in warfare and belonging to "Volksliste III"* was striking. The latter were not Germans but had originated from countries occupied during the war. Their reliability was doubtful. In addition, two Eastern† and two Georgian battalions were assigned to the division; I doubted that they would fight hard in cases of emergency. The following statement in the London *Daily Telegraph and Morning Post* of Friday, 1 September 1944 proves my point: "In the first days of the invasion one was struck by the unexpectedly high proportion of non-German troops among the units opposed to us."

The table of organization of the 709th Infantry Division on 1 May 1944 is given in Appendix A [at the end of this chapter]. It shows that no antitank companies were provided for the 729th and 739th Rifle Regiments, and no antitank battalion for the division. These formations were activated locally; that is, the Grenadier regiments were required to reduce the authorized strength of their companies and transfer personnel to the antitank units.

The division was placed under LXXXIV Corps, commanded by General der Artillerie Marcks. His CP was at St Lô.

---

* Ethnic Germans with foreign citizenship were registered in classified lists according to pure German descent, mixed descent, knowledge of German language, etc.
† Formed of non-Russian Red Army prisoners of war, or Russian prisoners formerly in the German labor service.

The mission of the 709th Infantry Division was to prevent an enemy landing in its sector. This sector extended from Le Grand Vez (northeast of Carentan) via Barfleur–Cap Levy–Cherbourg–Cap de la Hague–Cap de Carteret (west of Barleville).

In addition to this wide sector, there was the land front of Cherbourg, extending over about 65 kilometers. Cherbourg had been declared a fortress by order of Hitler in Spring 1944, probably for propagandistic and deceptive purposes. This declaration was based neither on the terrain nor on the condition of the fortifications. The defense value of Cherbourg had not been improved by any works during the German occupation. It consisted mostly of earthworks, extensive enough to justify Cherbourg being called a fortress by experts.

Cherbourg had less reason for being called a fortress than many other well-known localities on the coast of France. If a reliable encyclopedia like the 1943 Brockhaus calls Brest a fortress, states that Calais is strongly fortified, that Le Havre, Lorient, La Rochelle and St Malo are fortified, and that Cherbourg is a naval and commercial port only, there must have been good reasons for doing so.

The defense of Cherbourg against an attack by land was adversely influenced by the terrain. To the south and west the dominating heights are near the harbor; to the south they are about 1,400 meters distant, i.e. within easy machine-gun range. If these heights formed the main line of resistance, there was not enough room between them and the sea to bring sufficient of our artillery into position from which it could cover the zone in front of the main line of resistance, because the trajectory did not permit it. This may have been the reason for establishing and fortifying a land front at a distance from the main objective (the beaches) to be protected. It also caused the division to be widely spread out.

Proper defensive measures however, had not been taken; that is, to employ an adequate number of divisions for the defense of a 65-kilometer sector, and to fortify the landward front to resist the effects of modern arms. We had to be satisfied with field fortifications which reminded one of the position warfare in the autumn of 1914, or even more of the weakly fortified line of a cavalry screen. There was no continuous land front. It consisted of a number of islands of resistance, some of which were barely within sight of one another. When Hitler had Cherbourg declared a fortress in 1944, the commander, Generalmajor Sattler, remarked dryly, "A three-year-old boy does not grow a beard if you declare him to be a man and a town does not become a fortress by being declared a fortress."

When the fortress commander had to submit his written combat directive to the C-in-C West or to the Commander of Seventh Army a few weeks prior to the invasion, I, as Division Commander, made the following comment: "The land front has all the weaknesses of a bridgehead that is too wide. It is in danger of being penetrated at some point and of being rolled up from the flank or the rear."

The question may be asked why the construction of fortifications had not been intensified along the land front. This requires further explanation. The construction of the position was directed centrally by the Army. This task was chiefly attended to by Colonel of Engineers von Sciotta. It was decisive for the employment of building materials and labor, consisting chiefly of laborers of Organization Todt under the management of an architect, that the coastline formed the main line of resistance. The main efforts in the employment of labor were, therefore, made along the coast. The distribution of cement was directed by a higher agency, who classified the individual building projects according to their priority and who supplied materials for them accordingly. From time to time, meetings were held at Corps headquarters to fix the allotments of cement. These meetings were characterized as the "Concrete Exchange," because each branch of the armed forces—Army, Luftwaffe and Navy—tried to get as large as possible a share for itself. Beyond that it became apparent that Organization Todt preferred projects where as many cubic meters as possible of concrete could be used within the shortest possible time. A craze for record figures developed. This statement does not, however, imply an intention to belittle the merits of Organization Todt. It had to surmount great difficulties, had to work mainly with workmen of different nationalities, and frequently suffered from lack of materials or delayed delivery, particularly after enemy raids on the French railroad network had started.

The construction of the sea front was different. To call the coastline the main line of resistance was a violation of the German manual (FSR) for the conduct of field operations. According to this manual, a main line of resistance is part of a main defense area. This implies a certain depth of the defense zone, and this was lacking. If one had called it a "line of security along the coast," which indeed it was, instead of a line of resistance, probably the old principle that to attempt to secure everything results in no security at all would have been remembered.

Actually the so-called main line of resistance consisted of strongpoints, which were called islands of resistance if they were weakly occupied and bases if they were more strongly defended. Generally the main weapons in the strongpoints were two light machine guns, one heavy machine gun, one medium mortar, and one 75-mm field gun or 47-mm AT gun. The stationary weapons in the islands of resistance and bases were of varied models. They consisted of French, Dutch, Czech, Polish, and Russian guns, which made training more difficult, because the men had to know all these types besides their own German models. The distance between the islands of resistance and bases varied from 1,000 to 4,000 meters. Parts of them were secured by barbed wire and mines.

Additional protection against a landing consisted of the GHQ coast artillery, subordinate to the Navy, and the division artillery, which was also under the command of the Navy as long as it was combatting an enemy who had not yet effected a landing. The artillery, especially the GHQ coast artillery, was immobile, embedded in concrete behind loopholes, its field of fire being toward the sea.

By the middle of March 1944 the division had assigned the following units to the coastal main line of resistance:

919th Grenadier Regiment, less one battalion in division reserve;

729th Grenadier Regiment, less one battalion also in division reserve;

739th Grenadier Regiment (only two battalions strong) with the 795th and 799th Georgian Battalions attached to it; and

17th Machine Gun Battalion.

In addition, elements of LXXXIV Permanent Fortress Battalion (consisting of older men with limited fighting qualities) were in the area of Cherbourg.

The following units were assigned to the land front at Cherbourg:

Elements of LXXXIV Permanent Fortress Battalion; and

549th Eastern Battalion.

Additionally and behind the 739th Grenadier Regiment on the west coast of the peninsula, there was the weak 562nd Eastern Battalion, suitable only for the construction of field fortifications; it had arrived in a dilapidated condition.

The division had the following reserves:

One battalion of the 919th Grenadier Regiment;

One battalion of the 729th Grenadier Regiment; and

709th AT Battalion.

In and around Cherbourg there were agencies of the Navy, the personnel of the dockyards, of airdromes and of ships, guards for the launching installations for the V-weapons, personnel for sound detectors and searchlights, hospital personnel, Organization Todt labor personnel, etc., most of whom either were not fit for combat or were either not armed or else armed to a limited extent only.

The forward echelon of the command post (tactical group) of the 709th Infantry Division was at Chiffremont, about three kilometers east of Valognes, the rear echelon (supply group) at Hemeves, six kilometers southeast of Valognes.

The division's means of signal communication were increased by a wide stationary network of cables, which, although it was not very deeply laid, stood the coming test far better than expected.

Both the sea and land fronts were insufficiently mined. As far as I remember, up to April 1944, the entire sea and land fronts had been mined with only 132,000 landmines.

Antitank obstacles had been erected along the land front on the roads leading to Cherbourg. These obstacles, put up by order of Feldmarschall Rommel, were improved before the invasion and placed in the sea as an obstacle in front of the beach.

A novelty of these days, at least for me, who had up to that time been employed in the East only, was the flood of orders, directives, and regulations, which were continually showered on the troops. This paper flood impressed me more than the tide along the Atlantic coast. Higher headquarters concerned themselves with petty affairs of subordinate commanders; it became a problem for example, whether a machine gun was to be placed twenty meters more to the right or to the left. In such matters superior agencies were highly interested. In short, all the symptoms of position warfare on a quiet front made their appearance. A good example was the mania of the numerous technical staff officers to write voluminously. Not only did the orders of the superior field officers have to be respected, but also those of the Military Commander in France with all his subordinate agencies, those of area headquarters, and those of the military administration headquarters. If, for instance, the C-in-C of the Army wanted to have an old ramshackle hut removed to create a better field of fire, a written application had to be filed with the competent area headquarters, accompanied by a sketch. Such a state of affairs, for which, after all, the troops had to suffer, continued to exist, although it would have been worthwhile for higher headquarters to change this situation, instead of occupying themselves with petty interference in the concerns of the troops.

As commander of the 709th Division, with a sector more than 250 kilometers wide, I battled unsuccessfully for weeks to be relieved of the duties of judge of the personnel of Organization Todt. One day a laborer of Organization Todt on one of the Channel Islands, a man who was not subordinate to me, and who had illegally sold the wardrobe of his divorced wife during his home leave at Stettin, came before me for examination. As division commander on the Channel coast, I did not think it was my task to judge such cases. I therefore took this opportunity to file an application to change the judicial organization. My application was declined by the C-in-C West as a matter of "policy"— an argument which always serves to deny even the most justified request, and I had to continue to occupy myself with legal affairs for two hours daily. I mention this only in order to show how little understanding of things pertaining to the troops could be expected at that time in France from our higher headquarters.

Then, with a burst of propaganda, came Generalfeldmarschall Rommel's visit in February–March 1944.

Changes by Generalfeldmarschall Rommel

The appearance of Feldmarschall Rommel was accompanied by another flood of papers; I had the feeling that the chain of command was becoming still more complicated. "Who was the actual leader in the West?" That was the question asked by many of us. It was neither a military custom nor according to the "Führer" principle that two personalities should share responsibility. Up to that time, orders for the defense had been issued by the C-in-C West, Generalfeldmarschall von Rundstedt. Now, written orders were issued by Rommel, who also gave verbal orders on the spot, which were contradictory to the former orders. The opinion of Rommel was that, if an invasion could be prevented at all, the enemy would have to be beaten before he could land, that is to say on the water. On his first visit to my sector, Feldmarschall Rommel said. "Once the enemy has effected a landing, we cannot beat him, because his air force is superior." This opinion, called the "Rommel tendency," certainly had much in favor of it, because the bulk of the German forces were tied up in Russia and had already been bled white.

Rommel now demanded a tremendous effort in order to prevent the enemy from landing. He ordered:

a.   The erection of an uninterrupted chain of obstacles in front of the beach. They consisted of strong stakes to which mines were to be attached. These stakes were driven into the ground at such a distance from the beach that they were just covered with water at high tide. Rommel's idea was that the enemy would be able to land at high tide only. The landing craft would strike the stakes and cause the mines to explode, thus sinking the boats. The stakes had to be deeply driven in and embedded in concrete, so that the tide would not carry them away—a thing that happened frequently enough, chiefly on the west coast.

b. An increase in fenced-in minefields directly on the beach and in the rear area in locations threatened by possible air landings. As a preparatory measure areas were fenced in and provided with signposts. Rommel promised explicitly that "millions of mines" would be supplied. Their delivery, however, did not take place because of numerous and heavy air attacks on the French transportation system. If, subsequently, a long time after the invasion, mines were used on the western border of the Reich to a large extent, this was due to the fact that great quantities of them did not reach the Atlantic coast on account of transportation difficulties. Mines were so scarce that, despite my protests, I had to deliver up before the invasion, by order of the Corps headquarters, my mobile reserve of one thousand mines. Hence they probably were somewhere on a part of the coast which was not attacked, while they were missed badly during the fighting for Cherbourg.

c. The erection of dummy minefields on the beach and in the rear area against air landings. These minefields were fenced-in areas with signposts marked with a death's-head and the inscription "Caution! Mines!"

d. The erection of air landing obstacles in open country exposed to air landings, like meadows, pasture land, etc. There was an abundance of such areas, and the lumber for stakes, the so-called "Rommel asparagus," had to be cut first. This was a long, wearisome job.

e. Further flooding of the countryside.

This work left no time to train the troops, and it actually exhausted them. A further consequence was that the improvement of the land front was necessarily neglected. This went so far that not even the C-in-C of Seventh Army, Generaloberst Dollmann, could carry through the construction of a tower with six loopholes which he wanted to be erected in the eastern part of the land front, although the metal dome was already on the spot and needed only to be lined with concrete. As mentioned above, the tank obstacles erected on the roads leading to Cherbourg also had to be moved to the beach and rolled far enough into the sea to be covered with water at high tide. These tank obstacles came from captured French stocks, and were called "Rollböcke." Their transportation was difficult, but their absence later on was detrimental to the land front.

In addition, it must be stressed that Rommel did not want any local reserves, and crammed all and everything into the coastal main line of resistance. Even the mobile AT battalion of the division was placed far forward with its field of fire in front of the beach. The Feldmarschall said that the AT guns (Pak) could be withdrawn at any time if wanted at another place. As these guns were motorized, they could without doubt be shifted more easily and more quickly to another place than the local reserves, who moved on foot only.

Until the middle of May, the western part of the sea front of the Cotentin peninsula was only weakly occupied. The reasons were as follows:

a. There were not enough troops available.

b. The Navy had for a long time maintained the opinion that the frequent heavy seas running off the west coast made en enemy landing impossible. Moreover, it was to be assumed that the enemy would shrink from landing on the west coast, until he had eliminated the danger threatening from the Channel Islands of Jersey, Guernsey, and Alderney, which were occupied by German troops.

It is to be regretted that the Navy changed its opinion and declared that an enemy landing on the west coast was, after all, technically possible, and that Vauville Bay was particularly endangered. That the Navy changed its mind with regard to the west coast was all the more fateful since it thus met, so to speak, land-tactical theories half way. These land-tactical theories were that, as is desirable in land warfare, it is easier to overpower the enemy if he is pinned down at the front and attacked on both flanks. After the Navy had declared that the west coast was suitable for a landing, many people were haunted by the fear of simultaneous landings on the east and west coasts followed by attacks on Cherbourg from both sides.

On 11 May 1944, Feldmarschall Rommel again visited the sector of the 709th Infantry Division. On 19 April, 23 enemy planes had raided the Marcouf battery on the east coast; on 9 May the Morsalines battery on the east coast was destroyed by enemy air forces. The remains of the battery were shown to the Feldmarschall. The area was covered with craters, the guns had been buried, or else their wheels were sticking up into the air. As always during the last weeks, the enemy planes operated without interference from the Luftwaffe.

After his tour of inspection, the Generalfeldmarschall had a conference with Generaloberst Dollmann and the commander of LXXXIV Corps, General der Artillerie Marcks, at the soldiers' home in Urville-Hague. I do not know what the conference was about.

After the conference, however, an order was given that the 243rd Infantry Division, commanded by Generalleutnant Hellmich, which up to that time had been kept in reserve, should be assigned to the west and northwest coasts, with its right wing at the northwestern corner of the land front of Cherbourg.

In addition, a static projector regiment, less one battalion, and a completely obsolete Panzer company of the 101st Panzer Training and Replacement Battalion were assigned. They had about twenty-five 37-mm guns mounted on captured French tank chassis. Already in Winter 1941/42 this caliber had proved to be totally useless against the Russian T-34 tank, because its projectiles ricochetted from the armor-plating. AT guns with 37-mm calibers were, therefore, jokingly called "Tank Knockers" an early as the

Winter of 1941/42. Moreover, part of these so-called tanks could not move far before coming to a dead stop. They were, therefore, to be employed only for firing at landing craft.

Furthermore, two Czech 83.5-mm antiaircraft guns with a range of about 16 kilometers were removed from the fortress area of Cherbourg, where they had been emplaced with great care and trouble and transferred to the 243rd Infantry Division for employment on the west coast. In their old position they had been of value because of their 360-degree traverse. Unlike most of the guns used at Cherbourg, they could fire at targets both on the sea and on land. The concern about the west coast, therefore, used up forces, which, if kept in reserve as before, would have been very useful during the first phase of the enemy landings.

Even the completely obsolete Panzer company could have been employed against enemy troops landing from the air. The 243rd Infantry Division had been trained by numerous field exercises and had also been made mobile. It had not been worn out like the static 709th Infantry Division by continuous coast guard and labor service during the last months.

Through the assignment of the 243rd Division, the 1st Battalion of the 739th Grenadier Regiment and the 795th Georgian Battalion (less one company) were released to the division. One company of the latter battalion was also assigned to the 243rd Infantry Division in spite of my protests, and remained with it on the northwest coast. Not until the start of the invasion was this company released by the 243rd Infantry Division, after its parent battalion had already been overpowered in the jump-off area of the enemy air landings. The 3rd Battalion of the 739th Grenadier Regiment was ordered by Corps to occupy the area around Height 180.2, southwest of Cherbourg, using its heavy weapons to combat air landings.

The 795th Georgian Battalion (minus one company) was transferred behind the southeastern seashore. It was in the jump area of the enemy air landing and must have been overpowered on 6 June, as from that date on no news was received from it. In an enemy pamphlet, which was shown to me during the battle, the commander of one of the companies of this battalion, a former Russian general staff officer, was portrayed as giving orientation to an American officer by means of a map. My request, telephoned to the commanding general before the invasion, to employ the Georgian battalion on the coast, and replace it in the rear area by a German battalion, had been declined for the reason that Generalfeldmarschall Rommel did not want to use foreign formations like the Georgians on account of their unreliability. This example also shows how orders from above interfered with the internal affairs of the troops. Neither an army nor a division commander was allowed to exchange two subordinate battalions.

During the above-mentioned visit of Generalfeldmarschall Rommel, I proposed on 11 May to destroy the harbor of Cherbourg thoroughly and to use all available forces for this purpose: engineers, Organisation Todt and a rock-drilling company. My proposal was based on the study of the experiences gained at Salerno, on intelligence reports of the concentration of numerous airborne units in England, and on the repeated heavy bombing of battery positions and sound locators on the Cotentin peninsula.

After my proposal had been bluntly declined by the Feldmarschall, I again submitted it in the evening to the commander of the Seventh Army, who passed the night at my headquarters. I reasoned as follows: "It is likely that the enemy will land from the air on the Cotentin peninsula with strong forces in order to support his landing from the sea. All reports agree that the enemy has completed his preparations in England. If the harbor of Cherbourg is immediately demolished, it will frustrate at the last minute the program of the enemy."

Generaloberst Dollmann agreed with me and I had the impression that he was convinced of the soundness of my ideas. In the same evening he told his first general staff officer, Oberst Helmdach, to apply by teletype for permission to destroy the harbor. The request was declined. I cannot say how far the Navy was responsible for the refusal.

The harbor of Cherbourg should have been destroyed by the middle of May regardless of the few ships in it, which in any case were good for nothing. Taking into account the demolitions at the harbor carried out after the start of the invasion, under pressure of the enemy, one may justly ask: How much better could the harbor of Cherbourg have been destroyed if the demolition had been started by the middle of May, when it would not have been under enemy pressure and if all available labor had been employed at the most important points. There were great amounts of large-caliber shells of French origin for demolition purposes. The next question is: How would the High Command of the Allied invasion forces have been influenced by the report that effective demolitions in the harbor of Cherbourg had been carried out by the middle of May? Perhaps such a measure would have delayed the start of the invasion.

Before the invasion, the Seventh Army assault battalion* was transferred as reserve of the army to the area west of Le Vaste. The battalion had a light field howitzer battery, which was brought into position near Ste Marie-du-Mont.

In addition there were the two heavy 456th (mtz) and 457th (mtz) Artillery Battalions under Regimental Staff Seidol (mtz). They were in position but remained as reserve of the army group.

The bulk of the attached 100th Smoke Battalion was in the area of Morsalines and one battery of the battalion on the southern boundary of the division sector.

Appendix A
709th Infantry Division, Static Division, 15th Wave

Total strength: 10,536
                   1,784 "Eastern" elements
                    333 Foreign volunteer auxiliaries

---

* Sturmbataillon AOK 7 – a special assault battalion with heavy firepower at the disposal of armies.

Status: 1 May 1944

Infantry

Organic units: 3 Plat of 15th Co are Pers for
static L AT guns

Artillery

Pending arrival of regular T/E weapons, Btrys are
equipped with static MGs, etc.
Static L field howitzers 14/19 (Czech)

Signal Troops	*Engineers*	*AT Troops*
Admin Units	*MT Troops*	*Sup Troops*
MP	*Vet Troops*	*Med Troops*

1. *German weapons* (not included in T/O)
   - 7,800 rifles
   - 58 Model 41 rifles
   - 451 rifles with grenade equipment
   - 720 SMG
   - 1,301 pistols
   - 262 signal pistols
   - 72 MG with mounts
     (3 for each Co of 729th and 739th
     Grenadier Rgt; 12 released by I Bn,
     739th Rgt and assigned to coast defense
     rgt)

2. *Captured weapons* (not included in T/O)
   - 72 81.4-mm Mort (French) (3 per Co of 729th
     and 739th Grenadier Rgt; 12 released by
     I Bn, 739th Rgt and assigned instead of
     the withdrawn L Mort; 36 to coast defense)
   - 634 rifles (French)
   - 3 pistols (Russian)
   - 42 SMG (Russian)
   - 81 auto rifles (Russian)
   - 322 rifles (Czech)
   - 1,183 pistols (Polish)
   - 160 pistols (Belgian)
   - 19 L MG (Russian) employed by:
     MT Colm 2   Butcher Co 1

Horse-drawn Colm 4   Division Surv Det 2
Sup Flat 3   Surg Hosp 1
Ord Plat 1   Mtz Amb Plat 1
Baker Co 3   Vet Co 1

APPENDIX B

The Assault Battalion of the Seventh Army

1) Organized in 1943 as an instruction unit for the service school of the Seventh Army.

2) Organization:

Battalion Staff

Staff, Company, consisting of: 1 platoon heavy mortars

1 platoon antitank guns

1 platoon 20-mm antiaircraft gun

1st to 3rd Companies like grenadier companies.

4th Company (heavy)

     consisting of: 2 heavy machine gun platoons.

1 light infantry howitzer platoon

1 infantry engineer platoon

1 light field howitzer battery

Coast Artillery Sector Cotentin

by Generalmajor Gerhard Triepel

In December 1943, the artillery for defense of the Cotentin peninsula was reorganized and new numbers were assigned to regiments, battalions and batteries of the coast artillery.

East coast: The sector from the mouth of the Vire river to Barfleur was under the 1261st Coast Artillery Regiment.

North coast: From Barfleur to Cap de la Hague stood the 1769th Artillery Regiment (Divisional Artillery of the 709th Infantry Division), plus a battalion of Naval Artillery.

West coast: From Cap de la Hague as far as Port Bail—six kilometers south of Carteret— stood the 1262nd Coast Artillery Regiment.

On December 1943, the concrete constructions were not finished except for a few batteries. With increasing energy, we began now to improve batteries and command posts. The telephone network—for which cables had been dug in, two or three meters deep—was extended. By the end of February, troops and headquarters were moving into shelters which were provided for them.

Beginning in April, several batteries—in concrete emplacements on the east coast— were hit with pattern bombing, mainly at night. First to be bombed was the Marcouf naval battery, which had been rebuilt for 21-cm guns. The next objectives were batteries such as the 5th, 1261st Regiment (guns of French origin, caliber 10-cm) emplaced at VI Decosville; the 6th, 1261st Regiment (guns of French origin, caliber 15.5-cm) emplaced at Morsalines; the 7th, 1261st Regiment (guns of French type, caliber 15.5-cm) emplaced at Gatteville; the 9th, 1261st Regiment (guns of French origin, caliber 9-cm) and the 10th, 1261st Regiment (guns of caliber 17-cm), both emplaced at Pernelle; and the 1st, 1261st Regiment (Russian type, caliber 12.2-cm) emplaced at St Martin de Varreville.

Some of these batteries were bombed several times. Losses were only slight. Concrete shelters were made up of ferro-concrete held fast, without exception. Those which had been bombed several times showed cracks. Some of the guns were damaged. The gun positions at Morsalines (6th Battery, 1261st Regiment), at Pernelle (10th Battery, 1261st Regiment), and at St Martin de Varreville (1st Battery, 1261st Regiment) were so badly battered that all these guns had to be brought up to another firing position. Even cables were damaged by bombs, and several days elapsed before the damage was repaired.

In all its sectors, the 1261st Heavy Artillery Regiment was reconnoitering positions which had been built up to strength in improvised fashion and that for the Heavy

Artillery Detachment 456 as well as 457 (equipped each with 12- to 15-cm howitzers, along with one Russian gun battery, 12.2-cm).

Searchlights were installed in all sectors: on the east coast near Foucarville; near Quineville, La Hougue, and near Barfleur; and on the north coast, namely east and west of Cherbourg and near Omonville la Rogue and Cap de la Hague, and on the west coast south of Jobourg, north and south of Flamanville, at Pointe du Rosel and near Carteret. These searchlights were mainly allotted to naval batteries, and to those of which the greater part were intended for defense against targets on the sea.

Batteries were provided with an ample supply of ammunition (about three to four units of fire), and also with emergency rations and water. Several batteries had smoke-producing apparatus to be able to lay a smoke screen, should one be required. For a close-in defense, batteries were provided with small guns as well as machine guns, which were surrounded by barbed wire. A larger number of dummy batteries was available. Near each battery was put up one dummy battery. The one assigned to the 1st Battery was badly damaged by bombs, during the night of Whit Sunday.

The beach was everywhere blocked with obstacles and mines. All fields which had been suitable for the landing of gliders were protected against this threat by trunks which were dug in and partly provided with wire. However, these trunks were mostly too weak and the space between them so large that they failed to achieve their end.

Because of difficulties in supplying ammunition, of which too many kinds had to be manufactured, it was necessary, even after 6 June 1944, to provide various batteries with some other guns. Equipment of telephone and radio, likewise, was deficient to some extent. For instance, radio equipment which was urgently required by the artillery of the 91st Infantry Division did not arrive there until a few days before the invasion took place.

Preliminary Report on the 243rd Infantry Division on the Cotentin Peninsula

by Hauptmann Herbert Schoch

Organisation of the Division

The combat formation of the division consisted of the 920th, 921st and 922rd Grenadier Regiments, the 243rd Artillery Regiment, the 243rd AT Battalion, the 243rd Engineer Battalion, the 243rd Signal Battalion, the 243rd Replacement Training Battalion, and the 243rd Division Combat School. The supply troops consisted of the 243rd Ordnance Platoon, the 243rd Bakery Half-Company, the 243rd Butcher Half-Company, the 243rd Static Army Ration Supply Depot, one horse-drawn column (emergency) the 2/243rd Heavy Truck Column, the 243rd Command Staff of Supply Officer, the 243rd Supply Platoon, and the 243rd Field Post Office. A few officers, noncommissioned officers, and enlisted men of the former 243rd Veterinary Company were assigned to the 920th Grenadier Regiment.

The 922nd and 921st Grenadier Regiments each consisted of three battalions, the 920th Grenadier Regiment of two battalions. The artillery regiment was the 243rd Artillery Regiment and comprised the Staff Battery, two light battalions (three batteries of 76.2-mm guns each), and one heavy battalion (four batteries of 122-mm guns). The engineer battalion consisted of the engineer battalion staff and two companies each of nine rifle squads. The signal battalion consisted of the staff company, one telephone company (mtz), and one radio company (mtz). The AT battalion consisted of the battalion staff, one company on self-propelled mounts, two assault gun companies, and one antiaircraft artillery battery. The replacement training battalion originally consisted of four, and subsequently of five, companies. The division combat school was about a full company strong.

The 243rd Infantry Division was assigned to LXXXIV Corps, Seventh Army, Army Group B.

The division had been prepared for the invasion by means of many exercises, advanced combat practice firing in the countryside and at the coast, day and night alerts, and march exercises, as well as by means of the thorough military and political training of the soldiers. Four hours' time were required to alert the division. The division reserve consisted of the replacement training battalion, a few coast defence units, and the personnel of the division combat school.

At the beginning of the invasion, the division had been stationed in the area Cap de la Hague–Portbail. About half of its units were right on the coast, and the remainder three to four kilometers inland on the nearest heights. The units on the coast were to prevent a landing from the sea, and those on the heights a landing from the air.

By the middle of April, when the division arrived in this sector, the coastal fortifications consisted only of pockets of resistance, mostly occupied by Eastern battalions. These pockets of resistance were on an average at a distance of four kilometers from each other. Their equipment consisted mostly of captured arms. In each pocket of resistance there were two light machine guns, one heavy machine gun, one medium mortar, and one 75-mm field gun or 47-mm Pak. In important areas, two to three pockets of resistance were combined. They were generally from 300 to 500 meters inland from the beach and surrounded by a simple barricade of wire. Only the combined pockets of resistance were close to the beach. They had at first been camouflaged, but after two years the camouflage had worn out. Along the beach, minefields had been laid in a belt about 16 meters wide. In places, this belt had been reinforced.

The following officers were in command:

Division Commander:	Generalleutnant Hellmich
920th Grenadier Regiment:	Oberst Klosterkemper
921st Grenadier Regiment:	Oberstleutnant Simon
922d Grenadier Regiment:	Oberstleutnant Müller
Artillery Regiment:	Oberst Hellwig

Tactical Organization and Preparation
for Combat at the Beginning of the Invasion

The 243rd Infantry Division, originally transferred to France as static division, had been retrained as a partly motorized and tactical reserve division by order of Generalmajor von Witzleben (the first commander of the division) and Generalleutnant Hellmich, with the concurrence of Corps.

At the beginning of the invasion, the partial motorization had not been altogether completed. However, officers, noncommissioned officers, and enlisted men had received thorough training, so that there was a good standard of preparedness, combined with high spirits and sound morale. The armament (including new arms such as the Model 42 machine gun and the recoilless antitank grenade launcher) was normal. The 920th Grenadier Regiment was an infantry regiment and horse-drawn. The 921st Grenadier Regiment, with 1st and 3rd Battalions, had been reorganized since January 1944 as a bicycle regiment, whereas the 2nd Battalion was on foot and had been assigned to coast defense. The 922nd Grenadier Regiment, organized like the 921st Grenadier Regiment, had been reorganized into a bicycle regiment late in Spring. What has been said about the Grenadier regiments also applies to the other units of the division.

In addition, antitank obstacles in the shape of stakes with explosive charges attached to them had been set up. It had been intended to increase the depth of the minefield, but this had not been done.

Shortly after the arrival of the division, an uninterrupted system of positions with frontal cover for heavy and light infantry weapons had been erected. The positions were on the edge of the beach, and covered one another with flanking fire. Their garrisons partly lived in the positions, and partly near them, in tents and wooden shelters. One company occupied a sector of from four to six kilometers, with planned supporting fire by the artillery. The artillery had mapped barrage fire zones in front of the MLR. The division had also just begun to develop the advance combat area and to place pole obstacles in the areas exposed to air landing attacks, but when the invasion began this had not yet been fully carried out.

The officers had been made acquainted with the terrain of the Cotentin peninsula by a large number of tactical rides and field exercises. The GHQ coast artillery batteries Nos 1051, 1052, 1053 had been instructed to cooperate with the division.

In addition, there were stationed on the Cotentin peninsula the 91st Infantry Division in the area Carentan–Ste Mère-Église, and the 709th Infantry Division on the east coast of the Cotentin peninsula adjacent to the north of the 91st Infantry Division. The command post of the 243rd Infantry Division was, at the beginning of the invasion, at Château Malesay near Briquebec, and the command post of the 921st Grenadier Regiment at Les Meanil, 3 kilometers southeast of Barneville. The location of the command posts of the other units is no longer remembered.

History of the 21st Panzer Division from the Time of Its Formation until the Beginning of the Invasion

by Generalleutnant Edgar Feuchtinger

I. Formation and Training

The formation of the 21st Panzer Division could not be compared to that of any other Heeres Panzer Division. Its foundations were batteries they had built themselves from self-propelled gun carriages belonging to the 227th Artillery Regiment. These were made after the Western Europe campaign, 1940–41, from captured British and French armored tractors and German 105-mm guns. These guns were particularly successful in battles in the Waldrow area, and south of Lake Ladoza, and their rate of fire compared very favorably with that of the German assault guns.

As a result of these successes, the order was given in the Summer of 1942 to build two artillery groups in German workshops near Paris. On 1 October 1942 the Armored Artillery Brigade (self-propelled gun carriages) was formed from these groups. It consisted of two armored artillery regiments, each of which had six batteries of six guns each, five batteries having Heavy Field Howitzers 13 (150-mm) and one battery light field howitzers (105-mm), and one assault gun battalion which had four batteries of ten guns each, six of which had 105-mm barrels and four of which had 75-mm barrels (Antitank Gun 42). The two artillery regiments had French Lorraine tractors for the gun carriages; the assault gun battalion had Hotchkiss tanks. All gun carriages were armor-plated with steel from the German steel mills at Krefeld and Hanover, the work being carried out in their own plants. The tanks having gone rusty as they had been left out in the open for two years, they had to be dismantled and cleaned completely, and generally the parts of two or three tanks were required to build one new tank of as good as new quality.

Special vehicles for the communication and ammunition units, baggage trains, convoys and workshops, and ordinary transport trucks, were made in similar ways. The distribution and number of vehicles corresponded on the whole with the composition of the German assault gun batteries or assault gun staffs.

The commanders and battery commanders were good, but the junior officers, NCOs, and enlisted men were not so suitable. The NCOs and EMs were taken from static batteries on the coast and on the Atlantic islands. They were too old, and useless for an armored command. This Armored Artillery Brigade had originally been formed

114

so that it could be used in the center of gravity of a Panzer army in order to provide the tanks with a little more artillery protection, as the tractor-drawn artillery could not as a rule follow right behind advancing tanks, due to difficulties presented by the terrain. In difficult terrain it had often been observed that, at the crucial moment, the tanks had to go into battle without the necessary artillery protection. This resulted in heavy losses, and the success of the action was often jeopardized, if not forfeited altogether. Even when they had succeeded in more or less keeping up with the tanks, it was a frequent occurrence for tractor-drawn artillery pieces to fail to be ready right at the start of the engagement to direct effective fire on targets which quickly appear in tank battles.

The Armored Artillery Brigade could not be put to the use for which it had been created, as the 1st, 6th, 7th, and 10th Panzer Divisions, which were in the West in late Fall 1942, were called to the East and to Tunis, respectively, by strategic events on these other fronts. Thus the brigade received orders with its regiments to fake new Panzer divisions, and was spread over Normandy and Brittany for this purpose. When southern France and Toulon were occupied, large parts of the brigade were able to put the road capacity and powers of endurance of their vehicles to the test. The distances of several hundred kilometers were covered in a few days, more or less without incident.

In the Winter of 1942, one regiment was taken from the brigade, which, being a motorized artillery regiment, became a Heeres-Artillerie regiment. The self-propelled gun carriages of this regiment were handed over as mobile reserves to twelve static divisions that were employed on the coast. In the beginning, the brigade was responsible for the maintenance and the initial training of these batteries. In March 1943, the brigade was converted into the "Schnelle Brigade West" in place of the missing artillery regiment. For this purpose it received an additional Panzer Grenadier regiment, a reconnaissance battalion two companies strong, a reinforced engineer company, a reinforced signal and radio company, a company of medics, and two supply and replacement companies. To organize Panzer battalions, orders were given for those remaining captured French Hotchkiss or Somua tanks not already transformed into static defenses or shipped to the East to be collected laboriously from all over France. Thus a Panzer division of average mobility arose from wreckage and old iron.

Due to several weapons invented by the division itself, and a corresponding complement of vehicles, the division in the end had the most heavy weapons of any one division in the Army, and, corresponding with a chart for the formation of Panzer divisions published by the Organization Branch of the Army, was the only division to have its own organization besides the "Grossdeutschland." Even at the time of the invasion, the formation of the division had naturally not yet been completed. Particularly the Panzer regiment had been treated rather badly, as it was only able to exchange its antiquated Hotchkiss and Somua tanks for German Mark IV tanks a few weeks before the invasion. The division was not equipped with Mark V tanks (Panthers). At the start of the invasion the 1st Battalion had eighteen tanks per company and the 2nd only twelve tanks per company.

The division, which had thus been formed very slowly and regrouped often, suffered considerably where its training was concerned.

The original allocation of NCOs and men to the division was similar to the formation of the brigade. The first elements came from surplus personnel from other divisions. Obviously the replacements were not always satisfactory in those circumstances. Only in the course of many months did the division succeed in obtaining better personnel through the replacement and training unit of its Ersatzwehrkreis VI (area of Günster) and getting rid of part of the unsuitable matériel. The order calling for the formation of the division stated that all members of the former 21st Africa Armored Division now in Germany were to be transferred to the division. In this way the division got a small but good cadre of experienced veterans (about 2,000 men). Naturally these men, many of whom only joined the division at a late date, were no full compensation. If, despite all this, a bearable standard of training had been reached by the time the invasion started, it is only thanks to the willingness of the division, its good spirit, the fairly good officers and there in particular the commanders. Particular credit for the standard of training has to be given to General der Panzertruppen Frhr Geyr von Schweppenburg, to whom the responsibility for the division's training had been transferred.

A great disadvantage, which affected all divisions in the West that were not classified as static, was a continuous change in the station. Another disadvantage was that the division was twice stationed in Brittany, where Panzer unit training was as good as impossible owing to the unfavorable terrain.

In the eleven months from July 1943 to the invasion, the division was stationed in the following places:

1. Area around Paris.
2. Area around Rennes
3. Area around Orléans.
4. Area around Paris and Le Havre.
5. Transfer to Austria (consisting of journey there and back by railroad).
6. Area around Rennes.
7. Area around Caen.

Hand in hand with this training period, which was continually being interrupted, went the preparations for the expected enemy landing. This was not only bad for the staffs of units, but also for the troops themselves, as they had more and more to do with work on defensive measures, such as the consolidation of field fortifications and the erecting of "Rommelspargeln" (upright poles with sharpened pointed ends knocked into the ground at short intervals to impede airborne landings) and so forth. In the last weeks before the invasion, when the division was in the Caen area, one-third of the division had been built into the coastal defense fortification system and had been subordinated in the tactical aspect to the static infantry divisions.

II. Preparations

1. Reflections on concentrations

The 21st Panzer Division knew that, due to its composition of vehicles, it would be far more likely to be committed in the West than in the East. Despite this, the creation of spare parts depots and a particularly well-equipped and far-seeing spare parts echelon opened possibilities for all sorts of employment.

In March 1944, the division was transferred to Hungary, but this transfer was rescinded when the division had gone half way, and it was turned round and started on the return trip. This transfer had temporarily taken the mind of the divisional staff off its particular suitability for commitment in the West.

During the long wait in the West, the leaders of the division had given serious consideration to the problem of the best employment of a Panzer division in case of invasion. Apart from that, as already mentioned, it had suffered a lot from the continuous change in the strategic intentions of its superiors due to the frequent changes of station.

To its superiors, the staff of the division always represented the viewpoint that a Panzer division should not be standing in readiness near the coast. Such a disposition would, however, be justified if it had been ascertained that the invasion would take place in this locality. In that case, however, the division would have to be as near to the coast as was possible, if they were at the same time to be just outside the area which would be subject to pattern bombing on coastal defenses. Under certain circumstances, such a concentration of tanks could even have changed the invasion plan, as was proved by the 21st Panzer Division on the occasion of trying out their special weapons on 1 June 1944. Tracks of armored vehicles seen going towards the coast near Lion-sur-Mer (aerial photographs) caused the Allied High Command to assume that armored reserves had been put ready just at that point, and resulted in talks concerning a possible shifting of the sector to be attacked. The CG of the division heard this from the G-2 of the Canadian Army in the course of talks about the history of the war in POW Camp II in England.

Assembling in readiness any farther away would necessitate a longer march to reach the enemy once he had landed, but that had to be put up with. The staff of the division stressed that, under all circumstances, it should have the possibility of attacking the enemy, once landed, in his weakest spot with its full assembled weight, regardless of any strategic considerations which would be a matter for the higher command.

There were, however, two prerequisites to hitting the enemy with the full weight:

a.   Terrain favorable for tanks.

b.   That the division would not be kept in readiness for any tactical purposes.

Not in readiness for defensive purposes means to put the division in readiness in such a way that at the time of an enemy landing, or in case of any tactical parachute landings, no parts of the division would immediately be involved in the fighting.

This view, held by the divisional staff, was supported by its immediate superior, Frhr Geyr von Schweppenburg, and defended by him before higher superiors. The divisional staff itself spared no pains to fight for its views before its highest superiors, both before the Supreme Commander West and before Feldmarschall Rommel, who appears to have been the actual exponent of holding Panzer divisions in readiness for tactical purposes. He was determined that the would-be invading enemy should not set as much as one foot on land, and feared the air superiority of the enemy when moving up the Panzer divisions. As the landings were, however, not to be expected along the entire Western front in any case, the mass of the Panzer divisions would naturally have to be moved up a considerable distance in any event, and, by tactical employment at the wrong point, farther still. However, the division which was directly affected by the landing would lose its concentrated striking power by being at readiness in small groups and by a similar tactical commitment. That is what happened to the 21st Panzer Division on invasion day.

Areas in which the elements of the 21st Panzer Division were at readiness at the time of the invasion: After its return from Hungary, the Division had been at readiness in the Rennes area. From 1 May 1944 on, it was at readiness in the Caen area.

Billeting areas:

II Bn, 125th Panzer Gren Regt: northeast of Caen, east of the Orne;

II Bn, 192nd Panzer Gren Regt, 1st Co 155th Panzer Art Bn, 200th Panzer Jäger Bn: north of Caen, west of the Orne;

305 Army AAA Bn: in position north of Caen;

125th Panzer Gren Regt with 9th and 10th Co, IV [sic], 200 Assault Gun Bn: Vimont–Cagny area, southeast of Caen;

I Bn, 125th Panzer Gren Regt: Vieux–Fume–St Sylvain area;

22nd Panzer Regt: Falaise area;

I Bn, 192nd Panzer Gren Regt: area around Carpiquet–Fontaine–Etoupefour, west of Caen;

Staff of 192nd Panzer Gren Regt, with 9th and 10th Cos: Thury–Harcourt area;

2nd Bn of 155th Panzer Art Regt: St André–Fontenay area, south of Caen;

III Bn, 155th Panzer Art Regt: Beurgueous–St Aighan area, south of Caen;

220 Panzer Engr Bn: St Rémy–Clicy area;

200 Assault Gun Bn: Falaise–Conde area;

21 Recon Bn: area north of Conde;

Division reinforcement troops: Argentan area;

Administrative troops: Falaise area;

Divisional staff with Signal Bn: St Pierre area

2. Organization in Case of Commitment

In preparing for the invasion, it was the division's mission:

    a.   To determine which roads were to be used to reach the area of commitment; and

b. To reconnoiter the area of commitment (terrain and roads of approach) for the individual cases of commitment in the Channel coast area and the Netherlands, Abbeville, Le Havre, Caen, Cherbourg, Brittany (St Malo, Brest), Nantes, and Bordeaux.

In preparing for the invasion, the greatest attention was to be paid to Le Havre, Caen, Cherbourg, and Brittany.

Preparation of the troops for these cases was made with attention mainly to these points:

a. That the troops were alarmed with the greatest possible dispatch;

b. That the readiness of the troops to march would be in echelon, so that some units could achieve top speed readiness at the cost of others;

c. That the troops could easily be moved into the roads of approach in the various directions by fixing time, roads and point of departure;

d. Composition of the march groups; and

e. Allocation of replacement depots for individual cases.

Concerning the last point—that is, which replacement depot was responsible for whom—the division had, without success, suggested to the respective quartermasters that they split up the few large depots, so that they could be brought nearer to the front and built up in the depth of the coast. At the time of the invasion, this would have shortened the distance which the supply columns had to travel, and, in the main, would have eliminated the danger from the air both for the depots and for the troops moving the supplies. This suggestion was turned down with the comment that it would be impossible to carry it out, as there were allegedly not enough forces to guard them. There was great fear of the activities of the French Resistance movement in case of invasion.

After only a few days of fighting at the beginning of the invasion, the division's supply columns already had to cover long distances. Roughly a week after the invasion began, the artillery ammunition had to be picked up from near Rennes in Brittany, and ten days after that it came from as far afield as the Soissons area, east of Paris. Gasoline replacement lines encountered similar difficulties. Gasoline dumps near the front were as good as non-existent. Shortly after the start of the invasion, the large gasoline dump near Paris, containing the largest part of the gasoline destined for the Western front, was bombed from the air and burnt out within a few minutes. Later on, gasoline had to be picked up from the supply trains at the railroad, which in turn also suffered heavily from air attacks. The situation concerning infantry ammunition replacements was somewhat more favorable, but all types of special ammunition were difficult. Supplies of food came up without any trouble.

3. Training

In preparation for an invasion, these points were particularly stressed in the training program:

1. Individual training:

Good shooting with all weapons, particularly tanks, including antitank weapons;

Special training for riflemen;

Camouflage, cover, use of entrenching tools;

Training courses in small units;

Technicians' courses;

Driving courses (including tank driving). Over 50% of the men needed as drivers had had no training in driving.

2. Training in units:

Night fighting in unit strength, motorized marches with enemy air superiority:

    a. Marching in the dark;

    b. Marching and keeping large distances apart;

    c. Regulating traffic (employing MP detachments and trained officers and NCOs drawn from the combat troops).

Attacking with air support, cooperation with the Luftwaffe (including radio communications);

Artillery shooting in cooperation with liaison planes;

Both attack and defense, with the imaginary enemy, using British tactics;

Crossing mined terrain;

Special-unit training for individual weapons, special demonstrations of all branches, including engineers, antitank guns, signal troops and so forth;

Combined weapons training, firing tactics;

Cooperation of tanks, assault guns, Panzer grenadiers and artillery;

Trial and training shoots with the weapons designed and built by the division (multiple-barreled rocket projectors and single rocket projectors).

Just as the many moves of the division, and its constant employment on building projects, were detrimental to the training of the division, so it was a great disadvantage that the troops, or at least the combat elements, constantly had to be ready for action. In some periods the Supreme Commander West ordered some alarm stage every day. This mistake was never rectified, despite the numerous times that the division informed higher headquarters that the continuous sounding of some high alarm stage not only dulled the troops in that direction, but also considerably disturbed their training. Whenever the weather was anywhere near favorable for an invasion, a high alarm stage was ordered. Concerning that, the division considered that the alarm system should in any case be such that it could function at all times, and that sentries should pay full attention to their duty as a matter of course, so that no increase of readiness should be necessary.

The German High Command's lack of understanding for the need of good, solid, basic training was a mistake which it made throughout the war and which showed in all theaters of war. The organization of a bunch of recruits into a unit was sufficient for the High Command immediately to throw them into battle. No consideration was given to training and the consequent welding of one unit as such, which is so necessary in battle.

Another great difficulty in the training of the 21st, as in many other divisions, was that 15% of the replacements were so-called "Volksdeutschen" (German nationals from abroad), many of whom did not even have a proper control of the German language. Their sentiments varied. For many of them elementary school classes in German had to be started. Some of them were enthusiastic soldiers and helped to master the difficulties they brought with them themselves. A smaller number were very disturbing to the soldierly spirit. Their uncooperative attitude, often springing more from personal worries than from individual nationalism, was understood by their superiors, and they were assigned specially qualified personnel officers. But neither they nor the staff of the division, nor any higher authorities, ever succeeded in getting at the roots of their troubles. These were that in many cases the dependants of these "Volksdeutschen" had had their livelihood or their property taken away by the political authorities, or else had been deported or imprisoned by them. The military, right up to the OKH, was powerless to do anything about it.

Despite all its troubles, the standard of training of the 21st Panzer Division was sufficiently high at the time of the invasion.

The 352nd Infantry Division

by Oberstleutnant Fritz Ziegelmann

A. Initial organization of the
352nd Infantry Division in the St Lô Area

After the defeats suffered up to October 1943 on the southern sector of the Russian front, a reorganization of infantry divisions was ordered by the Army High Command in France and Belgium after 1 December 1943. As Senior General Staff Officer, I had to report on 5 December 1943 in St Lô to the staff of the 352nd Infantry Division, which was about to be newly organized.

About 5 December 1943, that part of the 321st Infantry Division which was to be rested arrived from the East in that area of St Lô where the reorganization was to take place. Among others there were the divisional staff, grenadier regiment staffs, artillery regiment staff, personnel for one grenadier battalion, personnel artillery battalion, elements of a communication detachment, and units of the service of supply. The organization of the division was to be completed by 31 January 1944, according to the Order of Battle of a Type 44 division.

Definite orders were not available for later commitment after the organization of the 352nd Infantry Division had been finished. It was generally felt that, from 3 January 1944 on, a commitment in the East was to be counted upon. The training of the 352nd Infantry Division was carried out according to Eastern combat principles.

The organization itself proceeded very slowly, especially in equipment. Since I had been Quartermaster of Army High Command 7 from October 1942 until November 1943, and was acquainted with the organization questions of this period, the slowness of reorganizing the 352nd Infantry Division was obvious to me. Conversations with various superior authorities I knew led to no positive result. The chief reasons for this were the lack of matériel—beginning in the year 1944—and the labor shortage in Germany. (The effect of the bombing raids was becoming stronger.) This was a strong check upon the training program of the 352nd Infantry Division.

Thus it was possible, for example, to begin with the artillery training only at the end of February 1944, since the delivery of sighting devices and harness pieces was not possible before the middle of February. Until the beginning of March, each soldier had been able to throw only two hand grenades and shoot during three rifle and machine-gun exercises. The training of relief drivers had not been possible until 1 May 1944 because of the fuel situation. There were also personnel difficulties during the training

122

period. The 14th companies of the grenadier regiments were only set up in February 1944—the first time as "Panzerschreck" (bazooka) companies. Replacements consisted chiefly of young people (class of 1925/26). Almost all these people, being physically of limited capacity as a result of the shortage of food in Germany, were fit only for limited military duties. Marches over 15 kilometers led to high casualties. A proposal of the division to grant these people a milk allowance was ignored. The purchase of milk from the country, in which the French peasantry was very helpful, succeeded in correcting the dietary deficiency of these young people.

The officers corps was composed of 50% of inexperienced officers. 30% of the noncommissioned officer posts were vacant on 1 March 1944, because of the lack of competent noncommissioned officers. The total strength of an infantry division Type 44 amounted to around 12,000 men, which included around 1,500 Hiwis (Russian voluntary labor).

During the initial period of organization, the division received the order from 1 January 1944 on, in case of alarm (employment in Holland, Belgium and France), to keep ready a combat team (one grenadier regiment, one artillery battalion, one engineer battalion, elements of a signal battalion, supply troops, and the operations staff of the division).

The commitment of this force was mobilized and was practicable at twelve hours' notice (by foot and rail). From 1 March 1944, the same measures were made available for the whole division, practicable at eighteen hours' notice.

To sum up, it can be said that the 352nd Infantry Division was at full strength and fully equipped by 1 March 1944, but the training in the three months of organization was, however, because of the slow supply of men, ammunition and weapons, only carried out properly during the last month. It had so far progressed on 1 March 1944 that company and battery training could be considered satisfactory, if not judged too harshly. Formation training (battalion, regiment), however, did not take place. The monthly reports of the division on this matter were not heeded by the OKH.

As a general staff officer, I had the impression that it was only of importance to the High Command Headquarters to announce as soon as possible that another division had been re-formed and was at their disposal. Whether the division was able to accomplish its missions through having had the necessary training under modern conditions was not of interest. How tasks were to be accomplished was entirely the business of the division's command. This mistake led very often to the destruction of a division during its first days of fighting.

B. Commitment of the 352nd Infantry Division in the Coast Defense Sector of Bayeux

Because of the inspection tour of Fieldmarshal Rommel, the new Army Group B began its activity in January 1944; therefore, the 352nd Infantry Division was ordered early in March to commit, as an artillery reinforcement, its 1352nd Artillery Regiment on the coastal front in the area west of Bayeux.

The artillery regiment served tactically under the 716th Infantry Division. However, in matters of training they were still subordinated to the 352nd Infantry Division. On 15 March 1944, Headquarters LXXXIV Army Corps ordered the 352nd Infantry Division to take over the coast defense sector at Bayeux from the 716th Infantry Division. The orders for other tactical employment for the 352nd Infantry Division stayed in force; unit training was to continue.

The 352nd Infantry Division had the following missions:

1. Defense of the coast defense sector of Bayeux;
2. Improvement of the battle sector;
3. Training of the unit for battle.

To fulfill all tasks satisfactorily was for the newly-formed division not easy. It had believed, until then, it was to be employed in the East. It had been possible to improve manpower conditions in the division, in particular with regard to the young people, but an abatement of working energy was soon noticeable. On an average, the soldiers worked nine hours daily, with additional three hours daily for instruction.

In detail, the following picture of the 352nd Infantry Division becomes discernible:

1. Defense of the coast defense sector of Bayeux

The strength employed in the Bayeux sector (reinforced 726th Grenadier Regiment without II/726th Grenadier Regiment) was taken over. The former battalion sectors became regimental sectors, whereby the hitherto employed battalions of the reinforced 726th Grenadier Regiment retained their former mission, i.e. occupation of the battle installations on the coast (MLR) and the formation of small attack reserves. Two regimental staffs of the 352nd Infantry Division took over one battalion (now regiment) sector each, and the regiment on the middle sector relinquished one battalion (916th) as reserve to the right regiment sector. A reinforced grenadier regiment of the 352nd Infantry Division (the 916th Grenadier Regiment and 352nd Fusilier Battalion, and—from 20 May 1944—the 915th Grenadier Regiment and the 352nd Fusilier Battalion) was corps reserve.

Through a very exact terrain study, and influenced by combat experiences in Sicily and Italy, and by the detailed map exercises and conferences of the Commanding General of LXXXIV Army Corps, General of the Artillery Marcks, we decided on our plan of organization. It became gradually clearer that an invasion might occur which in particular would concern the sectors of the 352nd Infantry Division that summer. We were supported therein by information in the German press about Russian's demands for an active, decisive participation of the Western Powers in the war. This view was supported by the strict censorship ordered in England, the curbing of diplomatic privileges, and of resistance to enemy landing craft on the south coast of England—according to a report of the German Wehrmacht—and by the cancellation of all furloughs for all commanding and general staff officers from March on. Careful attention to the tides also indicated that the highest command reckoned with an invasion soon. From a conversation my division commander had in May with Field Marshal Rommel—whom he knew very well—he seemed to expect the beginning of the invasion in early August. Rommel himself was on leave on 6 June 1944.

The distribution of our own forces was definitely determined by the possibility of the enemy—by isolating the Cotentin peninsula—coming into possession of the spacious Cherbourg harbor and, with additional forces from the captured bridgehead, of undertaking the push for Paris, the main junction of communications in France—of beginning the push to the south and south-east. In the sector of the 352nd Infantry Division, the main thing was to reinforce the left wing (Vire mouth, southeastward of the Cotentin) and to strengthen with reserves the danger points of the landing sectors (sectors by St Landeul and Arromanches). The Corps reserve, kept mobile on the right division wing (sector south of Bayeux), was, therefore, in a position of readiness because it had to reckon with the withdrawal of the assault reserve of the 21st Panzer Division lying to the east.

The grouping of the reserves was a hobby of Field Marshal Rommel. It was his opinion that he could destroy the enemy with an attack in front of the MLR—consequently, in the water. All heavy weapons of the infantry were incorporated in the defensive installations, or had joined new combat installations (field strength). On the occasion of his visit in May, I was reproached because I did not bring the reserves (rifle company without heavy weapons) close enough to the coast. He wished every soldier to be able to concentrate his fire on the water. My query, that the width of the division sector (53 kilometers) and the weakness of our rearward constructions made possible to this enemy an infiltration through the less heavily occupied sections, and that, to counter this, assault reserves were necessary behind the lines, remained unanswered. I saw clearly that, in an attack, our positions on the beach (MLR) and the rearward main combat area would come under the heavy fire of naval artillery and the effect of the enemy air forces.

A release of the assault reserves for counterassaults was impossible under these conditions during the daylight hours.

My Chief of the Division agreed with me: the Commanding General also had the opinion that we must find a compromise solution. Therefore, these reserves (rifle companies) were ordered nearer to the MLR so that some of them could concentrate their fire off the shore, and a counterattack would still be possible with the remainder in depth.

In May a mission again made necessary exact terrain reconnaissance and emplacement work. Hitler gave orders to hold each foxhole to the last man and last cartridge. An abandonment of the battle area during engagement was thus impossible. In the division battle area were:

Points of resistance (one squad/group);

Strongpoints (platoon to company);

Organic groups of strongpoints (1–2 companies).

Could, for instance, the crew of a pocket of resistance abandon their battle positions to help a neighbor, and would a recognized and bombarded battery (strongpoint) be allowed to take up a new firing position? No solution was offered by the higher commands. An innovation was introduced by the Rommel order declaring the battle sector—the divisional sector—a fortress area. There was a sea front (former MLR on the beach) and a land front (10–15 kilometers to the rear, parallel to the sea front) in the 352nd Infantry Division sector fronting south. In this fortress area (length of the MLR, 100 kilometers) were to be quartered the entire troops of the division, as well as the supply troops. Besides their problem of supplies, the latter were to defend the land front, where an attack by air-landed troops had to be reckoned with. It turned out that this could not be done because the supply troops had their quarters further south (the supply areas of the army lay far to the rear). Taking into consideration that the 352nd Infantry Division only had disposal of one issue of ammunition (with the exception of the permanent installations) because of their special duties, the above measures could only be described as insufficiently thought out.

To cope with local unrest and to arrest bailed-out air crews, "hunting patrols" on bicycles or motorcycles were organized in each regimental sector. Through their employment, a small number of air crews were handed over to the interrogation service of the Air Force in Caen.

2. Improvement of the Battle Area

The improvement of the coast defense sector of Bayeux on 20 March 1944 was to be counted as "below average." With the appearance of Field Marshal Rommel, there arose in these territories an activity which gave work to many "local administrative offices." Often ordered in haste, a lack of experience and matériel often developed, but improvement during this period really took place and rendered the invasion more difficult.

(a) *Installation of obstacles in the coastal outpost area (steep and shallow coastline).* It depended first of all on barricading the danger areas. Assuming that enemy landings would only take place at high tide, obstacles of all kinds were erected upon the interior beach, so that their upper parts projected. "Tschechen" hedgehog defenses, pile-driven stakes of metal, and concrete as well as wooden trestles were set up here and partly charged with deep water or surface mines and HE.

It turned out that in the course of time these obstacles filled up with tidal sand and had to be dug out again. During the storms in April, the mass of these obstacles were torn out and the mines exploded. It was necessary to begin again. Considering that the wood had to be cut in the "Forêt de Cerisy" after permission had been granted, that it had to be carried at least 30 kilometers in horsedrawn vehicles (lack of fuel), had to be logged by circular saw (limited supply) and rammed by hand (which took a long time), and was particularly difficult on account of the rocky foreground of the "Grandcamp," results were still surprisingly good.

In the second half of May, the possibility of a landing at low water was discussed. The construction of obstacles to the seaward of the former coastal obstacles was begun. But it was impossible to build these obstacles in proper depth. In this chapter belongs also the blocking of the steep coast by Longues and St Pierre du Mont. We reckoned in these sectors with the employment of enemy commandos who could climb up the steep cliffs with their special equipment. On both steep gradients, old 24-cm shells were embedded by the engineer battalion which, after touching a trip wire, came rolling down and, with an effective splinter range of 600 meters, exploded over the water. Every 100 meters there was placed, on the steep gradients, one roller grenade by 1 June. A final innovation was the employment of "Goliathen tanks" ("Goliaths") a remote-controlled small tank with explosive action. These weapons arrived only on 5 June and were not used.

b. *Completion of the permanent battle installations (concrete) and installations built by the troops* With the completion of permanent battle installations, it became evident that Rommel's authority was not enough. The decisive factor was the cement supply. This came in four different ways: Air Force workers, Navy, OT, and fortress engineers worked side by side, often overlapping. It showed again that over-organization may become a menace. Analysis (July 1944) showed that, of the battle installations in the division sector:

15% were bomb-resistant

45% were splinter-proof

Almost half of the battle installations were outmoded and, at most, improvised reinforcement.

A faulty distribution of building material was the order of the day. It happened in the division sector, for instance, that the Air Force built a section in concrete, while the infantry with their heavy weapons were in poor earth emplacements (flooding). With the invasion, the concrete shelters were of no use to the Air Force and the ground holes were no longer occupied by soldiers.

c. *Improvement of the mine belt along the coast and the flooding of certain area.* The mines, laid two years previously, could no longer be claimed to be detonatable. A new allotment of T mines (effective against tanks) did not arrive. Up until 1 July we laid about 10,000 S mines (effective against men). For the plans of the Field Marshal to become practicable, the installation of a mine belt 5 kilometers deep would be needed, consisting of 10,000,000 mines (100 meters – 150 mines) for the divisional sector (about 50 kilometers wide).

The general situation did not allow the realization of these plans for even one divisional sector in the "Atlantic Wall."

As an improvisation in the "fortress sector" (seaward front—land front), the flooding of some districts by damming up streams was considered. These measures were accomplished by the engineers with as much consideration as possible for farming (cattle-breeding, fats). But, as real obstacles, they lost their effectiveness during the warm days of May.

The preparations for blasting the bridges were delegated to the regimental commanders. After the training of the infantry by the engineer battalion, the objectives were determined, explosive material prepared, and the responsibility for action settled in writing.

d. *Installation of obstacles against air landings.* It was important to deny parachute troops and troop-carrying gliders open spaces in the "fortress area," and in the south this applied primarily to the area round Bayeux. As a second center of gravity, the Vire estuary was considered, and, as a third center of gravity, the sector south of the landward front. The first mission was fulfilled by the division, the other missions only to some extent. The fixing of wire between 2 meter long piles dug into the ground was left mostly uncompleted for lack of wire.

e. *Construction of the land front.* For the improvement of the landward front, the population was called up. This was, however, undertaken by an inadequate number of men because of other important work done in the name of the German Military Government. The unit was obliged to do this work itself. The former second-line positions (fronting upon the coast) were filled up, and new works built fronting vice versa.

3. Training of the Troops for Fighting

The time to train the troops for battle was short, and was on an average about three hours daily. Individual training was pushed ahead, as was firing practice in sharpshooting at sea targets, and instructions in unit training (counter-attack).

In taking over the sector, we were surprised that the reinforced 726th Grenadier Regiment was very backward in training, because of the continuous surrender of troops to new formations, and a lack of initiative in the officers and NCOs in training the remainder. In addition, the corps of NCOs was composed of elements which hoped to survive the war without having been under fire, whereby the trustworthiness of troops for the East was very doubtful.

The lack of equipment for practice and drill made itself felt; by way of example, the monthly allotment for the fourteen new companies was five rounds of "Panzeschreck" once a month for sharpshooting. In consequence of constant lack of fuel, the training of the drivers could not be essentially improved. The trucks (named Otrag), which were supposed to transport the corps reserve (reinforced 915th Grenadier Regiment), were in bad shape because the French drivers were lazy and matériel for repairs was lacking.

Impressed by the planning conferences of the Commanding General, I held a map exercise with all the adjutants and special missions staff officers, where the situation corresponded with the facts of 6 June 1944. Also, the officers were suitably instructed. I must mention the practical training of the corps reserve (reinforced 915th Grenadier Regiment), which practiced the counterattack from the Seulles flatland on Crépon.

To sum up, it can be said that:

a. Apart from a series of small questions, which remain obscure, the tactical organization of the 352nd Infantry Division was prepared for an enemy attack.

b. In the short time, the improvement of the battle area had made progress in spite of many difficulties, but could not be considered "good."

c. The training of the troops was continued, but not completed.

Generaloberst Alfred Jodl.

Generalfeldmarschall Wilhelm Keitel, pictured here with Hitler and the visiting Turkish chief of staff, 7 December 1943.

Generalfeldmarschall von Rundstedt (foreground) in conversation with General Lohr.

Generalfeldmarschall Erwin Rommel.

Generalleutnant Karl Wilhelm von Schlieben.

Above: 'Dragon's teeth' tank obstacles. Large numbers of these obstacles were planned for the Atlantic Wall, but shortages of concrete and time led to other types of obstacles being substituted.

Below: Steel obstacles along the Atlantic Wall. By 1944, shortages again led to wooden obstacles, topped with land mines, being used instead.

Right: A tower incorporated into the defenses of the Atlantic Wall. The Wall made use of existing fortifications whenever possible, as here in this wartime propaganda photograph.

Above: Less picturesque, but militarily more significant, was this nineteenth-century fort, part of Cherbourg's defenses.

Below: A German wartime painting of a 240mm coast gun in what may be Battery Hamburg, near Cherbourg. The only other such weapons were deployed at Le Havre.

Right, upper: Battery Hamburg, near Cherbourg, after its capture.

Right, lower: Atlantic Wall defenses near Cherbourg.

Left: A German *Goulashkanone*, or field-cooker. The German static divisions in Normandy were especially short of this vital piece of equipment and could not be fed once they were forced out of their original coastal positions.

Above: The Allied bombing campaign against French transportation in the months before and after D-Day presented the Germans with an insoluble problem with regard to both operational mobility and logistics. Attacks were first concentrated against rail yards, but attacks on bridges often proved more effective.

Below: German defenders employing a captured French 75mm gun. This gun, modified for use against tanks, is well camouflaged: a skill for concealment helped counter superior Allied firepower.

Above: German telephonists at work. Despite Allied bombing and attacks by the French Resistance, the Germans retained excellent communications on the ground.

Below: A German wartime sketch of an artillery observer team in action. German tactics on D-Day relied on such observers being able to concentrate firepower—both from coastal guns and batteries inland—against the beachheads. Their failure to do this helped doom German attempts to resist the invasion.

Above: A German sketch of an 88mm gun in direct fire mode.

Below: A camouflaged coast defense artillery emplacement.

Above: German artillery and infantry weapons in Normandy showed little standardization and included a broad range of German and captured equipment, for which resupply was often impossible. However, some airborne units were fortunate enough to be able to make use of these recoilless 105mm guns.

Below: A German paratrooper in training. Von der Heydte's 6th FS Regiment was jump trained and, while it did not carry out any parachute operations during the campaign, this capacity contributed to the unit's remarkable cohesion.

Above: Men of the US 1st Infantry Division take cover on Omaha Beach.

Below: The body of a US soldier rests next to a German underwater obstacle on Omaha Beach. With a contact mine attached to its top, such mass-produced timber obstacles were submerged at high tide.

Above: The large numbers of tanks landing on D-Day surprised many of the authors, especially on the British and Canadian beaches. Less successful were the US 'Duplex Drive' M4 Sherman tanks, as pictured here at Utah Beach.

Below: A contemporary map showing Allied gains on D-Day.

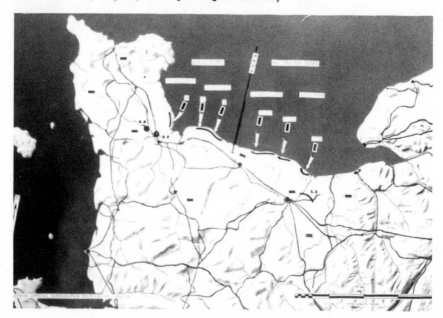

Employment of the 711th Infantry Division on the Invasion Front: Preparation

by Generalleutnant Joseph Reichert

Preliminary remarks

This work is being written after more than 2½ years and without references. Therefore, it cannot claim to be fully accurate as to dates and figures. During the whole period, the writer was commander of 711th Infantry Division.

I. History of Preceding Events

The 711th Infantry Division was a newly organized division, 15th Wave. As to its strength and equipment, the division had been originally organized only for occupational purposes. It disposed only two infantry regiments (three battalions each but minus the 13th and 14th Companies), one light artillery battalion, one engineer battalion (consisting of two companies), one antitank battalion (of two companies), one signal battalion (comprising two companies), and the most essential supply troops.

At first the division was employed as an occupying force at the line of demarcation between the occupied and the unoccupied part of France, and later on as a fortress division at various places on the Atlantic coast in France. When I took over the division on 1 April 1943, it had already been employed for a long time as the left wing division of the Fifteenth Army, in the same coastal sector between the Seine and the Orne in which it was located also at the time of the invasion.

The sector of the division was considered so-called intermediate terrain—that is, terrain which was not directly threatened by enemy large-scale landings, particularly as there was no large harbor which could be effectively used strategically. It was assumed, however, that some of its parts could also be involved, in the event of an enemy landing near Le Havre or Cherbourg. In the former case, the enemy would probably occupy the highlands between the Seine and Touques; in the latter that between Touques and Dives, if for no other purpose than in order to prevent an attack from there against the flank of its landing forces.

The key point of the entire division combat sector was, therefore, Mt Canisy (south of Deauville), controlling both the apparently endangered highlands east of Touques and east of the Dives. It was, therefore, especially fortified and equipped with artillery.

The type of terrain which offered the most favorable landing possibilities to the enemy was located between Trouville and Villers-sur-Mer and between Houlgate and the left divisional boundary. The other coastal area was either a steep coast or a swampy district like the mouth of the Seine from the right divisional boundary near Berville as far as Honfleur. The mouth of the Seine itself also seemed unfavourable for a landing, because of its ever-changing state of being choked up with either sand or mud as well as the possibility of the immediate effect of the Le Havre fortress, which was well equipped with relatively strong artillery.

It was the task of the division to prevent any enemy landings—the MLR being the coastal line at high tide—by a counterattack to throw back again into the sea any weaker enemy forces which might have invaded the coastal line or to seal off stronger forces which might have succeeded in penetrating until the arrival of necessary reinforcements.

According to this mission, and considering the probable enemy intentions, as well as the suitability of the terrain features, the positions were improved either as concentrated fortress areas or simple field fortifications. In the same manner, forces were deployed and heavy weapons emplaced as far as they were available.

The weapons of such a weak division by themselves would have rendered the defense of a coastal sector of 45 kilometers completely illusory. Therefore, a quantity of permanent weapons and permanent equipment was assigned to the division as well as to each division employed on the coast. These consisted mainly of captured weapons (guns of 50 to 150-mm caliber, antitank guns, MGs, mortars, and flamethrowers), which, except for the 150-mm guns, had to be operated entirely by the infantrymen of the division. Thus practically almost the entire infantry which was employed in the strongpoints on the coast handled either artillery or heavy infantry weapons.

In addition to the standard armament of the troops, an infantry strongpoint disposed one to four 50-mm guns mounted on trucks, one to three antitank guns or 75-mm LAK and two to five MGs or mortars. Each strongpoint was provided with ammunition and supplies to last for several weeks. From the available French 150-mm howitzers, there were formed four batteries of four guns each and incorporated into the division in such a manner that at first, through command channels, one artillery regimental staff and two mixed artillery battalions were organized from the personnel of the artillery battalion available according to the Order of Battle. It resulted tactically in the employment of one artillery group east on the mountainous terrain east of Touques and one artillery group west on the range of heights east of the Dives. The main strength of artillery firepower was represented in the main coastal artillery 1255th Battalion, with three batteries of six French 150-mm guns and one French 100-mm gun battery consisting of four guns, to which another gun battery of 150-mm caliber with four naval guns was added later on.

For the conduct of battle on the coast, it was generally ordered that the battle on the whole was to be conducted from open fire positions. For the single firing positions, the possibility of all-around fire was demanded. The fortifications which had to be improved had to serve as protection for the heavy weapons and personnel of strongpoints against the bombardment from the sea and from the air which generally preceded an enemy landing. Direct firing through loopholes was permitted only for single, specially important flanking positions.

According to the MLR as ordered (high tide line), the type of terrain (mostly vaulted slopes) and the covered terrain (the lengthy villages close to the beach), most of the strongpoints had to be also set up in the immediate vicinity of the beach. In addition to the completion of the flanking defense works, which were considered as particularly important, the following priority was established for the improvement of the fortified positions: shellproof shelters for crews of the strongpoints as well as for antilanding guns and antitank guns (garages), command posts for the staffs, emplacement of the Army's coastal artillery, and partial emplacement of the divisional artillery.

At about the turn of the year 1943/44, the threat of an invasion became more acute, perhaps owing to available news from England. The troops became aware of it on account of the now commencing inspection tours by Field Marshal Rommel, who had been given extraordinary powers and who brought new life into the work of construction of the so-called Atlantic Wall, progressing, it is true, steadily, but nevertheless slowly.

By this time the improvement in the divisional sector progressed to such an extent that the entire garrisons of the strongpoints, although rather crowded, could be put up in shellproof quarters. The same applied to the bulk of the antilanding and antitank guns, as well as to all of the regimental and battalion staffs. The construction of a few pillboxes for the Army coastal artillery had begun.

A continuous wire entanglement extended along the whole coast. The terrain between individual strongpoints and further inland of them was mined. Automatic barrage fire of the artillery as well as fire concentrations in front of individual sectors were fixed and tested in practice with live ammunition. Fire concentrations in front of sectors which seemed particularly threatened and also on land could be quickly put into effect by means of codewords. Also, with the neighbors to the left and the right the protection of the lines of demarcation was organized and practiced. The garrisons of the strongpoints were being constantly trained for their tasks and the reserves instructed for employment in any imaginable situation.

The general training was now almost completely neglected. The whole division, including the supply units and the rear services, became construction troops. In a few months, at a working speed increased tenfold, a continuous, strong system of obstacles in several rows came into being close to the beach in front of the whole coastal sector for protection against an enemy landing at high tide. Shortly before the beginning of the invasion, at single places, there was under construction yet a second obstacle line—so called "nut-cracker" mines, which were sunk into the water by boat in front of the dry ebb-sector, for protection against an enemy landing at low ebb.

Moreover, all large free areas up to a depth of 15 kilometers which seemed to be suitable for an air landing were strengthened with piles. The work on concrete construction by Organization Todt had to be continued during spare time. The demand for an all-round defense by all weapons was abandoned; instead, an increased construction of flanking pillboxes for KWK and LAK, and at least concrete-reinforced protection to the sea, was demanded. This work, which had been done hither to only by Organization Todt, had now to be accomplished also by the troops.

Single enemy planes appeared now and then to take photos. It was certain that enemy espionage was as active as ever, as the population had not yet been evacuated. (This was proved after the invasion by captured British maps, which contained markings for each weapon in the individual strongpoints.) But there was neither a fighter-bomber attack nor were bombs dropped on places of construction. The pillboxes for the Army coastal artillery increased more and more, were being stripped, and guns were being mounted. Until about May the entire coastal sector was completely peaceful. But the invasion psychosis—I considered it as such at that time—continued. The reserves had to leave their barracks and were to be deployed in field type shelters or natural caves near the coast ready for an immediate counterattack. All vehicles and motor vehicles had to be dispersed and to be dug-in splinterproof. The same applied to the sheltering of horses.

A second line, one to two kilometers in the rear of the strongpoints, was improved in a field type way, also switch positions along the Seine, Touques and Dives. Against possible air landings, a constant observation service extending over the entire sector of the division was being organized. A second position, ten to twenty kilometers off the coast, was established in the form of strongpoints in a field type way. Minefields and dummy minefields were being laid in depth, and mine obstacles being prepared on the roads. The Dives and Divette were dammed up and the whole Dives valley flooded as far as deep into the hinterland.

All billets were improved to serve as strongpoints. A provisional mobilizing of the division, preparations for which had already been made at the initial organization, was practiced.

Some hundred Dornier projectors (Do-werfer) were installed toward the probable landing centers of gravity near the coast, two mortar companies being formed and employed for a more effective concentration of the fire on the steep coast between Villers-sur-Mer and Houlgate. The divisional artillery was reinforced by one detachment of medium field howitzers, 130-mm on self-propelled carriages, the antitank company of the division was enlarged into an antitank battalion by mobilizing a further company, and for each infantry regiment one strong antitank platoon was formed comprising five antitank guns. In addition, thirty to forty 20-mm antiaircraft guns were allotted to the division and distributed among infantry and artillery.

Although the improvement of the position was by far not yet completed, and I realized that, presumably, every coastal division that would be affected by the invasion had to be written off in the long run, I believed nevertheless that, in conjunction with one armored division located in the vicinity of Lisieux, with which all possibilities of a commitment had been agreed upon, I would be able to fulfill my task. On the other hand, I personally was not at all convinced that an invasion across the Channel would take place, not even when at the beginning of May the first heavy bombs started to fall—

probably intended for the 100-mm Army coastal batteries between Villerville and Trouville. As the majority of the bombs fell into the sea and only a few villas along the beach had been destroyed, I considered the whole thing at first as an unsuccessful emergency bombing release. I realized my mistake only when, after a few days, the coastal batteries on Mt Canisy were bombed, on which occasion two pillboxes which had only just been completed were shot to pieces and rendered useless. The same happened to all the four Army coastal batteries, some of which were attacked two or three times during the course of this time. The first attacks also brought losses; the guns, however, remained intact. Minor damage which occurred could be repaired within a short time. Also, a 150-mm battery of the divisional artillery was hit; however, neither losses of men nor of matériel occurred.

Because the bombardments extended along the whole Channel coast, without any indication of a special center of gravity, no conclusions could be drawn as to where a possible invasion was planned. The simultaneous air attacks against the French railways and railroad stations at the same time impeded completely the bringing up of supplies. The whole situation was further characterized by air attacks on the Seine bridges, the objective of which—at the most—was to prevent the German troops from crossing the Seine either from east to west or vice versa.

Thus, everything could be considered as a preparatory stage for an invasion across the Channel, what it actually was and as it was understood by higher German commands—all the more so as we knew about the strength of all the forces which were concentrated on the southern coast of England—but all this did not give us a clue as to where the invasion would take place. I was personally more inclined to suppose that everything was a huge bluff—just as our Atlantic Wall was from the point of view of defense—with the object of helping the Russian ally to tie down strong German forces. Even so, the harassing of supply lines attained its end and I considered the Western Powers to be rich enough to afford such a tremendously deceptive action.

By the Spring of 1944, developments on the Eastern front had already turned out so unfavorable for us that, if one did not believe in a German magic weapon, one could see the end coming anyway. Besides, an invasion in Europe had already been made by the Anglo-Americans in Italy and also gained ground there. I could not imagine, therefore, that especially the British would risk their fleet once more for a new large-scale operation before the end of the war, and considered a new landing in the rear of the German forces in Italy as more likely, be it on the east or west coast of Italy or on the south coast of France.

That the V-1 and V-2 launching bases which were being built along the whole Channel coast, and which were threatening England, would urgently necessitate an invasion there I did not believe either, as this threat could already be counteracted sufficiently by a corresponding employment of the superior air force alone.

If, however, the invasion across the Channel was planned in earnest, then it very likely would take place only as a result of pressure on the part of the Russian ally, as also the German press repeatedly reported. In that case one would hardly take the risk of launching it at an operatively decisive place, in the knowledge that a kind of Atlantic Wall really existed where one was expected, but rather at a place where conditions were easiest for the attacker and where the risk for a landing was slightest.

Thus I expected a possible invasion across the Channel on the Cotentin peninsula, with the serviceable harbor of Cherbourg, which offered a good opportunity of landing and had the shape of a peninsula, facing an enemy who practically had no navy at its disposal. Furthermore, it would soon offer covered flanks and thus make it relatively easy to hold a bridgehead, until enough forces could be landed, in order to start decisive operations in conjunction with the extremely superior air forces—even if at first this area would prove to be a quite unfavorable operative one—and then launch the decisive advance.

The Seventh Army, by the way, also expected the invasion to take place against the Cotentin peninsula. That even the higher command figured on the possibility of an invasion at that point appears from the fact that, during the last months prior to the invasion, a number of fresh divisions were brought up to that front, by which the individual divisional defense sectors were considerably reduced.

At any rate, the landing on the Cotentin peninsula was only thought of as a secondary action. However, we rather awaited the main offensive to take place north of the Seine, as proved by the hesitant measures to bring up reinforcements from the area north of the Seine after the actual start of the invasion. In case the enemy had sufficient forces at his disposal, this idea of accomplishing an operation of such decisive importance for the issue of the war could certainly not be ignored.

The 346th Infantry Division to 4 June 1944

by Oberst Paul Frank

The 346th Infantry Division was organized in October 1942 as a Festungs (fortress) division intended only for duty in the fortifications of the Channel coast. During 1943, it functioned as such in the St Malo fortress area on the northern coast of Brittany. In December 1943, it was withdrawn and re-formed as a mobile reserve division (Type 1944). In the midst of this reorganization, it was transferred to the Fifteenth Army as the army reserve. It was held near Camanches in the region, south of the mouth of the River Somme. Towards the end of January 1944, it was transferred to Belbec, northeast of Le Havre.

In this position, the division had the following missions:

a. Prevention of airborne landings behind the Le Havre fortress;

b. Immediate counterattack of a seaborne invasion between Fécamp and Le Havre and at the mouth of the Seine;

c. Preparation for a transfer at short notice to other positions on the Channel coast (probably to the north).

In the fulfillment of these missions, the following steps were taken:

a. The Division was divided into regimental and battalion Kampfgruppen to cover all areas that seemed to lend themselves to airborne attacks. Artillery and infantry weapons were so emplaced to put heavy fire on such areas. Mobile assault forces were held ready for a concentrated counterattack. Air landing obstacles were erected. A divisional alarm system was established, providing four interchangeable communications nets. Close liaison was maintained with the Commander 17th LW Feld Division, who was the sector commander. In emergencies, he would issue orders for the 346th Infantry Division also.

b. In accordance with Genfldm Rommel's conviction of the difficulty of large-scale movement in the event of enemy attack, the division was moved up immediately behind the coastal defenses, with the forward elements five to eight kilometers inland. In the event of simultaneous landings along the whole coast between Fécamp and Le Havre, the 17th LW Feld Division would control the Fécamp sector and the 346th Infantry Division the Le Havre sector. The following preparations were made: the division artillery was included in the coastal fire plan, assuming the widest possible fields of fire; to each infantry regiment was

151

attached a reinforced Fahrradgewegliches (bicycle infantry) battalion; and to the division was attached a motorized battalion, a pioneer (engineer) battalion, two mobile light artillery batteries and a Panzerjäger (antitank) battalion with a Sturmgeschütz (SP assault gun) company.

c. All the division combat echelons were rendered mobile by the use of trucks and buses. (The vehicles were standing by, either with the individual units themselves or within the division area.) Two infantry battalions were equipped with bicycles and motorized combat vehicles. Only the heavy artillery battalion was horsedrawn. Reconnaissance parties were sent out, with primary importance placed on the area to the north as far as the mouth of the Somme. Judging from the reports and directives coming from higher headquarters, there was little possibility of the division being committed south of the Seine. With neither bridges nor bridging equipment, a crossing of the Seine was considered most unlikely. Nevertheless, the division had investigated the French civilian ferries, secured them against sabotage, and prepared for lack of cooperation from the French ferry operators by appointing auxiliary operators from amongst the divisional engineers.

On the basis on reports from higher headquarters, the division expected the main effort to come north of the Seine. These reports emphasized that British units were being trained for fighting on steep coasts and that the open country north of the Seine was basically more favorable for an airborne assault. Higher headquarters warned of the possibility of a series of diversionary landings in the south.

As army reserve, in search of operational possibilities, the division had done a great deal of reconnaissance in and around the coastal defenses. The staff's resulting opinion was that the Wehrmacht would have difficulty in defending the coast. The reasons for this were:

a. Although a great deal of construction had been done, it was nowhere complete.

b. Even sufficient construction would not compensate for the inadequate number of men and weapons (to occupy the entire coast).

On the eve of battle, the transformation to a normal mobile division was not yet complete. Senior officers were well schooled in mobile operations, but most of the junior officers were young and inexperienced. Although the division was for the most part up to strength and was comparatively well trained, almost one-third of the enlisted personnel were older men no longer entirely suited to a major battle. The division still lacked a complete light artillery battalion, as the long-awaited German howitzers had not arrived. The French howitzers that were used instead had a lower rate of fire, and were inadequately supplied with ammunition. Furthermore, the Aufklärungs KP (Divisional Reconnaissance Company) was still missing. The level of training was good. Leaders were trained in mobile antitank tactics. The morale was excellent, with the only questionable troops being the Ost battalion (composed of Russians, Poles, etc.) and the approximately 10% Volksdeutschen from Volksliste Three.

Organization of
the 6th Fallschirm Regiment

by Oberstleutnant Friedrich, Freiherr von der Heydte

At the end of September or the beginning of October 1943, Hitler, influenced by the fact that elements of the 1st Battalion of the 7th Fallschirm (FS) Regiment* had effected Mussolini's liberation, approved a plan proposed to him by Göring which called for a large-scale increase in the number of parachute troops. Until the Fall of 1943, German parachute forces comprised one corps (XI Air Corps) consisting of two divisions. Göring's plan called for increasing the parachute forces by the end of 1944 to the strength of two armies, totaling 100,000 men, to be placed on a par with the Waffen SS in regard to personnel replacements, weapons, equipment, and training. Göring probably had in mind the possibility of a future struggle for political power within the inner circle, and intended to use the parachute forces to counteract the influence of the Waffen SS, since he had failed in his plan to make such use of the Luftwaffe field divisions.† In this connection, it is interesting to note that, shortly after the order was issued to develop the parachute forces according to Göring's plan, Himmler succeeded in inducing Hitler to approve the activation of a parachute regiment within the framework of the Waffen SS.

Expansion of the airborne forces was begun without delay after approval by Hitler. The 3rd and 4th Divisions were to be activated immediately. The 1st and 4th Divisions were to constitute I FS Corps, and the 2nd and 3rd Divisions II FS Corps. In October 1943, shortly before being transferred from Italy to Russia, the 2nd Division assisted the activation of the 3rd Division by giving up the 6th FS Regiment, which was split into separate cadres and deactivated.

In November 1943, orders were given to activate a new 6th FS Regiment, with the former Ia‡ of the 2nd FS Division as commander. Since the 2nd FS Division was at that time committed at the Russian front, the new regiment was for the time being subordinated directly to the Parachute Army.

---

* 7th Parachute Regiment. The abbreviation FS is used throughout the remainder of the manuscript in connection with the unit designations.
† Excess German Air Force personnel were organized into field divisions for duty with the ground forces.
‡ Operations officer. This is the German equivalent of the US Army G-3. In a division he also acts as Chief of Staff

The initial organization of the new 6th FS Regiment was undertaken during the first days of January 1944 at the troop training grounds at Wahn. Activation, equipment, and training of the regiment were supposed to be completed by 1 April 1944. The regiment was organized along the general lines of an army infantry regiment. It was composed of three battalions, each consisting of three rifle companies and one heavy weapons (heavy machine gun and heavy mortar) company, one mortar company (the 13th), one antitank company (the 14th), one engineer platoon, and one bicycle reconnaissance platoon. In June 1944, the engineer and bicycle reconnaissance platoons were expanded to form the 15th and 16th Companies. In the summer of 1944, an antiaircraft defense company (the 17th), a motor transport company (the 18th), a supply and maintenance company (the 19th), and a replacement training company (the 20th) were added to the regiment, while the 13th to 17th companies inclusive were combined to form the 4th (Heavy) Battalion. Each battalion had one signal communication platoon and one supply platoon in addition to the companies already mentioned. The supply platoon was responsible for the establishment of a battalion ammunition distributing point, and the transportation of ammunition from this issuing center to the front line by means of carrier units. The regimental staff also had at its disposal a signal communication platoon as well as a motorcycle messenger platoon and a parachute servicing platoon. The parachute servicing platoon packed the parachutes for the entire regiment, and saw to it that they were kept in serviceable condition. The total wartime strength of the regiment was slightly more than 4,500 officers, noncommissioned officers, and enlisted men.

The personnel replacements of the regiment at the beginning of 1944 were of high quality. One-third of the officers and about one-fifth of the noncommissioned officers were battle-tried parachutists, some of whom had fought in the battalion of the regimental commander in Crete, in Russia, and in North Africa. The enlisted personnel consisted entirely of young volunteers averaging seventeen and a half years in age. Four months of training sufficed to weld the regiment into a unified whole, adequately prepared for ground combat as well as airborne operations. The regimental commander, who was known to be opposed to the training methods used by the parachute schools, was given permission to complete the jump training of the men himself; for this purpose, one squadron of Junker 52s and one flight of Heinkel 111s were assigned to him at Wahn and placed under his command during the four training months, with the result that every member of the regiment was enabled to make nine jumps, including three night jumps. About 10% of the men were eliminated in the course of jump practice.

The regiment was, in general, better armed than the Army infantry regiments. Since each rifle squad was provided with two machine guns, in contrast to one in the Army, the firepower of the parachute companies was considerably greater than that of an Army rifle company; likewise, the firepower of the FS regiment's heavy weapons companies, which had twelve heavy machine guns and six heavy mortars each, was somewhat greater than that of the Army heavy weapons companies. In contrast to the Army and Waffen SS, the equipment and training of the regiment enabled it to employ all of its heavy machine guns in concealed firing positions—a factor which proved effective in the subsequent fighting.

The 13th Company was at first equipped with twelve so-called chemical projectors, 105-mm mortars with a range of 3,500 meters. Unfortunately, these mortars were no longer being manufactured, so that it was impossible to obtain replacements, and it became necessary to substitute medium mortars in some cases and heavy mortars in others. The 14th Company comprised one 75-mm antitank platoon with four guns and three Panzerschreck (bazooka) platoons with six bazookas each; later on, this company was also equipped with Püppchen (heavy antitank rocket launchers). All personnel of the regiment were trained to use magnetic antitank hollow charges and Panzerwurfminen (hollow-charge antitank grenades), as well as Panzerfausts (recoilless antitank grenade launchers).

The 15th Company, by way of experiment, was provided with several Einstoss-Flammenwerfers (para-flamethrowers), which proved very effective. The 17th Company, after its activation in the summer of 1944, was equipped with twelve 20-mm antiaircraft machine guns and four 20-mm triple-barreled guns.

The regiment's communication system was considerably better than that of an Army regiment. The signal communication platoon of each battalion had four telephone subsections and six radio sections, each equipped with one "Dora"* instrument (later called a "Gustav"); the signal platoon of the regiment had four telephone subsections and one switchboard team having a 12-line switchboard, and six radio sections with one "Berta" instrument each. In addition, there were two radio sections with one pack receiver each; each radio section also had one 35-watt instrument (for communicating with aircraft) and one 70-watt instrument (for communicating with ground forces during airlanding operations). The heavy weapons companies had their own communication sections, including telephone and pack radio subsections.

The regiment's motor transport was inadequate. On average, each company had only two trucks. When the Allied invasion began, the regiment had a total of seventy trucks with a total capacity of slightly more than one hundred tons, but among them were more than fifty different types of manufacture – German, French, Italian and British.

The regiment commander, in his last operations report before the beginning of the invasion, evaluated the regiment's combat efficiency as follows: "The regiment is completely fit for airlanding operations, but only conditionally fit for ground combat because it does not have enough heavy antitank weapons and motor transport."†

---

* Codename for a type of pack radio.
† It is not quite clear why the regimental commander evaluated his unit as being completely fit for air landing operations, but only conditionally fit for ground combat. One surely presupposes the other in the case of systematic training, which the regiment had received. In matters of supply, the regiment was naturally always dependent on the support of the Wehrmacht.—Pemsel.

II. Situation of the Cotentin Peninsula prior to 6 June Invasion

On 1 May 1944, after barely four months of training, the regiment received orders from the Air Force operations staff, bypassing the headquarters of the Parachute Army, to move to the area of Army Group Rommel in France, bringing with it its entire airlanding equipment.

At Army Group headquarters, the regimental commander was informed that his regiment was being detached and assigned to LXXXIV Corps at St Lô. He was, however, unable to learn why orders had been issued to bring the airlanding equipment.

Generalleutnant Marcks was the Commanding General of LXXXIV Corps, and Lieutenant-Colonel von Siegern was his Chief of Staff. Corps headquarters and the prearranged command posts were located at the northern edge of St Lô, on the road to Carentan. Corps was in charge of the coastal defences of the entire Carentan peninsula and the area on both sides of the Vire estuary; as far as the author can recall from a remark made by Generalleutnant Marcks, this covered a coastal strip of about five hundred kilometers.

With the exception of the 91st Grenadier Division and the 6th FS Regiment, all the divisions of the corps were committed to the defence of the coasts at the time the invasion began.

The regiment received orders from Generalleutnant Marcks to assume responsibility for defence measures against parachute and airlanding troops in the area Lessay (incl)–Périers (incl)–Raids (incl)–St Georges-de-Bohon (incl)–Meautis (incl)–Baupe (excl)–Monte Castre (incl), that is, the southern part of the Cotentin peninsula. The area to be protected was over twenty kilometers in width and almost fifteen in depth. The road distance from the western to the eastern border of the area was almost thirty-five kilometers, and from the northern to the southern border nearly twenty kilometers. Corps advised the regimental commander that the defence measures, planned and directed by Army Group Rommel, required that the troops were to be scattered through the area, and that small strongpoints were to be established from which the surrounding country could be controlled. Allied parachute units, no matter where they landed, would encounter a handful of well-placed, combat-ready German soldiers. In view of the advantages which such an arrangement offered, the dispersal of the regiment and the difficulty or even impossibility of concentrating its scattered units for rapid employment had to be risked.

The regimental commander was under the impression that the commanding general of LXXXIV Corps was not in complete accord with this order from Army Group Rommel.

This was not the only case of disagreement between Army Group and its units; such dissension was apparent during the first days in Normandy. The Army Group also differed from Army and Corps on the conduct of operations in the case of an invasion—or, at least, such was the impression of the regimental commander at the time. During a visit to regimental headquarters, Feldmarschall Rommel, who had known me since the

North African campaign, summarized his views concerning the proper strategy approximately as follows: "The coast should be our main line of resistance for the following reasons: the enemy must be destroyed before he even sets foot on land; once he has succeeded in establishing himself in a beachhead it will be very difficult for us to drive him out again; the invasion will already have been half-way successful."

This idea was at variance with the views of General Dollmann, who expressed himself to the regimental commander as follows: "In view of the thin line of coastal defense, we will scarcely be able to prevent the enemy from establishing a beachhead. It must be our task then to bring up all our forces as rapidly as possible to this beachhead in order to crush the enemy during the first days, while it is still weak and before the enemy has had a chance to extend and improve his position." General Marcks appeared to be of the same opinion.*

The various members of the German command group in the West also disagreed on the location of possible and probable points of Allied landings. General Marcks expected the landings to take place north of the Vire estuary and on the eastern coast of the Cotentin peninsula (as the author recalls, in the Coutances area), and found support for this assumption in maps which were carefully kept up-to-date and which showed the focal points of enemy air reconnaissance in May 1944. At the top level, it was evidently expected that landings would be concentrated north of the Seine estuary, approximately in the Boulogne area.

Apparently, the members of the command group were in agreement only in completely underestimating the potentialities of the Allied parachute and airlanding forces. It was the general opinion that paratroopers would prefer wide open spaces. When Generaloberst Student, the Commanding General of the German Parachute Army, objected to this conception on the grounds that modern paratroopers were also prepared to jump in wooded areas and villages, his objection was dismissed on the ground that he was boasting.

The obvious dissension prevailing among members of the higher command on questions of supply had the most disastrous effect. Two views were in conflict. Those who believed that the Allied air force would destroy all supply lines and railroad stations demanded that supply depots be established on a large scale in the rear of the forces. Others expected the attacks of the Allied air force to destroy immediately any depots set up prior to the start of the invasion, since their location would undoubtedly be betrayed to the Allies by the civilian population, and wanted the supply bases located as far as possible from any prospective front.†

---

* The facts concerning the disagreements over fundamental problems of defense which existed between Field Marshal Rommel on the one hand and Generaloberst Dollman and General Marcks on the other, have been aptly presented.—Pemsel

† The statements with regard to the dissension on questions of supply existing among members of the higher command, and the explanation therefor, are not based on fact. In this case, everyone was completely aware of the fact that the decentralization of the depots was a matter of necessity. As far as the effectiveness of enemy

The troops available for a defense against an Allied landing were not comparable to those committed in Russia. Their morale was low; the majority of the enlisted men and noncommissioned officers lacked combat experience; and the officers were in the main those who, because of lack of qualification or on account of wounds or illness, were no longer fit for service on the Eastern front. I should, of course, add that this is the personal opinion of a regimental commander who was transferred to Normandy in May 1944, and that his impressions were gained from attendance at training maneuvers and tactical rides during the first days of combat. It is possible that his experience was particularly unfortunate. It should not lead to any generalizing.

The situation with regard to the weapons and equipment of the forces in Normandy was nothing short of deplorable. Weapons from all over the world and from all periods of the twentieth century seemed to have been accumulated, in order to convey the impression of a mighty force. Later on, at Carentan, in the sector of the 6th FS Regiment, four different types of mortars (ranging in caliber from 78 to 82-mm) of German, French, Italian, and Russian make and seven kinds of light machine guns were committed on a front barely two kilometers wide.

In order to make LXXXIV Corps mobile to some extent, or at least to make sure of essential transportation facilities for the units, each regiment of the corps was ordered to brand or otherwise mark horses and vehicles belonging to French civilians; these horses and vehicles were, however, to be left with their owners and were to be utilized only in case of an Allied invasion. It was, I believe, quite obvious to troops with combat experience, from the lowest ranks up to the regimental commander, that this order could not be carried out. Such orders were not conducive to improving combat morale or faith in victory on the part of the troops.

The top-level command itself did not appear to have any great confidence in the troops in the West. Certainly only lack of confidence could account for one of Hitler's orders, which lower headquarters repeated but did not implement. This was the order issued in May 1944 which required every "strongpoint commander" and every independent commander to give his written word of honor not to desert in case of an Allied invasion. Like many other "Führer" orders issued at the time, this one was transmitted by the higher commands without comment. It was not enforced. When the commander of the 6th FS Regiment refused to give his word of honor or to compel his officers to do so, his refusal was readily passed over by his superiors.

The most disheartening comments were those made by General Marcks during a conversation with the author following a training maneuver in the Cherbourg area, when he described the situation as follows: "Emplacements without guns, ammunition depots without ammunition, minefields without mines, and a large number of men in uniform with hardly a soldier among them."

---

espionage and enemy air raids was concerned, it was immaterial whether the depots were located at the coast or deep in the interior. The shifting of depots in the long run always involved a problem of transportation facilities, which were never available in sufficient measure.—Pemsel

The 2nd Panzer Division: Preparation

by General der Panzertruppen Heinrich, Freiherr von Lüttwitz

1. When and where did you expect the invasion? Why?

The 2nd Panzer Division was located in the area near Amiens. Naturally, the point of view directed itself toward the coastal region, where the division's employment was held as the most likely, and for that reason arrangements had been already made. This sector was approximately located between Ostend and the estuary of the Seine. Landing possibilities on the coastal region were not too bad; besides, this was a coastal region which could be reached quickly from England. Therefore, it was believed that a landing in this coastal area was the one most likely. This belief was also strengthened by the fact that the bulk of the V-1 launching sites were located here; surely, their destruction must have been of major importance in the event of an Allied landing. Generally speaking, everybody was oriented and knew the nature of the shores—that it was of no importance great enough to hinder or endanger an invasion in that prescribed place. According to experimental reports, which were received, and which concerned the developments of maneuvers on the English west coast, there was proof enough that all material installations, their arrangements, and all other technical obstacles could be overcome and mastered. Besides, it was clear that the permanent possession of a useful harbor became, in the second phase during a landing operation, of utmost importance.

An invasion north of the Somme seemed for some reasons to be especially valuable, so that, in the hinterland, the industrial center located at Lille–Douai could shortly thereafter be occupied. By this, on one side the weakening of German potential would be achieved; on the other hand, it would offer a jump-off base for a further attack in an eastern direction, toward the Rhine and Ruhr.

It was expected that an enemy thrust into the industrial region would be followed up with an open rebellion of the workers' masses in this area. The civilian population of northern France remained up to now completely calm and cooperated willingly in all matters and military needs. However, in case of an invasion, their attitude remained unknown, and had to be doubted. Nevertheless, these doubts had not been confirmed. Not until later, in the Ardennes, did I hear of one act of violence in which the division was involved. At that time, about 11 or 12 June 1944, a gang of Maquis was stopped west of Paris in a truck which belonged to one of the medical companies, and took the men on the truck with them as prisoners.

159

The French civilian population was attracted through the good rates which were offered for setting up emplacements of obstacles—the so-called "Rommel asparagus", which served as a precautionary measure against an airborne operation. Later in the course of the division's fighting, the civilian population was also always ready to furnish shelter for the division or to arrange it.

At Christmas 1943, the first divisional elements arrived from the East, coming into the area Cambrai–Arras, the last elements arriving by January 1944. The division's entire equipment was left behind on the Eastern front, but by the time it arrived here, it had been freshly reinforced and newly equipped.

During mid-February, the division received its first alert and orders, which called for preparations for a swift march, aimed either against an airborne enemy, or a counterattack against such enemy forces that succeeded in piercing the "Atlantic Wall." The division was later transferred to an area west of Amiens, on both sides of the Somme river. The division's bulk was located on the southern bank of the river. With the arrival of Spring, the time of the invasion had to be reckoned with: it was getting nearer. It was believed that the invasion would take place just within the divisional sector; therefore, the division's preparedness to march from the time of receipt of the first alarm was set to 1½–2½ hours. The state of readiness was increased to encounter airborne operations to such an extent that by the end of April 1944 nearly all the guns and machine guns were in position along the outskirts of the town. The division could be alerted by a special radio communication net, so that every company could be on standby within a matter of a few minutes.

From mid-February, the timing of the invasion was calculated daily. By mid-April it was generally believed that an invasion was imminent. The exact time of the invasion was not known.

2. Did you ever consider, especially, whether the defenses along the coastal sector were sufficiently built up? Give the reason why.

The 2nd Panzer Division was not assigned and in charge of any coastal sector and was therefore not responsible for the coastal defenses. But in the Spring it was still being busily employed on the extension works in the fields near the coast, and the tidal region, as well as on constructions in the "area behind the front."

Organization of the
3rd Fallschirm Division

by Generalleutnant Richard Schimpf

The initial organization of the 3rd FS Division was ordered by the Oberbefehlshaber der Luftwaffe (Commander-in-Chief of the Luftwaffe). The area of Chalons-sur-Marne–Bar le Duc–Joinville was fixed as the place of assembly. Division headquarters was at Joinville. At the beginning of January 1944, I was assigned as commander of this division and took over the command. The division was in every respect subordinated to II FS Corps, which at that time was located in Melun. The troops arrived gradually in separate transports, at a strength of about 500 each. They consisted of young, still insufficiently trained men, all of whom had volunteered for parachute troops service and were, on average, from 21 to 22 years old. Their fighting spirit and morale were accordingly excellent, and a uniform standard of fighter was secured. The cadre, the subordinate commanders, and the individual troop commanders were, for the most part, assigned from among the experienced and battle-tried leaders of the former parachute troops. This gave a good basis with regard to personnel and training of the division, if only enough time could have been made available for the proper training of the young replacement troops, who were most eagerly interested in their work. The distribution of equipment unfortunately did not proceed as quickly as would have been desirable, considering the comparatively rapid arrival of troop replacements. During the last days of January, the transfer of the division into the Bretagne was suddenly ordered. There, their organization and training were to be completed. The transfer into the area around Mons d'Arrée and Houlgate was executed by railroad transport.

Although the transfer was undesirable at first, as it delayed the organization of the division and caused considerably less favorable supply conditions, the new assembly area was far superior, particularly because of its downright ideal training conditions. The thinly populated area, hardly used for farming, offered everywhere the best training possibilities, even for shooting with live ammunition. Besides, there were no unwholesome diversionary influences in the line of amusements, such as were usually found in France.

While moving into the new area, the division also received a combat mission, in the event that the enemy, during an invasion in the Bretagne, would try to establish a Voxfeld*—difficult to win back—by landing paratroopers and airborne troops in the

---

* In this case, possibly an air head.—Ed

open land around the heights of Mons d'Arrée, which was quite favorable for parachute landings. For such a contingency, the division was assigned to the Corps HQ of XXV Infantry Corps. However, the previous assignment to II FS Corps was not altered. The mission of the division in this area was to prevent an airborne operation by annihilating airborne troops before they were able to become tactically effective. Accordingly, in the assignment of troop billets, this mission was taken into consideration, and plans were formulated to quickly reach all places favorable for jumping and airborne operations, and particularly to arrange to cover them with fire. For this reason, some units, especially artillery and Flak, were quartered in temporary barracks on the dominant heights of Mons d'Arrée, and a permanent air signal service was established. However, on the whole, this possible combat task did not overburden the troops, and only slightly delayed their training, which, for the time being, was of course the main task of the division.

A much more serious handicap in this connection was the fact that the furnishing of equipment, especially weapons and motor vehicles, did not proceed with the necessary speed. Attempts to overcome this disadvantage by various improvisations were successful to a certain extent, at least as far as the training was concerned. The training to make them qualified soldiers made good progress, because of the enthusiasm shown by the young troops, the qualified and experienced officers, and the favorable training conditions. Therefore, by the beginning of the invasion, this training had been brought up to such a high level that the troops were qualified to hold out and meet the extraordinary requirements of the invasion battle, which lasted for months, without a rest. In a report of the First US Army captured during the Ardennes fighting, these accomplishments of the troops were admitted and given credit.

With regard to the peculiarity of parachute troops, the instructions consisted first in the training of individual fighters for guerrilla warfare, considering terrain and weapons; later, it was extended to training for combat at company and battalion level. By instructing the subordinate commanders in the art of map maneuvers, their ability to make tactical decisions and the technique of command were strengthened. In order to prepare the division for commitment in accordance with its specialization, and to awaken and develop an espirit de corps among the troops, jump training was finally carried out by continuously detaching troops to the parachute training schools in Lyon and Wittstock. By the beginning of the invasion, the bulk of the division had already passed through these courses of instruction, which lasted from three to four weeks.

By 6 June 1944, a general estimate of the degree of preparation for action could be made as follows:

Personnel: With few exceptions, 100%.

Training: Ready for any combat action, so long as it did not require special preparations.

Weapons: With certain restrictions, about 70%; MG 42 and antitank weapons were especially lacking.

Ammunition: Satisfactory. Three to six basic loads were available for the weapons on hand.

Mobility: For a fully motorized division it was insufficient. Only about 40% of the required motor vehicles were available, some of which were fit for service to a limited extent only; the spare parts situation was very poor; and there was no uniformity in types of vehicles. The amount of fuel was insufficient for the available vehicles.

III Flak Corps

by General der Flakartillerie Wolfgang Pickert

The general missions of III AA Corps were supporting the Army against the enemy's aerial and ground attacks, by a concentrated commitment of the AA regiments or of the entire AA Corps at the focal point. To be in a position to carry out this mission, the corps was fully motorized, and its commanders and officers were specially selected. In this combination it was unique. (The other AA Corps always contained a number of non-motorized units also, and were thus not fully mobile.)

Up to about 26 May 1944, the batteries of III AA Corps were mostly emplaced, in superimposition, next to locally permanent AA batteries, on airfields and on V-weapon installations. Here they were emplaced in immobile, never varying commitment, without any practical training in the impending special combat missions for the repulse of an invasion. Administratively, the Corps was directly subordinate to Air Force Administrative Command Headquarters (Luftflottenkommando) 3 in Paris. Operationally, the AA batteries committed were subordinate to the Air Force Administrative Command Headquarters (Luftgaukommando) Western France Command Post at Étampes; likewise territorially and regarding supplies.

At the time of my assumption of command, about 24 May 1944, and after I had been oriented as to the main missions of the Corps, I immediately endeavored to get the AA Corps out of this rigid commitment. I wanted to train and harden the men for their new tasks by a continually changing mobile commitment in areas over which there was heavy enemy air activity. I succeeded in obtaining permission for this, at least for the greater part of the men. So, three regiments were committed on both sides of the mouth of the Somme river in the coastal area. The fourth regiment had unfortunately to be assigned to the Bayeux–Isigny area a few days later. This area was subjected to particularly heavy air attacks, and did not dispose sufficient locally emplaced AA batteries for its defense. Thus, on the evening of 5 June 1944, two AA regiments were committed north of the mouth of the Somme river, between Montreuil-sur-Mer and north of Abbeville, one regiment in the Le Tréport region, and the fourth regiment as previously indicated.

The troops, though generally adequate, were inexperienced in combat and had grown soft in the West. During the time that now followed, they learnt a lot that was to be useful to them in their mobile engagements, about reconnaissance, camouflage, and digging in, and about gunnery against an aerial enemy, under ever-changing conditions.

The officers were young, fresh and select, but also had only little combat experience. They had no knowledge of cooperation with the ground forces, and of taking a hand in ground combat, or they had been unused to it since 1940.

Both officers and men, staffs and troops were invigorated by the new mission, which substituted mobility and flexibility for the hitherto prevailing torpidity. This short period of preparation for the heavy battles that were to come paid off well (later).

Corps Command post: east of Meaux. Forward Corps Command post during the commitment astride the mouth of the Somme: immediately south of Amiens.

PART THREE
D-Day: Invasion

Was this really the invasion? Not simply an airborne raid? These were the questions the authors of these documents were asking early on 6 June. Even when the amphibious landings were well under way, it remained uncertain whether this was a diversion for a main assault elsewhere.

The US 82nd and 101st Airborne Divisions were dropped inland behind Utah Beach and astride the Meredat river. While many of these paratroopers were lost and the vast majority far dispersed from their intended drop zones, this allowed the airborne troops to both disrupt the German response and, as these documents will show, become the *de facto* security zones for the beachheads.

Because of the confusion caused by the airborne invasion, the response of the German 709th Infantry Division—its commander absent at a high-level wargame—was sluggish against the paratroopers, as was the supporting 91st Luftlande Division. Utah, on the eastern flank of the Contentin peninsula, and defended by a single battalion of the 709th Infantry Division, was taken with light casualties. The German resistance against the advance from Utah Beach in the days to come, despite the fighting of units such as Kiel's and von der Heydte's regiments, was never as effective and cohesive as it was against the advances from Omaha and the British beaches.

There was nothing sluggish about the German resistance on Omaha Beach. The fighting was a near-run thing, despite the fact that the 352nd Division's three battalions were spread thin. However they lacked the reserves—either misdirected against the paratroopers or in the British sector—to push back the first heroic advances off the beach. By the end of the day, the American beachhead at Omaha was nowhere more than 2,000 meters deep, less than a fifth of what had been planned. But, for the Germans, the time where even a small force—the only force they could muster—could have made a difference was long past.

The British airborne forces proved, despite their dispersal, to be an effective flank guard. The seizing of "Pegasus Bridge" across the Orne blocked lateral German movement and preserved the bridge for the Allied advance. On their beaches, the British and Canadians also encountered strong resistance from strongpoints and units of the 716th Infantry Division. However, the collapse of resistance in some of the 716th Infantry Division sector along the British beaches—the Ost battalions melted away— led LXXXIV Corps to commit its tactical reserve of the 352nd Division's

Kampfgruppe Meyer to that area rather than to Omaha, where they could have proved decisive.

While the road to Bayeux was open (it fell the next day), the advance on Caen was slowed by counterattacks by the 21st Panzer Division's Kampfgruppe Luck and continued resistance by the remnants of the 716th Infantry Division.

Seventh Army headquarters did not put its subordinate units on alert until 0215, and gave no decisive and bold commands to the forces in contact. LXXIV Corps was only able to have more of an impact by its commander, General der Artillerie Marcks, leaving headquarters to organize counterattacks. Marcks had been promised by General Dollman, Seventh Army commander, that, in the event of invasion in the vulnerable Caen sector, armored reserves would be instantly made available for a counterattack. However, the Germans, incorrectly assessing the direction, size, and success of the invasion, failed to do this.

D.C.I.

OKW War Diary: 6 June 1944

by Major Percy E. Schramm

On 6 June, the invasion began after weather conditions had delayed the operation for 24 hours. The way had been prepared through attacks against the coastal defenses and the hinterland. The landing took place in the area between the mouth of the Seine and Cherbourg, as expected by the German High Command (shown by the transfer of the 91st LL Division, 6th FS Regiment, and Panzers to the Cotentin peninsula). The operation was prepared by the jumping of parachutists belonging to British and American airborne divisions. At 0100 hours, following this landing, which partly took place through clouds, a landing from the sea started at low tide at 0300–0330 hours, unaffected by the foreshore obstacles. The enemy supported this action with fire from his medium and heavy units.

Our own batteries started firing, and some of the parachutists were immediately annihilated; the enemy, however, succeeded in gaining a foothold on the beach and forming pockets of resistance in the rearward area. It finally became evident that the British attacked on both sides of the Orne while the Americans attacked at the mouth of the Vire and on the Cotentin peninsula.

In order to support the divisions fighting at the coast, the 12th SS Panzer Division, as the first division, was brought up to Lisioux and the 21st Panzer Division thrown into battle west of the mouth of the Orne. The latter was hampered in its efforts to move up by parachutists who had jumped near Caen. The 91st Infantry Division was committed in the St Vaast area, and the Panzer Lehr Division, which together with the 12th SS Panzer Division had been kept as OKW reserves, was released. Motor torpedo-boats which were moving up from Cherbourg were greatly hampered by heavy seas, caused by a wind velocity which even in the bay reached 4–6; destroyers, moving up from Le Havre, were able to release their torpedoes.

That this was the long expected D-Day was evidenced by the fact that Eisenhower's orders were published, followed by speeches by the enemy's prime ministers. It was not as yet clear, however, if this was only the first push designed to tie down our forces or if it was already the major assault. It was surprising that sabotage did not increase noticeably. It was therefore assumed that the enemy at first would attempt to pinch off the Contentin peninsula with the intent to capture Cherbourg, in order to simultaneously or subsequently attack Fifteenth Army with the forces held in readiness in southeastern England.

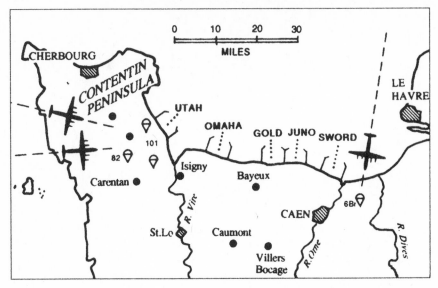

The D-Day Assaults

The situation east of the Orne had been mopped up by the 711th Infantry Division on the evening of the first day, while to the west of the mouth of the river a 10 kilometer long bridgehead had developed, which so far was only very small. The 352nd Infantry Division, employed at this point, was able to seal off the area without any help.

The 709th Infantry Division was able to squeeze the Americans together, but was unable to annihilate them since they were currently reinforced from the air. Since it could not be ascertained whether or not the enemy had landed also at the west coast of the peninsula, the 17th SS Panzer Grenadier Division was (reportedly) released from the OKW reserve (this report later proved erroneous).

OB West on D-Day

by General der Infanterie Günther Blumentritt

Q: When were you alerted to the imminence of invasion? By whom?

A: OB West was not alerted. In view of the uncertain situation in 1943–44, OB West and the armies ordered constant "special attentiveness" and a rapid series of alert stages. We had no naval or aerial reconnaissance, and no information from our espionage agents. For us, the English southern coast was an impenetrable sphinx. Rumors and scattered reports did not give us specific information on the time and place of the landing. A permanent alert of the troops was not possible, since training and rest were equally important.

Q: When were you informed that the invasion had started (give hour and minute, if possible)? Did this notification include locality of invasion?

A: On 5 June 1944, approximately between 2200 and 2300 hours, OB West intercepted a coded radio message from England to the French Underground. We did not know its meaning. In any case, this message deserved special attention, and, consequently, it was transmitted to Army Group B and the armies for their information. Fifteenth Army had also heard the message and ordered "Alert II" (the highest alert stage). Seventh Army gave "Alert II" somewhat later; as far as I know, LXXXIV Infantry Corps ordered the alert independently. About midnight, OB West received a much more distinct message (from the London broadcasting station, I believe), directed from England to France. OB West heard of the events as follows:

a. On 6 June 1944, about 0015–0030: The first paratroop jump at the mouth of the Vire, near Carentan and later near Lisieux.

b. About 0100–0200: Further jumps

c. About 0100–0300: Jumps also on the west coast of Normandy (false report).

d. About 0600: The beginning of the bombing and artillery fire on the invasion front, and therewith the start of the landing. Between 0600 and 0800, it was apparent that the landing would take place approximately between the Orne and the Vire. Not so clear was whether this was the actual invasion, a secondary operation intended as a diversion or a feint, or only a local operation to gain a foothold in France by first taking the Normandy peninsula with Cherbourg.

On 7 or 8 June 1944, our troops captured a complete plan of operations of an American Corps [V Corps—Ed.] with all political and military objectives. This

171

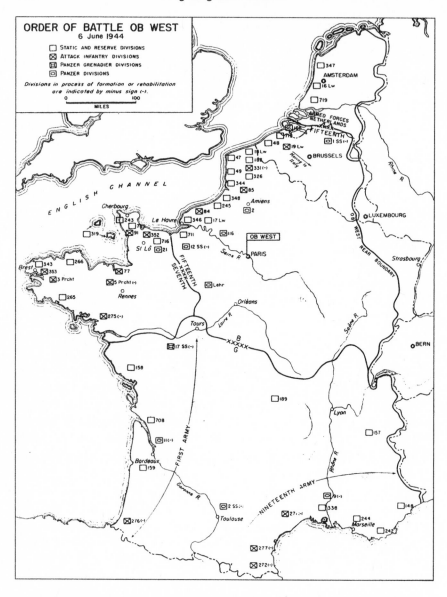

overall plan gave us a clear picture of Allied intentions and the time phases of the first operations in Normandy. The capture of this plan had no practical effect on the Allied military operations since, even though we knew the Allied intentions, we were unable to do anything more than had been done already. Politically, Appendix I of the plan was interesting to us because it gave a clear statement of political objectives, confirming the agreement with Russia—although this was not specifically mentioned in the plan.

Q: What were the first orders received by you from the next higher headquarters immediately after the invasion? By whom?

A: By midnight, there was naturally high pressure at OB West headquarters. There were innumerable telephone calls, teletype messages, requests, orders, and reports to OKW, Army Group B, Third Air Force, Navy Group West, WB NDL, Militärbefehlshaber for Belgium and Northern France, and the German Embassy in Paris (as well as the French government at Vichy). There were requests for the French government to issue proclamations (agreed upon in advance) to the people, urging the French to keep the peace and warning against revolts, sabotage, and obstruction of the German defense measures. There were also requests for the French police to ensure that these measures were carried out. Between 0100 and 0300, OB West independently issued orders to alert the OKW reserves for movement. A request was made to OKW for the release of the Panzer Lehr and 12th SS Panzer Divisions. Between 0300 and 0400, on the independent decision of OB West, one Kampfgruppe from each of the two divisions was moved toward Lisieux and Caen. Between 0400 and 1600, OB West sent repeated urgent requests to OKW for permission to assume control of the two Panzer divisions. Until 1600, these requests were denied, with the inference that the Führer was not yet certain that this was the "real" invasion; he feared the main landing would take place on the Channel coast (Fifteenth Army).

Between 1500 and 1800, the first orders were issued for the predesignated divisions on the fronts not under attack to send (according to the prearranged plans) regimental groups to Normandy. The highest alert stage was put into effect in all German commands in the West, including Army Group G (First and Nineteenth Armies). Before the beginning of the actual invasion of the coast, all commands had been instructed on the measures to be taken; now these measures commenced to be effective. I cannot give the full details without references.

About 1600, the OKW reserves were released, and, in the evening of 6 June 1944, these reserves moved toward Normandy. Orders were given to all headquarters to drive back by counterattacks those enemy forces which had landed. Genfldm Rommel, who was on leave near Ulm, was recalled and arrived in La Roche-Guyon on the evening of 6 June 1944. On the night of 5/6 June 1944, Seventh Army had cancelled the wargames to which many commanders had been ordered. (Thereby, the Commander of the 91st LL Division was shot by American paratroopers while on the return trip in his vehicle.) By 0600, all commands were informed, all possible countermeasures were in process, and the West was alerted.

Q: Give the exact location and disposition of all units of your command on 6 June 1944.

A: OB West Headquarters (von Rundstedt) was at St Germain, west of Paris; the staff of Army Group B (Rommel) was in La Roche-Guyon on the Seine, 40 kilometers northwest of Paris. Seventh Army (Dollmann) was at Le Mans, Fifteenth Army (von Salmuth) at Tourcoing, and Third Air Force and Navy Group West in Paris. The troops in Normandy were under Seventh Army. The Seventh Army, under Army Group B, was the first affected by the invasion, because of the commitment of LXXXIV Infantry Corps in Normandy.

Q: Give your mission, the mission you assigned your subordinate commanders, and the time sequence planned.

A: The mission assigned OB West by the Führer was to hold the coasts and to prevent a landing. The MLR was the high tide line. All available batteries and supporting weapons were to repel the invasion on the sea before a landing could be made, or to eject those forces already landed in front of the MR. All commands were instructed accordingly.

Q: Give any new orders or any changes made to the old orders occurring during the course of the campaign, together with reasons and subsequent developments. Criticize plans and orders.

A: By 8 or 9 June 1944, in spite of the commitment of the 12th SS Panzer and Panzer Lehr Divisions under I SS Panzer Corps, and in spite of bringing up the first, inadequate reinforcements, we did not succeed in repelling the invasion or in defeating those forces which had landed. It was evident to Genfldms von Rundstedt and Rommel that the invasion was successful. In a few days, we realized that our forces and means were not strong enough to reverse the situation. This was reported to OKW, and the envisiaged reinforcements were brought up from fronts not under attack—however, only insofar as the movement was permitted or ordered by OKW; that is, by the Führer himself. The Führer reserved for himself the authority to move each individual division. After a few days, when the Allies succeeded in joining the inner wings of the two beachheads in the vicinity of Arromanches, thus establishing one large beachhead, it was even more obvious that all counterattacks would be futile.

In the first two days, it appeared that the 91st LL Division and elements (regimental groups) of the adjacent coastal divisions would be able to encircle the American paratroops near Carentan and cut them off from the sea. The attempt did not succeed, however, since the paratroops received a steady flow of reinforcements from the sea. The reinforced 91st LL Division was hard pressed in turn, and suffered heavy losses. As the situation seemed threatening, Genfldm von Rundstedt requested a conference with the Führer. Up to that time, all orders read, "counterattack" in order to throw back the landed enemy. However, the reinforcements necessary for this purpose arrived very slowly because of the demolished railroads and bridges, the Resistance movement, the Allied air supremacy, the limited mobility of the horsedrawn infantry divisions, and the lack of fuel and transportation. The Allies landed troops faster and in greater strength than we could reinforce our own.

The Beginning of the Invasion and the 346th Infantry Division

by Oberst Paul Frank

During the evening of 4 June 1944, the following message came to Division from the Corps Ic: "V-Mann [agent] reports invasion between Cherbourg and Le Havre on 5 June 1944." Since similar reports had been received before and had been unfounded, the staff attached little importance to this communication; nevertheless, a Class I alert was ordered for the night of 4/5 June 1944. When nothing happened, the unreliability of the V-Mann reports seemed to have been demonstrated once more. However, since the following night, with its full moon, seemed particularly suitable for airborne operations, the division was kept alerted.

About 0100 on 6 June 1944, word came by telephone from Corps that paratroops were dropping into the area of the division on our left (711th Infantry Division). Reports began to pour in concerning various aspects of the enemy action:

a.   Remarkably strong enemy air activity;

b.   Air bombing of coastal gun positions;

c.   Sound locator units reported the approach of large, slow-flying air formations and seaborne units.

From these reports, Division concluded that this was a major operation in which the airborne invasion would certainly be followed by a landing from the sea. Further, it was believed that this landing was probably already in progress. Since a large part of the air formations passed over Le Havre, it was at first expected the landings would also be made in this area. However, by an immediate study of captured maps, it was established before dawn on 6 June 1944 that the areas of enemy interest all lay south of the Seine; this was confirmed at daybreak, when it was observed from Le Havre that the whole enemy fleet concentration lay further west. This, added to the lack of every type of enemy bombardment north of the Seine, led the division to expect an early transfer to the threatened area.

Corps retained the opinion that the landings in the south were diversionary, and that the principal landing would take place in the area (just) north of the mouth of the Seine, and probably even farther north.

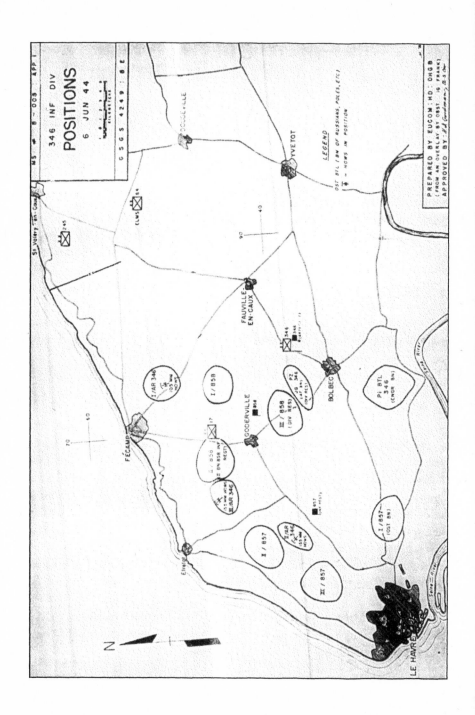

The 711th Infantry Division and the Airborne Invasion

by Generalleutnant Joseph Reichert

For the division, the time up to 5 June 1944 was passed in strenuous construction work by day, on guard duties at night at different stages of alertness, according to the weather conditions and the arrival of news from the V-men. As heretofore on 4 June, in consequence of a report from a V-man that the invasion was to be expected on 5 June, a full-scale alert (Alarmstufe I) was ordered for the night of 4 June. However, during the night, as well as on the following day, perfect quiet prevailed again. For the following night, as far as I can remember, the second stage of alert was ordered, during which half of the men had the right to sleep with their clothes on.

As on the whole day of 5 June, the following night until just after midnight passed completely quietly. We were still in the Casino [Officers' Mess] of the divisional staff until about 0030 hours on 6 June, and were just about ready to retire, when an exceedingly loud noise of motors of single planes, flying apparently very low over our quarters at tremendous speed, attracted our attention. The fact of the air activity as such, at that time, was not surprising, because our own and the enemy's busy air routes of incoming and outgoing planes lay directly over us, which was used nearly every night. It struck us as strange, however, that the planes were flying so low; we had the feeling that they might almost touch the roof.

It was a full-moon night and the weather was fairly stormy, with low-hanging black clouds, between which several low-flying planes could be distinctly observed, flying no particular course but moving in a circle around the divisional command post. Just after having entered the house again, in order to arm myself, I heard cries outside of: "Parachutists!" Dashing again into the open, I still saw a few parachutes landing near the divisional command post. In the meantime, the 20-mm antiaircraft guns which were employed in the strongpoint had opened fire.

Immediately after the alert had been given, the strongpoint was occupied by clerks, messengers, drivers, orderlies, etc.; the guard company which had been on duty hitherto had had to be dissolved a few days before, to reinforce the front troops. Considering the extent of the strongpoint (about 700 meters in diameter), the garrison was extremely weak. Whilst the IIa organized the direct defense of the strongpoint, I ordered the Ia to alarm the whole Division sector and reported to the superior command, LXXXI Army Corps at Rouen. The entire wire net was intact. In the meantime the first prisoners—

177

two parachutists who had landed in the strongpoint itself—were taken, who, however, could not give exact details as to the purpose of the undertaking, and probably did not want to. In the meantime enemy air activity, and with that also the defensive fire of our 20-mm antiaircraft guns, had stopped, so that everything seemed to be peaceful again.

I, on the other hand, realized that it was a sure sign of the beginning of the invasion, which we had expected for a long time, no matter whether it was planned at this point or whether the air operation was only a feint. The first impression was that it was an attempt to wipe out the command post. As a first measure, therefore, I ordered the nearest reserve troops—an engineer company located near St Arnould—to reinforce the strongpoint of the divisional command post.

The following few hours passed very slowly and we expected the attack of the airlanded enemy at any moment, although the reconnaissance patrols sent into the immediate terrain did not contact any enemy. Only nervous firing by the strongpoint forces, with no battle experience, at returning reconnaissance patrols took place. When on 6 June, at about 0300 hours, the engineer troops arrived, an immediate danger to the divisional command post had been eliminated. In the meantime, from reports coming in from the regiment etc., I had received the impression that all of the troops were ready for defense along the coast; that in the remaining area adjoining the coast as east of Touques—also in the farther hinterland—everything was quiet and under control, whereas the presence of a great number of parachutists and landed supply-carrying gliders had been ascertained in the area between Touques and Orne, mainly on the left part of the divisional sector and between Dives and Orne. Against these forces, the fighter commands and the local reserves had already been committed. Connection to the left neighboring unit was maintained everywhere.

In connection with my deliberations made previously about the possibility of an invasion by the enemy, I arrived at the conclusion that the enemy invasion would be made on the Cotentin peninsula, and that the airborne troops who had already landed were to take possession of the higher terrain between Touques and Dives, so as to prevent the effect of enemy fire from there against the left flank of the invasion area.

Therefore, it appeared to me that the right divisional sector to the east of Touques was safe enough to permit me to take the responsibility of transferring the reserve battalion located there, still at night, into uncertainty—or at any rate into the endangered area, all the more so as, in view of the enemy air activity which had to be expected, a transfer during the daytime would meet with the greatest difficulties owing to the few Touques crossings and the open terrain that had to be passed.

I ordered, therefore, this battalion also to move into an area directly to the east of the divisional command post to be at my disposal, so as to be able to employ the latter as became necessary either against the landed enemy airborne troops or against an enemy who had to be expected from the sea. Just after dawn, this battalion, too, reached the area as ordered without encountering enemy resistance.

Besides, the artillery was set up to direct concentrated fire in front of the left wing of the divisional sector.

. . . Although the enemy airlanding had been unsuccessful at that time, its effects later became quite annoying. I have never been able to comprehend the object of the enemy airlanding in the divisional sector at that time. Probably the prisoners' statements were correct—that some elements had lost their route and become lost owing to the lack of flight commanders. This is also probably the reason why the fighting qualities of the troops, whose physical condition struck us very favorably, had such little effect. The portions which were employed in the bridgehead to the east of the Orne, and which were efficiently controlled, fought in an excellent manner both during the attack and the defense.

Likewise, I do not quite understand why the Allies made the airborne landing prior to the invasion from the sea, because the place of airborne landing was too near the coast for a feint, thereby neutralizing the element of surprise.

Commitment of the 1058th Infantry Regiment and AOK Assault Battalion 7

by Oberstleutnant Günther Keil

The Hessian-Thüringen 919th Infantry Regiment had roughly been deployed before the invasion as follows:

1st and 2nd Battalions at the coast from the mouth of the Carentan Canal to La Belle Croix (inclusive);

Georgian Battalion, subordinate to the regiment, lying in reserve east of Ste Mère-Église;

3rd Battalion of the 919th Infantry Regiment on the hills northwest of Quineville, west of La Belle Croix (inclusive) in the second line.

Regimental units:

13th Company of the 919th Infantry Regiment (infantry gun company) with two platoons northwest of Hebert, northwest of Ste Marie-du-Mont.

Mission: barrage fire toward the sea.

One platoon (Lt Saturnus) at Cauvin.

Mission: to fight enemy airborne landings on the plain north of the Carentan Canal.

14th Company of the 919th Infantry Regiment:

One heavy AT platoon at the coast in the area of the 1st Battalion;

One medium AT platoon at the crossroads northwest of Ste Marie-du-Mont;

One medium AT platoon in the area of the 2nd Battalion on the hills northwest of Quineville, west of La Belle Croix.

16th Company of the 919th Infantry Regiment:

Three platoons for operating the AT guns employed in the nests of resistance and the strongpoints;

One light AAA platoon on a hill west of Quineville.

Headquarters Company:

Signal platoon on the advance command post on the hill west of Quineville in the pillbox signal center;

Engineer platoon at the command post of the regiment;

Company leader and motorized column in Montebourg.

Command post of the regiment: quarry near Hill 69 (road triangle north of the road Montebourg–Quineville, half-way between the two villages named).

Advance command post: pillbox signal center on hill west of Quineville.

Before the invasion, the 1058th Infantry Regiment, 91st Division, was committed as follows. One battalion, possibly the 3rd, of the 1058th Infantry Regiment was committed at St Conte du Mont–Angeville au Plain, with the mission of preventing enemy airborne troops from landing on the broad plain north of the Carentan Canal. The Panzerjäger Company of the 1058th Infantry Regiment and the Division Training School, consisting of one infantry platoon, were committed in a hedgehog formation at the Carentan–Ste Mère-Église, Chef du Pont–Ste Marie-du-Mont crossroads, with the mission of blocking the roads against enemy tanks. One battalion, commanded by Moch, was committed on the hills to the north of Montebourg, with the mission of defending the hills against airborne landings.

One battalion, as I recall, was committed between Valognes and Cherbourg, with a mission regarding which I have no information. The location of the regimental command post is also unknown to me. The 1058th Infantry Regiment formed a part of the 91st Division, and the battalion and the Panzerjäger company in the rear of my sector—the battalion at St Conte du Mont and the company at Montebourg—had both at the same time been ordered to cooperate with me.

During the night of 5 June 1944, at 24 hours, enemy parachute troops made a jump over my command post at the quarry at Hill 69 north of the Quineville–Montebourg highway. The parachutists were taken prisoner. From the maps in the possession of the captured parachutists, it was evident that the main locality for the drop would be Ste Mère-Église.

At 0200 hours, a special mission staff officer of the Georgian Battalion, located east of Ste Mère-Église, and a messenger from Christ Engineer Company, 790th Engineer Battalion, from Emondeville, arrived at the regimental command post and reported that thousands of parachutists had jumped, and that their units had been surrounded. Previous to this time, I had not made so serious an estimate of the situation, because I had believed that in this hedge-covered terrain the parachutists would have difficulty in orienting themselves and that some would even land in the wrong spots, like those who had jumped near my command post although they had been marked for Ste Mère-Église. Moreover, at first I did not believe that it was a matter of a drop by complete divisions, but that it was a question of operations by fairly large task forces; and, even after the arrival of the messengers, I did not consider the situation as serious as it actually was, because although both units reported that they had been encircled, the two messengers had been able to reach me without difficulty, the officer of the Georgian Battalion having even arrived by automobile.

After receiving the reports of the Georgian Battalion and the Christ Engineer Company, I requested the Operations Officer (Ia) of the division (Major Förster) to authorize an immediate attack by Moch's battalion against Ste Mère-Église. Major Förster received the release of the Moch battalion from Corps, and ordered the battalion to attack Ste Mère-Église at 0230 hours. I remember these facts very accurately, because

Division had no direct connection with Moch, but transmitted the orders to me. According to my calculations, Moch, whose battalion had been alerted at 2400 hours, and in any case was always ready for marching, could reach Ste Mère-Église at 0700 at the latest.

At 0700, however, I received a message from Captain Simoneit, commander of Headquarters Company of the 919th Infantry Regiment at Montebourg, saying that Major Moch and his battalion were still stationed at the southern exit of Montebourg. I then ordered Moch in the name of Division—Moch was not subordinated to me—to march at once against Ste Mère-Église. By 1000 a message from Moch's battalion reached me saying that the Azeville battery had been encircled, and asking whether he should liberate it. Since I had no contact with Division at that time, I again ordered Moch, on my own responsibility, to open his attack upon Ste Mère-Église. It must accordingly have been 1200, instead of 0700, when Moch made his appearance before Ste Mère-Église. This lapse of time had been sufficient to allow the American parachutists to take up firm positions, especially since the troop of Herman's AAA Regiment, of at least 200 men at Ste Mère-Église, was pushing southward toward the Panzerjäger company of the 1058th Infantry Regiment at the crossroads, instead of defending Ste Mère-Église. It was now impossible for Moch's battalion to take Ste Mère-Église.

It was impossible for me to take any action in regard to Moch's battalion, for the following reasons. In the first place, the situation in the sector of the 919th Infantry Regiment on our side was, on the morning of 6 June, still very obscure. There had been air landings in the 1st Battalion sector. There was no way of knowing to what extent the defense nests and support points were still holding out, because from 0100 there was no longer any contact with the 1st Battalion. The extent to which the enemy had advanced to the west and north after landing was also obscure. In-drops in the sector of the 2nd Battalion were to be expected, especially because enemy planes were repeatedly approaching Quineville itself. In this obscure situation, I could not leave the regimental command post. Moreover, situation reports, missions, and requests from the division were piling up on my desk. In the second place, I was not concerned, because the battalion was not under my command.

Commitment of the Assault Battalion

In the course of the morning, I was informed by the Division Operations Officer (Ia) that by noon the Army Headquarters 7th Assault Battalion would arrive on the St Martin d'Audouville–Coubière road by truck. I was ordered to move the battalion through St Floxel onto the road leading to Beuzeville-au-Plain. Half a company of the Panzerjäger Company of the 1058th Infantry Regiment, which had until then been operating in my sector southwest of Quineville, was to be attached to the battalion at the proper time.

The assault battalion arrived at the regiment at 1200 as I recall. Since the battalion commander had not yet arrived, the assault battalion was under the command of Captain Kaldauke. The battalion succeeded in advancing as far as the Georgian Battalion, and in joining the remnants of this battalion temporarily, and part of the battalion even succeeded in advancing as far as the church at Ste Mère-Église. However, since in the meantime Moch's battalion had been thrown back near Ste Mère-Église, and the enemy had been reinforced and was threatening to encircle the assault battalion, the latter had to withdraw toward the area southwest of Azeville.

One-half of the 709th Panzerjäger Company was started off on time in the direction of Azeville, where it was to join the assault battalion. However, against orders and without waiting for the assault battalion, it rode past Azeville, where it is reported to have advanced as far as the area northeast of Beuzeville-au-Plain and there to have been destroyed by the enemy.

As I learned in prison camp from Oberstleutnant Witte, head of the Division Instruction School of the 91st Division, the Panzerjäger company of the 1058th Infantry Regiment defended itself in its hedgehog position for several days, possibly until 8 June, and was then overcome by the enemy. Where the battalion at St Conte du Mont remained after the landing I do not know. It is certain that it did not fulfill its mission of hindering enemy airborne troops from landing. This is evident from the statements of Oblt Gluba, my company commander at Ste Marie-du-Mont. When we met again in a prison camp in England in 1946, Oblt Gluba gave me the following information from memory:

Oblt Gluba was commander of the 1st Company, 919th Infantry Regiment, the reserve company of the 1st Battalion. He was stationed in Ste Marie-du-Mont. Having given up parts of its personnel to nests of resistance, his company was reduced to one platoon of infantry, one heavy machine-gun group, and one medium mortar group. For three or four days, until 8 June, without food or ammunition supply, Gluba fought in the area of Ste Marie-du-Mont–Brucheville–Vièreville–Cauvin; then, having crossed the plain north of the Carentan Canal, and the canal itself, he joined the adjacent division. He tried repeatedly to make contact with the battalion at St Conte du Mont; at first he even intended to withdraw toward the battalion located at Angeville-au-Plain, but he was unable to locate any elements of this battalion.

The 1st Battery of Army Headquarters, 7th Assault Battalion, was not committed at the right wing of the 919th Infantry Regiment near the Carentan Canal (as General von Schlieben takes for granted in his report), but was committed northwest of Foucarville, with its train near Azeville. I know this definitely, because I drove to the battery position several times. It was attacked by parachutists as early as the night of 5 June and was destroyed on 6 or 7 June. It was merely involved in infantry fighting, and did not operate as an artillery unit. I know this from statements by the battery commander, Oblt Habel, who was in a prison camp with me.

On the right wing of my regiment, on both sides of Ste Marie-du-Mont, there was standing one artillery battalion of the 91st Division, consisting of a headquarters and two batteries; it was being activated. According to statements of Oblt Gluba of the 1st Company of the 919th Infantry Regiment, the batteries were attacked by parachutists in the morning of 6 June and destroyed.

If the parachute regiment of von der Heydte had been supported by artillery in his attack from Carentan, it can have been only the infantry gun platoon of Lt Saturnus of the 13th Company of the 919th Infantry Regiment. Well camouflaged, he was employed at Cauvin, having the mission to cover the plain north of the Carentan Canal under fire in case of airborne landings. According to the statements of Oblt Gluba, Saturnus has fulfilled this task for three days.

Oblt Gluba himself withdrew with his company on the second or third day to the position of Platoon Saturnus. When this position was attacked by tanks, the infantry gun platoon disabled several tanks. When all ammunition had been expended, the two guns were blown up. Saturnus and his gun crews, together with Oblt Gluba and the 1st Company of the 919th Infantry Regiment, withdrew to the adjacent division across the Carentan Canal.

LXXXIV Corps on D-Day: The Landing Battles

by Oberstleutnant Friedrich von Criegern

5 June 1944 passed without special events. About 2200 hours, it was apparent that enemy air activity became more lively than usual. In addition to the previously ordered degree of readiness, the corps commander at 2300 ordered alert for the entire staff. Apprehension led to the waking up of the Commanding General.

After it seemed, at first, as though expectations would not be fulfilled, at 0100 telephone messages arrived in quick succession. The 716th Infantry Division reported landings of enemy parachutists in the area east and northwest of Caen; the 709th Infantry Division and 91st LL Division reported the same from the area of Montebourg on both sides of the Vire river and along the eastern coast of the Cotentin peninsula. These messages were transmitted by 0130 to Seventh Army HQ. Even though these reports were not very clear, Corps concluded there would be air landings on a large scale and the beginnings of the invasion.

During the following hours, parachute landings were reported deep into the rear areas around Caen and Carentan. Troops located in the endangered areas reported that they had started—as ordered—to fight the enemy parachutists.

The 716th Infantry Division and 91st LL Division reported that, in the aforementioned area, the enemy had carried out landings with glider troops since 0320. There were air landings east of the Orne river at Revile as well as west of the Orne river at Benesville.

The command post of the 91st LL Division was attacked by airlanded enemy elements in battalion strength. The tactical group of the general staff section withdrew to the command post of the supply group staff section and continued to conduct battle from there. The commander of the 91st LL Division, Gen Falley, who had gone to Rennes for a map exercise ordered by the Army, was killed during the morning of 6 June when returning to the original command post which had been captured by the enemy. Already, by 0330 hours, the division could no longer communicate with troops committed in the area of Ste Mère-Église.

By 0600, two focal points of the enemy airlanding became apparent: the area north of the Orne river and the area of Carentan–Ste Mère-Église on the Cotentin peninsula.

The 6th FS Regiment received orders at 0600 hours to attack and annihilate the enemy in the area between Carentan and Ste Mère-Église. Prior to this, the 91st LL

Division—which since 0300 had been assigned to the Corps—received the mission to annihilate enemy elements near Ste Mère-Église through a concentric attack by two Kampfgruppen.

The 21st Panzer Division naturally received orders from the 716th Division to attack air landings east of the Orne river. The mission was executed by elements of this Panzer division.

After sea targets had been located, in spite of the fact that the locating devices had been severely damaged, landing fleets came into sight off the Calvados coast as well as off the east coast of Contentin. The 716th and 352nd Infantry Divisions reported that from 0530 enemy ship artillery opened fire against the coast from the mouth of the Orne river to Berniers-sur-Mer, near Arromanches, Colleville, and Grandcamp, and the beginnings of landings at the mouth of the Orne river.

At 0700, the 21st Panzer Division was assigned to the Corps by telephone from the Army. The Army agreed with the commitment of the division east of the mouth of the Orne river, which had already taken place. The subsequently arriving reports showed that the sea landings had been in progress since 0715. It seemed that three landing sectors became apparent: west of the mouth of the Orne river, east of Grandcamp, and along the east coast of Cotentin, east of Ste Mère-Église.

By 0900, the enemy had penetrated into the artillery positions of the 716th Infantry Division west of the mouth of the Orne river, and gained a firm footing near Asnelles and St Laurent. The rapid landing of tanks, reported near Asnelles, very quickly brought about a critical situation there simultaneously with those of the 716th Infantry Division west of the Orne river and in the sector of the 352nd Infantry Division near St Laurent-sur-Mer. The lack of depth to the defense and the lack of mobile antitank weapons were especially felt.

Now, Corps requested the commitment of the promised 12th SS Panzer Division, because the 21st Panzer Division was already employed east of the Orne river. Since the arrival of this division could not be expected on 6 June, orders were issued at 1000 to the 21st Panzer Division—most of their troops were still south of Caen—to advance and pivot west of the Orne river for a counterattack.

6 June: Cotentin Coast Artillery

by Generalmajor Gerhard Triepel

On 6 June 1944, around 0000 hours, on the east coast from Morsalines as far as the mouth of the Vire river, American airborne troops were jumping down. Simultaneously, pattern bombings were carried out over several places. In the region of Morsalines, an American captain and a number of parachutists were taken prisoner by the 2nd Battalion, 1261st Regiment. Contact with the battalion of the 191st Artillery Regiment at Ste Marie-du-Mont, and with the 1st Battalion, same regiment, at Foucarville, was lost. Thereafter, no report from these place came to regimental headquarters.

At dawn, the gigantic fleet became visible from south of the mouth of the Vire river far up to the heights of Barfleur. After that, numerous airplanes with gliders in two appeared from the east. They landed in the region of Ste Mère-Église–Carentan.

Several ships, which approached the coast, were fired upon by coastal batteries, and took off at once. The Marcouf naval battery and the 4th Battery (1261st Regiment at Quineville) opened fire on a small cruiser and sank it. The Marcouf battery was then taken under heavy fire from the enemy's naval artillery, and at the same time bombed by airplanes. Both of the guns—emplaced in concrete—were knocked out by direct hits through the loopholes.

Our batteries as well as strongpoints along the coast were constantly bombed by the air force. Even traffic on the roads was considerably harassed by fighter-bombers. Rocket bombs were very effective.

The 2nd Battery, 1261st Regiment (French type guns of 10-cm caliber, under concrete), opened fire against approaching motor boats, whereupon they turned back at once.

Parachutists appeared everywhere, to our discomfort. Our infantry attempted to clear up the terrain, but it was difficult to seize those parachutists, seeing that the ground with its unevenness offered only limited visibility.

The 2nd Battery, 1261st Regiment, fought against those paratroops who had assembled around the observation post located in a pillbox. After being fired on, these parachutists were chased away.

The 3rd Battery, 1261st Regiment (guns of French origin, caliber 15.5-cm)—in a firing position next to the one located at Fontenay, which was being built up—after opening fire against a ship, received such heavy fire from the enemy's naval artillery that within a short time it looked as though the battery had been plowed up. Two guns were damaged. Batteries 5 and 6 of 1261st Regiment also took a hand in the battle on the sea.

The 6th Battery, 1261st Regiment, was withdrawn from its concrete position, because the battery position, hit many times by pattern bombing, was turned into an area pitted with shell craters. It stood now northeast of Videcosville along a row of bushes, its front to the sea.

Even the 9th and 10th Batteries, located at Pernelle, as well as the 7th, were fighting against ships which could be seen within their range.

During the night, a large number of parachutists jumped into the battery of the assault battalion of the Seventh Army (light Russian howitzers), which was in the sector of the 1st Battery, 1261st Regiment, at Cibrantot. Bitter fighting took place with guns and hand weapons. The battery was lost, though some of the drivers made their way to the 2nd Battery, which was located nearby.

The guns of the naval battery of Marcouf that remained opened fire once more against an enemy ship. But this battery was knocked out by naval artillery in a short time.

Against troops who just jumped in the region of Ste Mère-Église–Carantan, a defense front was built up. From Montebourg in the direction of Ste Mère-Église, attacks were launched on both sides of the main road. Our attack did not progress beyond Ste Mère-Église due to the fact that it was carried out with forces much too inadequate and proceeding only a few hundred meters to the right and left of the road.

The 456th and 457th Motorized Artillery Battalions were employed in this combat area. They suffered losses by parachutists, upon reconnoitering and moving into position. Those batteries were repeatedly attacked by fighter-bombers without sustaining serious losses. While moving into position, the 2nd Battery, 456th Battalion, was ambushed and badly mauled by American parachutists.

The Invasion:
The 709th Infantry Division
by Generalleutnant Karl Wilhelm von Schlieben

Course of Events

A short time before, the division commanders on the Cotentin peninsula and the commander of the Channel Islands division received an order to participate in a wargame, which was to take place at Rennes, together with two subordinate commanders. As Chiffremont, near Valognes, was about 190 kilometers distant from Rennes, I, like other division commanders, left for Rennes late in the afternoon of 5 June together with the commander of the 739th Grenadier Regiment and the commander of the Seventh Army assault battalion. I had the permission of Corps Headquarters, to whom I had reported my departure.

6 June 1944

On 6 June, at 0530 hours, I received the following message at my hotel at Rennes through an orderly of the Kommandantur: "The wargame has been cancelled. You are requested to return to your unit." The orderly was unable to give me a reason for this change. The commander of the assault battalion, who was immediately sent to the Rennes Kommandantur, brought back the news that the invasion had started at 0100 hours. Where, he could not find out. We left immediately and found soldiers with local security missions in places that were completely free of the enemy, who told us of rumors that the enemy was approaching.

At Avranches, I think, we came to a stop after the second tire was blown out. This pause was used to get briefed by telephone by the commander of a regiment on special assignment, stationed on the west coast. I learned that a strong enemy force had landed from the air on the Cotentin peninsula, mainly in its eastern part. In order to safely reach my command post at Valognes, he advised me to drive along the west coast and then proceed via Briquebec. When we reached the Cotentin, we could see that the war had started. On the roads were motor vehicles disabled by bombs; the villages were empty, the inhabitants in hiding.

As I was leaving Valognes at about noon for my command post (Chiffremont), which was only a few kilometers away, I was stopped by a severely wounded German soldier, who told me that he had been under fire from the hedgerows only a few moments ago. I took the man with me, delivered him at the dressing station at Valognes and then left for Chiffremont, where I received the following information from the commander of the artillery, who had acted as my representative, and the first general staff officer:

1. Since 0100 hours there have been strong air landings continuing for hours, mainly in the area of Ste Mère-Église, behind the 919th Grenadier Regiment, but also in the Ferneile area, and near Cherbourg, Valognes, and Hemeves.

2. An immense fleet of fighting and transport craft is cruising off the east coast and has already landed men and equipment. The Marcouf heavy naval coast battery, embedded in concrete, had been put out of action by direct hits on the embrasures.

3. Nothing has been heard of the 795th Georgian Battalion, which was held in reserve at and around Berville. Furthermore, these is no news of the 1st Battalion, 919th Grenadier Regiment, committed along the southeast coast of the division sector.

4. Corps headquarters had committed the 1058th Grenadier Regiment, less one battalion, under the command of Colonel Feigang, and the Seventh Army assault battalion, formerly in army or corps reserve for a counterattack. The 1058th Grenadier Regiment belonged to the 91st Air Landing Division, a division of the 25th Wave.

The 1058th Grenadier Regiment, less one battalion, advancing via Montebourg, had the task of annihilating the airborne enemy and pushing on to the east to throw the enemy who had landed on the east coast back into the sea.

The Seventh Army assault battalion had been committed from Le Vast (16 kilometers northeast of Valognes) to Azeville (northeast of Ste Mère-Église).

According to the artillery commander, the attack of the assault battalion had made good progress. On the other hand, the 1058th Grenadier Regiment had not progressed beyond Montebourg. Replying to my question how much artillery had been assigned to the grenadier regiment, he told me that it had none. The reasons for the slow progress of this grenadier regiment, which had marched out early on 6 June, were as follows:

1. The commander of the 91st Air Landing Division, Generalleutnant Falley, had been killed by enemy parachutists on his return from the planned wargame at Rennes, in the immediate vicinity of his command post at Pont-l'Abbe. If he had been present when the 1058th Regiment, subordinated to him, had received its march order, he would surely have seen to it that artillery and perhaps also motorized units of his division AT and Flak companies were assigned to it.

2. The enemy resistance on the Montebourg–Ste Mère-Église road was favored by the hedges. A few well-hidden machine-gunners were sufficient to make serious difficulties for unarmored troops.

3. The enemy probably had considered the securing of the great Montebourg–Ste Mère-Église–Carentan highway as being one of his most important missions.

If the Seventh Army assault battalion had made quicker progress in the direction of Azeville, it might have met with less enemy resistance. This battalion likewise had no artillery. Its artillery was in position southeast of Ste Mère-Église, following the principle that artillery should be committed and not kept in reserve. This battery supported the 6th Parachute Regiment, commander Oberstleutnant von der Heydte, in its fight during the evening of 6 June. On 7 June, it was finished off by the enemy. The 5th Parachute Regiment, subordinate to the 91st Airborne Division, had been committed by Corps from the area southwest of Carentan, via Carentan against the coast north of Ste Marie-du-Mont. As I also learned later from Oberstleutnant von der Heydte, the parachute regiment was committed by Corps Headquarters without artillery. It may be that the strength of the enemy, the American 82nd and 101st Divisions, had been underestimated at first.

Even when taking into account the strong superiority in matériel and personnel, and preparations lasting several years without interference, together with the absence of the German Luftwaffe, one must admit that it was an immensely efficient Allied organization which brought about these results within a short space of time and during the short nights of the month of June. From further information given to me by the artillery commander and the first general staff officer after my return from Rennes, it could be clearly been that there was justification for asking the following questions:

   a.   Will further air landings or parachute jumps follow the enemy landing in the night of 5 June? Will the enemy jump or land in the immediate vicinity of Cherbourg, in the northeastern part of the peninsula (Pernelle Height) and on the west coast?

   b.   Where will the definite landing of the great mass of the ships sighted take place?

The anxiety with regard to these questions had been increased by reports concerning enemy forces being seen in the sector of the 729th Grenadier Regiment in the northeastern part of the peninsula, near Hemeves and Valognes, and near St Sauveur-le-Viconte at the rear of the land front of Cherbourg. The anxiety was justified because seven to eight airlanding or parachute divisions were said to have been concentrated in England.

Following the briefing on the situation, I telephoned the commander of LXXXIV Corps, General der Artillerie Marcks, informing him that I had returned from Rennes and resumed command of the 709th Infantry Division. At the same time I asked for the release of the 456th and 457th (mtz) artillery battalions, under the regimental staff of Lieutenant-Colonel Seidel, to support the 1058th Grenadier Regiment. My request was granted. The order to bring forward these battalions was given at once. Lieutenant-Colonel Seidel was ordered to report in advance to the commander of the 1058th Grenadier Regiment.

The Invasion:
The 352nd Infantry Division
by Oberstleutnant Fritz Ziegelmann

In the last days of May, there was increased activity of enemy air reconnaissance, which was also by night (night photography). I myself witnessed the low-level flight of single airplanes on the coast, which must have been of importance for reconnaissance (perhaps photographic reconnaissance), because an attack on objectives on the ground did not occur.

Messenger pigeon activity, which was more acute than before, is a special chapter, containing mainly statements with regard to rearward installations. They were only of importance for the enemy air force. But one message concerned us. The writer stated he lived in Criqueville, south Grandcamp, and gave information about 2/1716th Artillery Regiment; about new anti-aircraft units (1st Anti-Aircraft Regiment); and about increases in the construction of coastal zone obstacles near Grandcamp. He did not believe that a landing at Grandcamp would be successful.

During the last days of May, there were bombing raids on the army coast battery on the "Point du Hoc" (3/1260) and on the positions of 2/1716th Artillery Regiment which led to partial failure of the artillery; also on the direction-finder stations of the Air Force and Navy, so that these were not available for assignment, except to a limited extent.

Today, I know that we could have determined the boundary between the American and British invasion corps by means of the enemy air force's activity. Even if from other sectors (for instance, Calais) the same reports were found, it was obvious that the extension of the peninsula of Cotentin would be caught directly or indirectly in the invasion.

During the first days of June, an officer of the French Resistance movement was caught in Brittany and said that the invasion would begin in the next few days. This was true, if looked at "intuitively."

This information, because of the surprisingly strong enemy air force activity (low-level attack from the sea toward the east and west), led me to propose to my division commander that the troops be alerted with special regard to air landings. This was done.

On 5 June, shortly before midnight, I had gone to bed when at about 2400 hours the telephone rang and the special missions staff officer of Corps HQ, LXXXIV Corps, told me: "Enemy parachute troops landed at Caen, air raid warning Stage II." According to the alarm almanac, I had this order phoned to all of the subordinated units (regiments, and even battalions, in the sector of the 352nd Infantry Division), which was done by about 0200 hours.

There was no further report of the enemy by 0100 hours, except for that of brisk activity of his air force in the regimental sectors (low-level flights). Shortly after 0100 hours, the 914th Infantry Regiment (left) reported the landing of enemy parachute troops at the Carentan Canal hard east of the only emergency bridge west of Brévands. For further clarification as to the strength and intentions of these parachute troops, a supplementary report followed at about 0200 hours, to the effect that the enemy landed was estimated to comprise two companies, and that he was getting further reinforcements. The two rifle companies of 2/914th Infantry Regiment were employed in attack, to throw the enemy back across the Carentan Canal. The regiment requested the speediest bringing up of the 3rd Rifle Company (which was employed as guard company with HQ at that time), and it reported that small units of parachutists had dropped also east of the road from Grandcamp to Isigny, from where they were giving light signals. Fighter detachments of the 1st Anti-Aircraft Regiment were employed to fight these troops.

At about 0200 hours, the Staff in the c.p., after describing the situation of the sector of the 352nd Infantry Division, gave the following order:

"North of Port-en-Bessin, there are concentrations of enemy ships in sight. Major air landings have taken place in the Vire–low country south of Carentan; Corps Reserve (reinforced 915th Infantry Regiment) is immediately to march through the Forêt de Cerisy to St Jean de Daye. Regimental commander is to report to the c.p."

The 914th Infantry Regiment (left) was immediately ordered to send out patrols to discover the situation in the Vire depression south of Carentan.

At and after 0300 hours, the reinforced 915th Infantry Regiment 915 (2/915th Infantry Regiment and the 352nd Rifle Battalion on bicycles, 1/915th Infantry Regiment and regimental units on French cargo trucks) were on their way to St Paul Balaroy. As was to be expected, many of the French drivers claimed it was not possible to proceed further, due to engine trouble, and of course this held things up! After orientation on the situation at the divisional c.p., the Commander of the 915th Infantry Regiment (Oberstleutnant Meyer) was given the order at all costs to keep up his connexion with the divisional HQ. A radio station was allotted to the 915th Infantry Regiment.

At 0500 hours the situation of the 726th Infantry Regiment (right) and the 916th Infantry Regiment (center) was in no wise changed. Movements of ships previously reported in close proximity to the beach north of St Laurent proved false by this time. The report of the 914th Infantry Regiment (left) was that the fighting with the enemy parachute troops west of Brévands was very heavy, and the job of dislodging the enemy, perched in trees and behind hedges, had resulted in considerable losses on our side. The first prisoners of the 101st American Airborne Division were brought in there. Since no reports from the region south of Carentan were at hand yet, and telephone communication with the neighbor to the left (709th Infantry Division) was interrupted, the 914th Infantry Regiment (left) was given the order to take up communication also with the right wing of the 709th Infantry Division at Carentan. No noise of battle from the region south of Carentan was reported. On taking up telephone communication with the right neighbor (716th Infantry Division), we learned that the paratroops landed (north of Caen) were successively being reinforced and had apparently the intention of taking the Orne crossing at Benouville.

Near 0600 hours, shortly after sunrise, no fresh reports were at hand. It was expected—as low-tide was at 0525 hours on this day—that the picture before the divisional sector would probably greatly change at and after 0800 hours (when the tide started to come in again).

At about 0600 hours, the enemy suddenly started to cover the "landing-endangered" coastal sector around St Laurent and the background with the fire of heavy naval artillery. Shortly after that (between 0645 and 0700), the regimental commander who was responsible for this sector (Oberst Goth, 916th Infantry Regiment) reported the approach of a large number of enemy landing craft, some of which were also engaging with their weapons the fortified defense system.

The choice of the landing place, the strength, and the continuous naval artillery fire, as well as the large number of approaching landing craft reported again and again, gave rise to the idea at the c.p. that we had to deal here with a systematic landing by major forces. The invasion had really started!

After 0700 hours, the 726th Infantry Regiment (right) reported that, in the section of their right neighbor (an eastern battalion of the 716th Infantry Division), the enemy had landed on a rather wide front, and was advancing with tanks toward Meuvaine. A less strong attack—tanks as well—on the east border of Asnelles was repulsed. Shortly after that, the 914th Infantry Regiment (left) reported that no landing of parachute troops had taken place south of Carentan, but that, instead, north of there, further landings of parachute troops were going on, and that a landing from the sea had started on the right wing of the 709th Infantry Division, toward Andouville. There were no new reports of how the battle was going with the enemy paratroops landed west of Brévands.

The 352nd Infantry Division saw now clearly that a breakthrough by the enemy armored troops from Meuvaines to the south made it possible for them to turn to the west without great difficulties, so that at the same time the danger arose of rolling up the divisional front and losing the town of Bayeux.

The 352nd Infantry Division required reinforcements for sealing up the right flank which was being torn open; the main task here was to throw the enemy back into the sea from the region around Meuvaines, just as had been frequently practiced with the corps reserve (reinforced 915th Infantry Regiment).

In the course of a telephone conversation with the Corps commander, General of Artillery Marcks, shortly before 0800 hours, I described the situation and requested emphatically the return and subordination of the reinforced 915th Infantry Regiment, since from the latest reports received it no long appeared necessary to send it into the low ground of the Vire south of Carentan. Preparation of the reinforced 915th Infantry Regiment in the region east of Bayeux for the protection of the right divisional flank and a counterattack toward Crépon–Meuvaines appeared necessary. The Commanding General agreed to this proposal.

By 0900 hours, we succeeded in reaching the commander of the reinforced 915th Infantry Regiment and in giving him the order to lead his regiment back into the region around Esquay (east of Bayeux), with the addition: "Counterattack of the reinforced 915th Infantry Regiment, line of attack Crépon."

By that time, the situation at the front of the 352nd Infantry Division had developed as follows. The enemy had penetrated into the flank of the 726th Infantry Regiment (right) at Meuvaines and was advancing to Crépon. Portions of his detachments, and tanks as well, were advancing from Meuvaines to the west, but had been stopped by our 2/916th Infantry Regiment at the "La Gronde" stream. A minor attack from the sea on Arromanches had been repulsed. Asnelles, Arromanches, and the region hard south of it were lying under the fire of enemy naval artillery. The 3rd Battalion of the 1352nd Artillery Regiment, which stood south of that sector, covered the landing area east of Asnelles with continuous fire, and some of its elements moved forward against the enemy stuck fast at La Gronde. There existed no communication with the staff of the Eastern Battalion of the 716th Infantry Division, which had withdrawn to the south. The 916th Infantry Regiment (center) lay under continuous heavy naval artillery fire, which penetrated as far as the road from Bayeux to Isigny. Inferior enemy forces had succeeded in gaining a footing in the low plain of Colleville and Vierville.

I succeeded in establishing telephone communication with the troops in Pillbox "76" (Pointe et Raz de la Percée). The commander, whom I knew personally, described the situation in detail:

"At the water's edge at low tide near St Laurent and Vierville the enemy is in search of cover behind the coastal zone obstacles. A great many motor vehicles—and among these ten tanks—stand burning at the beach. The obstacle demolition squads have given up their activity. Debarkation from the landing boats has ceased; the boats keep farther seawards. The fire of our battle positions and artillery was well placed and has inflicted considerable casualties upon the enemy. A great many wounded and dead lie on the beach. Some of our battle positions have ceased firing; they do not answer any longer when rung up on the telephone. Hard east of this pillbox, one group of enemy commandos (one company) has set foot on land and attacked Pillbox '76' from the south, but after being repelled with casualties it has withdrawn toward Gruchy. . . ."

The regimental commander, who also had listened to this conversation, reported further that up till then we had succeeded in frustrating an enemy landing on a wide front. The rocket projectors emplaced at St Laurent had had a good effect. Countermeasures were being taken against the weak enemy, who had infiltrated at two places there. The 916th Regiment, however, had to report that the casualties on our side were successively rising in number because of the continuous fire of the enemy naval artillery and of the landing boats, so that reinforcements had to be asked for.

Oberst Goth reported, moreover, that a strong enemy commando operation was in progress against our main battery at Point du Hoc, where the enemy—in order to climb up the steep coast—had sent over rockets bearing rope ladders which rolled down the rocky wall. An assault detachment of ours (forty men) from St Pierre du Mont was at once sent out to Point du Hoc.

Near the 914th Infantry Regiment (left), a landing operation in a strength of one to two companies was repulsed west of Maisy in front of the obstacles of the coastal zone, and many enemy landing craft were set on fire, whilst the remaining ones withdrew to the west.

1/1352nd Artillery Regiment, which had an advanced observer west of the Carentan Canal, fought the enemy landings north of Pouppeville (sector of the 709th Infantry Division) with continuous fire. The reports of the engagements with the enemy paratroops west of Brévands said that we had succeeded in squeezing them into a narrow strip but that they were now defending themselves with extraordinary tenacity.

The commander of the 1352nd Artillery Regiment (Obstlt Ocker) supplemented the above reports on the basis of results obtained by his observation posts, and he hinted at the fact that the ammunition stock was already considerably lowered.

It was not possible to establish communication with the artillery carrier flotilla (A-Träger-Flotille) lying in the ports of Port-en-Bessin and Grandcamp for some days. The flotilla had departed during the night, except for a few artillery carriers at Port-en-Bessin, which were not maneuverable.

From the rear area, the Ib of the 352nd Infantry Division had no engagements to report. The local population, which, for the most part, had left the localities because of warning leaflets dropped by enemy planes, kept their heads down. The foreign workmen of Organization Todt moved, according to plan, toward Torigny.

The re-establishing of contact with the right neighbor, the 716th Infantry Division, told us that the enemy had succeeded in forming and widening out a bridgehead at the left wing of the division, and that he probably would reach the road from Caen to Bayeux that same day if the reinforced 915th Infantry Regiment did not speedily launch a counterattack. The Eastern Battalion which had been sent in there had not proved reliable. The left neighbor, the 709th Infantry Division, informed us that the enemy had succeeded in forming a bridgehead—to judge from his concentration of ships at sea— that we were to reckon with further landings. Against the air landings north of Carantan, the 91st Air Landing Division was employed. Further artillery support by the 352nd Infantry Division on the beach at Pouppeville was asked for.

On the basis of these reports, an estimate of the situation at 1000 hours with regard to the enemy was that he would form bridgeheads by landing at two points in the sector of the 352nd Division (Meuvaines and St Laurent), whence he would probably thrust forward to Bayeux. The Staff of LXXXIV Corps was informed of this situation, and I reported that the 352nd Infantry Division had in view to subordinate one battalion of the reinforced 915th Infantry Regiment to the 916th Infantry Regiment (center)—which was already weakened—so as to enable the latter to carry through an attack against the enemy who had broken in and was strengthening his forces. I further proposed to have the reinforced 915th Infantry Regiment (minus one battalion) launch a counterattack upon Crépon. I requested the subordination of 2/1716th Artillery Regiment and the still available elements on the left wing of the 716th Infantry Division, and, further, the commitment of the railway artillery battery standing near Torigny (southeast of St Lô). Corps agreed to the proposal submitted. At the same time, air support was requested for the counterattack planned by the reinforced 915th Infantry Regiment and against the steadily growing concentration of enemy ships off St Laurent.

At 1030 hours. the reinforced 915th Infantry Regiment received the order to direct 1/915th Infantry Regiment (the last march group of this regiment) to turn off, via Le Molay, to Surrain, and to subordinate it to the 916th Infantry Regiment (center). With its main body, the 915th Infantry Regiment had to reach the district around Villiers-le-See in order to launch the counterattack upon Crépon after the subordination of 2/916th Infantry Regiment and the remaining portions of the Eastern Battalion of the 716th Infantry Division.

The start of the counterattack was at 1200 hours. 2/1716th Artillery Regiment and 3/1352nd Artillery Regiment had to work together with the 916th Infantry Regiment. In addition, the 1352nd Assault Gun Battalion (ten assault guns) was subordinated to then 915th Infantry Regiment and brought up to Esquay (east of Bayeux). 1/352nd Antitank Battalion (twelve heavy antitank guns) was subordinated to the 916th Infantry Regiment (center) and brought up to Formigny. All of the staffs participating in the operation had received orders and instructions.

At about 1100 hours, the weather conditions changed. The sun broke through the clouds, and it was now high tide. The first enemy fighter-bombers appeared before long and started to paste the very widely spaced march groups of the reinforced 915th Infantry Regiment. The movements ceased, since more and more fighter-bombers appeared. The attempts of the 1st Antiaircraft Artillery Regiment, south of Grandcamp, were unable to deal with these air attacks, since this operational area was covered by several bomber squadrons, and many of the antitank guns had collapsed into their pits. Other bomber squadrons bombarded the positions of 1/916th Infantry Regiment (center), but without any visible success except for the morale effect. By this continuous activity of fighter-bombers at the coast, almost every movement on our side was made impossible. If the telephone lines to the regiments up till now had been intact, matters were changed from the very beginning of the enemy air activity, so that the radio section (sending in code) had to be set going. In order to relieve the 916th Infantry Regiment (center), the demarcation line to the 914th Infantry Regiment (left) was changed, and the latter was ordered to throw the enemy back into the sea at Point du Hoc by employment of forces of 1/914th Infantry Regiment. The 1352nd Artillery Regiment reported that security forces of 3/1352nd had stopped the enemy (infantry), who were advancing from Crépon toward Pierre Artus, hard east of the latter place, and that this artillery battalion had consumed all of its first issue of ammunition. An inquiry at the supply group of the 352nd Infantry Division elicited the information that we had not to reckon on a fresh supply of ammunition before a lapse of three more days! The last remaining stocks of the supply base at Bussy then were placed at the disposal of the 3rd Battalion, 1352nd Artillery Regiment.

After 1200 hours, the reinforced 915th Infantry Regiment reported that the attack upon Crépon could not start before 1400 hours on account of the brisk fighter-bomber activity. The 726th Infantry Regiment (right) had repelled another attack upon the La Gronde sector, and likewise a minor one from the sea in the region of the port of Port-en-Bessin.

The preparations for blocking and laying mines in the access roads to Bayeux were reported as being finished. In the sector of the 916th Infantry Regiment (center), the enemy—assisted by the high tide and his naval artillery, firing from the landing boats by tanks, and bomber activity—had succeeded in landing further forces; portions had penetrated from the west into Colleville, and further portions from the north into St Laurent and Vierville. In the villages, intense fighting took place on both sides. At the 914th Infantry Regiment (left), the reinforced company allotted to the main battery at Point du Hoc had not yet launched the planned counterattack. The situation in the region of Brévands was unchanged.

To judge from the utterances of prisoners taken by noon, there appeared to be employed:

At Crépon: the 50th British Infantry Division;

At Port-en-Bessin: an English Commando group;

At Colleville-sur-Mer: forces of unknown composition;

At St Laurent: the 1st American Infantry Division;

At Vierville: the 29th American Infantry Division;

Sharp west of it: an American Commando group;

At Point du Hoc: an American Commando group;

West of Maisy: American forces of unknown composition; and

West of Brévands: portions of the 101st American Airborne Division.

The opinion that the enemy would first of all try to conquer Bayeux prevailed.

Shortly after 1400 hours, the division received a radio message from the reinforced 915th Infantry Regiment that it had no communication yet with 2/915th Infantry Regiment, but that it would, nevertheless, start its counterattack on Crépon at 1430 hours. By that time, intense activity by fighter-bombers was going on, and several tanks felt their way forward from Crépon toward the south and the west.

At about 1500 hours, the reinforced 915th Infantry Regiment reported by telephone that the enemy anticipated our attack by overrunning our spearheads with his tanks—supported by fighter-bombers—and that he was now advancing toward the River Suelles in the south. The commander of the 915th Infantry Regiment fell at this time on the field of battle. The commander of the 352nd Rifle Battalion and the commander of the 352nd Assault Gun Battalion were missing. The troops had suffered heavy casualties, and now they were retreating. An attempt has to be made to recover the commander of the 915th Infantry Regiment, since he had been holding in his hands the map (1:100,000) containing exact details of the organizations on the coast.

During that afternoon the reinforced 915th Infantry Regiment was not able to reproduce a clear situation report. After reconnoitering the situation by officer patrols, the remnants of the 915th Infantry Regiment were subordinated in the evening of this day to the 726th Infantry Regiment (right), and the latter was ordered to set up a defensive front from Coulombs via St Gabriel, from here following the course of the Seulles to the west as far as Esquay; from there it would be linked to "Hill 64" (west of Batzonville), then follow the course of the Gronde beyond Asnelles. For this purpose, all the troops from Bayeux and portions of 3/1352nd Artillery Regiment were to be concentrated into combat groups and to be employed in preventing the enemy from breaking through to Bayeux on 7 June. In the sector of the 916th Infantry Regiment (center), heavy fighting continued throughout the whole afternoon. The enemy had succeeded in conquering Colleville and the district hard northeast of it, St Laurent (center) and Vierville (center). 1/915th Infantry Regiment had come up late in the evening, when it succeeded in breaking into the center of Colleville. Pillbox 76 reported the continuance of landings, including artillery, at Vierville, St Laurent, and east of it. For 7 June, the 916th Infantry Regiment (center) was ordered, after regrouping its forces at night-time, to narrow the enemy bridgehead by a counterattack via Vierville on St Laurent. For this purpose, the 352nd Engineer Infantry Battalion was subordinated to the 916th Infantry Regiment (center), and it was brought up via Bernesque, Aignerville, to Louvières. Moreover, the regiment was ordered to cooperate with two antiaircraft artillery battalions (one light and one heavy) of the 1st Antiaircraft Artillery Regiment, the employment of which (artillery against ground targets, and as antiaircraft combat artillery) had to be in the district north of Formigny. In the sector of the 914th Infantry Regiment (left), the reinforced battalion employed at Point du Hoc succeeded in the evening hours in encircling the enemy forces around the Point du Hoc strongpoint. The parachute troops west of Brévands were further narrowed in. At about 1000 hours, the regiment reported that it had found, among other things, a comprehensive order of the enemy—it was an order of V American Army Corps— in a boat which had drifted ashore west of Maisy.

Conclusive General Survey
with the 352nd Infantry Division on 6 June at 2200 hours

The enemy: The enemy had succeeded in forming three bridgeheads (namely, one northwest of Caen, another northwest of Bayeux, and a third north of Carentan) on 6 June. From the captured order (an order of the American Deputy Chief of the General Staff), which had drifted ashore, it was to be seen that the invasion had been started with three Corps, the 30th (e), the 5th (a), and the 7th (a) Army Corps. (The demarcation line between the 5th and 7th Corps was formed by the mouth of the Carentan Canal.) We had to reckon with an employment against us of at least two divisions of each Corps—a point later confirmed by prisoners—and presumably each division disposed an armored battalion. In connexion with the parachute divisions—one [?] division (e) north of Caen; one to two divisions (a) north of Carentan—we might very well presume that on 7 June the bridgeheads of the 30th (e) and the 5th (a) Army Corps were to be enlarged and united for the conquest of Bayeux, in order to thrust forward from this large bridgehead upon Caen and the Cotentin peninsula (bridgehead north of Carentan). Accordingly, we had to reckon with heavy attacks on the right wing and in the center of the sector of our 352nd Infantry Division on 7 June.

Our own and neighboring troops: In the right divisional sector (726th Infantry Regiment), all of the attacks on the coastal front had been repelled. The right flank of the division, however, was now almost unprotected, on account of the deep penetration of the enemy into the left wing of the 716th Infantry Division and the failure of our counterattacks upon Crépon, where the reinforced 915th Infantry Regiment had been defeated. An enemy attack made from here upon Bayeux would be successful if we did not in time oppose it with new forces.

In the sector of the 916th Infantry Regiment (center), the enemy had suffered considerable losses; by the effect of his heavy weapons, however, and with the support of air forces, he had succeeded in forming a bridgehead, the enlargement of which to a union with the 30th (e) Army Corps advancing east of Bayeux had in any case to be prevented. The last reserve (352nd Engineer Battalion) was, therefore, subordinated to the 916th Infantry Regiment with a view to narrowing in that bridgehead first of all after the necessary regroupings, and to remove it altogether by a counterthrust from the west toward the east. The intention of the division to employ to that end also the 352nd Replacement Training Battalion was not practicable, since the companies of this battalion were being reconstituted, but were not yet available, in the evening of 6 June.

On account of the lack of ammunition, the heavy harassing fire upon the bridgehead of St Laurent, which had been planned by the 1352nd Artillery Regiment for the night, had to be confined to a minor harassing fire. Consent to employ the 1st Antiaircraft Artillery Regiment—which suggested itself, since it retained an ample issue of ammunition—against ground targets, or as antiaircraft combat troops against tanks, had only been obtained after repeated telephone calls (which became necessary for deciding who was to be subordinated to whom), but, as this regiment had no fighting experience at all, the division did not feel sure as to its reliability.

In the left divisional sector (914th Infantry Regiment), they hoped to succeed in destroying the enemy forces landed at the Point du Hoc strongpoint on 7 June; an employment of the remaining portions of 1/914th Infantry Regiment (reserve) against the St Laurent bridgehead could not enter into consideration because of circumstances of space and time, all the more as enemy landings in the district of Grandcamp on 7 June were to be reckoned with. Destruction, or at least pressing back, of the enemy airborne troops west of Brévands via the Carentan Canal was taken in view for 7 June. LXXXIV Corps HQ was given a description of the situation according to this general survey by telephone on 6 June after 2200 hours, and for the carrying through of our purposes we requested them:

1. To bring up and subordinate to the division a new combat group for employment on its right uncovered flank;

2. To subdue the enemy north of the Seulles (right boundary of the division) and at the St Laurent bridgehead by night bombers (already requested in the afternoon of this day);

3. To support our counterattacks upon the St Laurent bridgehead by pursuit and bombardment airplanes (the fact was especially pointed out that on 6 June not a single German airplane was seen over the divisional area—except for two pursuit planes—which might give rise to a sense of inferiority among the men);

4. To bring up the guard company (1/914th Infantry Regiment) for mopping up the bridgehead west of Brévands; and

5. To supply the necessary artillery ammunition.

The requests under 2, 3, and 5 were rejected as not practicable, request number 1 was being considered, and number 4 was conceded. The discovery of the (captured) order of V American Army Corps was reported to Corps HQ and its special attention called to a sketch included with that order, from which it could be seen how the Allies imagined the moving up of German armored divisions to their positions (between Caen and Bayeux from the south toward the north, and from the east toward the west).

Evaluation of the Fighting Day (6 June)

Infantry, inclusive of reserves: On 6 June it has been shown that an enemy attack passing, at low tide, through the obstacles of the coastal zone with their mines and blasting charges, and through concentrated fire from all our positions, must needs result in failure. If the enemy succeeded—in spite of all the circumstances mentioned—in infiltrating his spearheads (which had been held back in a wide front at the obstacles of the coastal zone), and in forming a bridgehead in the evening, this success was to be ascribed primarily to the effect of the matériel and armament of his ground, naval, and air forces, which gradually brought about the breakdown of our battle installations, and these were to be designated as being only "average."

In general, the infantry in the permanent battle installations (concrete) was protected from the effect of enemy fire. But its field of view was limited, and for the rest the troops were rather isolated, especially since the telephone wire system (laid underground and insulated) was frequently interrupted, and could then only be repaired by specialists after painstaking work. Provided with sufficient supplies, this infantry persevered despite all that happened, and later on it again caused losses to the enemy. But so far as numbers mattered, these forces—as, for instance, in the combat installations bypassed—had ceased to count!

The infantry in the positions at field strength, without any doubt, contributed by the effect of their weapons to the casualties of the enemy in the coastal zone. At another time, on this infantry were also inflicted considerable losses by the continuous fire of the naval artillery and that of the landing boats, and especially later on by the enemy air forces.

The infantry employed as counterthrust reserve was too weak as to numbers, and had no heavy weapons. In bright daylight, a displacement became impossible for them because of the enemy air activity. The tactics of Rommel—"Let all weapons display their effect on the water"—might be correct; these weapons, however, ought to have been mounted in "permanent battle installations" (concrete), and in far greater quantity than was the case in the sector of Bayeux. As here an "Atlantic Wall" did not exist, there had to be at least some reserves in the rear. If this had not been the case, the enemy might even on 6 June have succeeded in forming a major bridgehead at this coastal front, and in thrusting forward from it.

The infantry employed as counterattack reserve (reinforced 915th Infantry Regiment), in my opinion, had taken the decisive part in the engagements on 6 June. Standing "at the ready" on the right divisional wing, and having frequently practiced an attack toward the northeast (Crépon), this reinforced regiment had to fall in—as ordered by Corps—first of all toward the west. Apparently, the report "Air landings south of Carentan" had not been immediately verified, for it was false! Now, the regiment was compelled to get over a distance of about eighty kilometers, twenty-five of which were to be marched—widely spaced because of the enemy fighter-bombers which had already started their work—and with the remaining fifty-five kilometers on bicycles or frequently breaking-down French motor vehicles. The enemy, moreover, attacking from Crépon toward the south, got a start on the overtired 915th Regiment (and its counterattack), which just arrived and was not ready for battle. If this unit had remained on the right divisional wing and from here fought the counterattack toward Crépon in the early morning, the right flank of the 352nd Infantry Division would not have been threatened by the enemy this day, and the withdrawing portions of the 716th Infantry Division would probably have been supported. The 30th British Army Corps then would not have so easily achieved success again and again on 6 June, and our own High Command would have arrived at different decisions.

Artillery and Antiaircraft Artillery: The artillery inflicted considerable loss of life upon the landing enemy by its volley fire, without having heavy casualties itself in its positions. Its activity, however, was reduced as soon as the enemy fighter-bombers took up their work. Within this branch of the service, most casualties occurred at the field observation posts, which could provide replacements, but not equipment, for 7 June (when there was about twenty per cent damage to equipment). If the artillery had had more than one issue of ammunition—as was the case with other front sectors—then it would have been able to display a greater defensive power. The report "Issue of artillery ammunition is not possible before 9 June" compelled us to handle ammunition as sparingly as possible.

This fact persuaded us that the enemy would succeed again in his plans for the next days, and we gained the impression that the conduct of battle in the event of an invasion had not been well weighed by our Supreme Command.

The Antiaircraft Artillery (1st Regiment) was, with regard to personnel and matériel, a strong weapon in the divisional sector. Its proper task, to fight the approaching of enemy planes—according to the opinion of the division—no longer entered into consideration, even if the regimental commander hinted at this now and again. By employment of its portions as a ground artillery and antiaircraft combat element (as meanwhile conceded), the division hoped especially to compensate for the lack of ammunition with the 1352nd Artillery Regiment. There were reported—as far as I can remember—as shot down by the 1st Antiaircraft Artillery Regiment, six fighter-bombers and two bombardment airplanes.

Antitank guns: The fixed antitank guns on the coastal front (defensive weapons against landings, antitank, antiaircraft, etc.) were fairly successful. The crews of the mobile antitank guns, which were less trained, were not specially successful. The 1352nd Assault Gun Battalion, on the occasion of the counterattack fought by the reinforced 915th Infantry Regiment, succumbed to the enemy tank superiority and fighter-bomber activity; its casualties amounted to fifty per cent. The total result was, as far as I remember, thirty tanks, sixty light combat cars, numerous armored vehicles, and fifty small landing craft.

Engineers: The 352nd Engineer Battalion, which had marched its 3rd Company to the 716th Infantry Division as ordered, had remained in the district of St Martin as divisional reserve and formed a new 3rd Company out of fortress engineers (senior soldiers). It made preparations for commitment on 7 June with the 916th Infantry Regiment (center).

Signal Corps: With the signal units, the repair and maintenance of the telephone network was no longer fully possible in the late afternoon. The divisional 352nd Signal Battalion was able to have repaired all damage done by its operating party. There did not occur any cases of sabotage at the permanent French network (most of the lines were switched into it). The radio monitor service, committed with the divisional staff, had recognized before long the enemy wavelengths of importance for the division, and had procured valuable information from the c.p. (reports on the situation of the enemy and so on), since the enemy sent his radio messages "in clear." But the enemy radio message intercepted "Report not needed obstacles demolition squads, since these are urgently wanted for other commitment" caused us doubts.

Supply units (road conditions): The establishment of supply bases at the back of every regimental sector had proved useful. Breakdowns in vehicles had been inflicted by fighter-bombers on supply journeys during the daytime, except for clearly marked medical ambulances, which were not attacked. It was necessary, therefore, to carry through the supply traffic during the short nights. The roads in the rear area of the divisional sector were mostly damaged.

Staffs (Command): Company and battalion command posts were so located that they were able to hold the command in hand by the means they had at their disposal. At the fighting fronts, however, because of the lack or the destruction of radio sets, messengers had often to march on foot, which caused delays. The regimental command posts were not touched by the fighting.

At the divisional command post, the transfer of the command staff to an improved c.p. was taken into consideration.

The enemy: The enemy led his troops according to orders issued beforehand, and which remained obligatory. Messages and orders necessary were sent by radio. Enemy messages were given "in clear," except for certain codewords. In the open terrain at the edge of the sea—on the coast—the infantry remained standing. The matériel employed by him was of excellent and decisive quality, which can be designated as unique and which at the end of the day had its due success, in terms of the actual damage as well as the moral effect of it on the German troops. On fighting for localities, the enemy, with his submachine guns and quick-reload rifles, was superior to the German troops which had only very few of the latter. It was striking to see on the first day, at the prisoner collecting point:

Good human stock (each soldier being amply provided with tobacco)!

Good small arms and plenty of ammunition;

Practical clothing and equipment (excellent maps, including panoramic maps of the field of view of the attacker—front toward the south—maps on handkerchiefs and so on);

Good, standardized motor vehicle accessories.

Casualties: Our own personnel losses in the divisional sector amounted on 6 June to about: 200 dead on the field of battle, 500 wounded, and 500 missing, which meant that about one-fifth of the total infantry fighting strength of 6,000 men had been rendered ineffective.

Extract from the Telephone Diary of the
352nd Infantry Division (Coastal Defense Section Bayeux)

D–Day

1.00 hours: LXXXIV AK to 352nd Infantry Division: State of readiness II. Parachutists jumped on 716th Infantry Division sector.

1.15 hours: Putting all units on the alert by telephone ended.

1.45 hours: Report from 914th Grenadier Regiment: From fifty to sixty enemy parachutists jumped near Carentan Canal south of Brévands.

2.00 hours: Report from 914th Grenadier Regiment: A new landing of parachute troops from thirty to fifty aircraft south of Brévands. Individual parachutists landed near 2nd Battalion of 352nd Artillery Regiment in the vicinity of Cardonville.

2.07 hours: Report from 916th Grenadier Regiment: No enemy contact yet on our sector.

2.09 hours: Call of the Ia on the Commander of 726th Grenadier Regiment: How is the situation? No enemy on the sector of Bessin.

2.13 hours: Ia of the Division reports to Ia of Gen Kdo LXXXIV AK: On the left wing of 914th Grenadier Regiment sector an estimated strength of one battalion parachutists near Carentan Canal southwest of Brévands. Individual parachutists, who evidently have missed their goal, are near Cardonville. Up to the time, on all other sectors quiet prevails.

2.14 hours: Report from Naval Commandant Normandy: Enemy sea targets located 11 kilometers north of Grandcamp.

2.15 hours: Report by Naval Commandant Normandy transmitted to 352nd Artillery Regiment.

2.35 hours: Information from our right neighboring 716th Infantry Division: Parachutists near Amfreville, Berville, Conneville, Herouvilette.

2.46 hours: Report from the 352nd Army Post Office: 2.35 hours two airplanes with troop-carrying gliders sighted, direction S–N.

2.48 hours: Report by the 352nd Army Post Office transmitted to 726th, 914th, 915th, 916th Grenadier Regiments.

2.55 hours: Report from 914th Grenadier Regiment: Approximately from eight to ten parachutists sighted near 4th Battalion of 352nd Artillery Regiment. Near Cardonville two parachutists with camouflage parachutes and in camouflage uniforms were taken prisoner. Apparently near Isigny landing of seventy paratroopers. Confirmation not yet on hand.

3.10 hours: Order from Gen Kdo LXXXIV AK (transmitted by Ia): Enemy parachute landing on either side of the Vire outlet. In the meadows south of Carentan, troop-carrying gliders landed approximately one company. Presumably they are going to advance to Carentan.

3.10 hours: 352nd Infantry Division keeps open the routes with its left neighboring 709th Infantry Division via Carentan and for this purpose moves Task Force Meyer to Isigny–Carentan. The task force is assigned to the corps reserve. The start of the movement is to be reported.

3.15 hours: Ia order to Obstlt Meyer, 915th Grenadier Regiment: The whole of the task force to be made ready and moved forward over the bridge west of Neuilly into the area Montmartin–Deville. The march is to be made in several columns and small groups. Readiness to march and the roll-call is to be duly reported.

3.20 hours: 01 Gen Kdo LXXXIV AK to the Division (upon inquiry): Order No 1200/44 g. Kdos (Führer order) is to be released.

3.22 hours: Report from 352nd Artillery Regiment: Since 03.20 hours 4th Battalion of 352nd Artillery Regiment is covered by pattern bombing. Strong air formations with troop-carrying gliders flying to the south.

3.25 hours: Ia of the Division to 914th Grenadier Regiment: Instruction concerning the bringing up of Task Force Meyer. Reconnoitering to be started against enemy troops

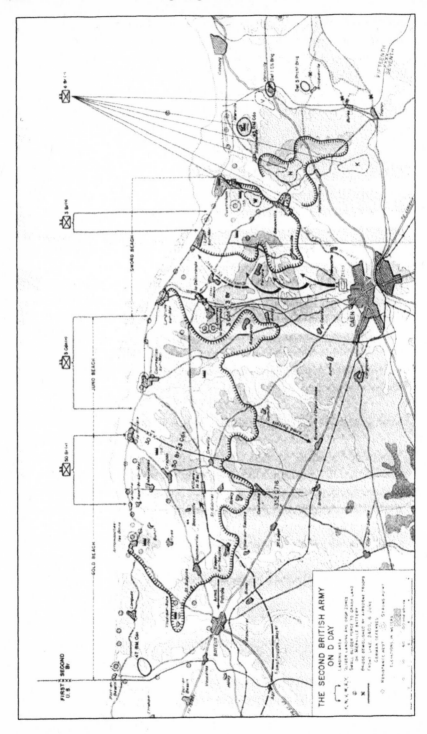

THE SECOND BRITISH ARMY
ON D DAY

landed in the depression south of Carentan.

3.30 hours: Report from 352nd Artillery Regiment: At present air attacks are being made on 4th Battalion of 352nd Artillery Regiment.

3.35 hours: Report from 916th Grenadier Regiment: Strongest bombing attacks on Le Guay, Point du Hoc and Grandcamp.

3.44 hours: Report from the Naval Commandant Normandy: One reinforced battalion of paratroops southwest of Brévands; here only a weak enemy detachment had landed. Bombing attacks are taking place continuously.

3.50 hours: Report from 915th Grenadier Regiment: Task Force Meyer ready to march. Roll-call at 04.15 hours.

3.53 hours: Ia reports to Chief-of-Staff Gen Kdo LXXXIV AK: Locating of sea targets has been disrupted at the time. March of Task Force Meyer to commence at 04.15 hours, one battalion to Carentan and two battalions into the area around Montmartin.

4.01 hours: Report from the Aviation Report Center Caen: On the sector of our right neighboring 716th Infantry Division, approach flight of strong four-motored formations with troop-carrying gliders heading south-west to Houlgate–Cabourg. Jumpings of parachutists near Morsalines, St Côme and Ste Mère-Église with the left neighboring 709th Infantry Division. Three prisoners captured, carrying maps of the Vire river mouth.

4.07 hours: Information from our right neighboring 716th Infantry Division: Current reinforcements in the form of airborne gliders and parachute formations east of Orne.

4.08 hours: Report from the Aviation Report Center Caen transmitted to 726th Grenadier Regiment.

4.19 hours: Information from Ic Gen Kdo LXXXIV AK to the Division: The situation at the Seine outlet is probably worse than with us; strong enemy parachute and airborne troops have landed there. Details are not yet known. At the time, enemy observes complete radio silence.

4.20 hours: Report from 915th Grenadier Regiment: Task Force Meyer—915th Grenadier Regiment and Fusilier Battalion (Artillery Battalion of 352nd Artillery Regiment)—is marching off and its arrival can be expected to take place in three or four hours. On the sector of 726th Grenadier Regiment, artillery fire can be heard.

4.30 hours: Report from 914th Grenadier Regiment: Report on the start and progress of the attack launched by the two battalions of 914th Grenadier Regiment against parachute troops southwest of Brévands. Details are not yet known. Near Carentan Canal the enemy is forcing his way from Le Moulin to the south.

4.34 hours: Report from 352nd Artillery Regiment: Landing craft have not yet been sighted ahead of Grandcamp.

4.35 hours: Report from 916th Grenadier Regiment: An American 1/Lt taken prisioner near St Pole Guay testified that along with the parachute troops also dummy dolls are being dropped, which explode when contacting the ground.

4.45 hours: Report from 726th Grenadier Regiment: Between 04.00 and 04.10 hours,

Defense Works Nos 44, 47 and 48 were bombed heavily.

5.02 hours: Report from 352nd Artillery Regiment: Off Port-en-Bessin one big and four smaller naval units were sighted. Ahead of Grandcamp light naval units are reported.

5.03 hours: Report from 352nd Panzerjäger Battalion: Single troop-carrying gliders were sighted at an altitude of 2,000 meters heading to the west.

5.06 hours: Report from 726th Grenadier Regiment: Defense Works, particularly near Arromanches, St Honorine and Colleville, in continuous air attacks, are covered with bombs of the heaviest caliber. Over Sully parachutists were observed, which probably were a crew which jumped from an airplane shot down.

5.10 hours: Report from 914th Grenadier Regiment: 2nd Battalion of 914th Grenadier Regiment brought in three American prisoners with aerial photos and maps of the Cotentin peninsula, particularly of the area around the mouth of the River Vire. For the time being, the prisioners cannot be forwarded, as enemy parachute forces have blocked the way.

5.15 hours: Ia exchanging information with Ia of the left neighboring 709th Infantry Division: In Carentan itself there are no enemy troops, but north of Carentan stronger parachute forces have been dropped. Ste Mère-Église is held by enemy parchute troops.

5.20 hours: Report from 352nd Artillery Regiment: Advanced observers of 2nd and 4th Battalions of 352nd Artillery Regiment report to have ascertained noises which probably originate from naval units, at approximate distance of two kilometers, heading toward the Vire outlet. Furthermore, 29 ships, including four bigger type naval units (at least destroyer or cruiser class) are reported to be observed at a distance of from six to ten kilometers heading toward Le Guay–Point du Hoc. Three or four aircraft have been shot down near Formigny; one pilot (a Pole) was taken prisoner. The number of landing craft off Port-en-Bessin has increased to fifty.

5.22 hours: Report from the Naval Commandant Normandy: Our naval units were firing at sea targets. One enemy ship blew up. Ia informed the Naval Commandant that about fifty landing craft, together with four bigger naval units, probably destroyers, were lying off Port-en-Bessin.

5.25 hours: Report from 726th Grenadier Regiment: 10 kilometers north of Port-en-Bessin, thirty ships have been observed proceeding slowly, keeping course to the west. Marine Battery Longue presumes them to be gunboats or destroyers.

5.27 hours: Report from 352nd Artillery Regiment: Off Port-en-Bessin, four bigger naval units. Close by the coastline, our own small naval units were observed.

5.32 hours: Report from 916th Grenadier Regiment: In the Bay of Colleville–Vierville, landing boats are nearing the beach. Farther on, bigger naval units have been sighted, keeping course to the west. A naval formation consisting of five men-of-war is heading toward the east; small landing boats have taken course landward. Apparently, the enemy enshrouds himself in a mantle of artificial fog.

5.35 hours: Ia reports to the Chief-of-Staff of Gen Kdo LXXXIV AK: Transmission of the report delivered by 916th Grenadier Regiment; in addition, five naval units have been observed further off from St Laurent, three of them units approaching the coast, together with a larger number of landing craft. Up to this time, twelve prisoners have been made.

5.36 hours: Ia reports to the Commanding General, Gen Marcks: Report identical to that made to the Chief of Staff.

5.37 hours: Report from 726th Grenadier Regiment: Between Defense Works Nos 56, 59 and 60 and ahead of Asnelles, numerous landing boats with their bows toward the coast are debarking. Naval units began to deliver fire on the beaches from their broadsides.

5.45 hours: Report from 914th Grenadier Regiment: North of Defense Work No 88, twenty-six landing boats, including bigger units, have been observed.

5.50 hours: Ia of the Division reports to the Chief of Staff Gen Kdo LXXXIV AK: Report by 726th Grenadier Regiment on landing boats ahead of Defense Works Nos 56, 59 and 60 and at Asnelles, also about firing of the beaches by naval units. The Commander of the Division suggests halting Task Force Meyer in view of the altered situation. The Commanding General agrees and orders the task force to be halted.

5.52 hours: Report from 352nd Artillery Regiment: Approximately from 60 to 80 fast landing boats are approaching the coast near Colleville. Our own artillery cannot reach these boats. The region of Maisy is kept under fire from heavy naval artillery; likewise Marcouf. The naval units on the high sea are too far away for our own artillery.

5.55 hours: Report from 916th Grenadier Regiment: Ahead of Vierville, forty-five smaller and middle-sized landing boats were observed, which opened fire on the coast.

5.56 hours: Report from 914th Grenadier Regiment: From ten to fifteen kilometers north of Defense Work No 88, three big naval units were observed, which delivered fire to the region of Maisy.

6.03 hours: Order transmitted by the Divisional Ia to 352nd Fusilier Battalion (it had switched in to the telephone network): Halt the Battalion; await further orders from the Commander of 915th Grenadier Regiment. Fusilier battalion located in the woods of Cérisy on the march road.

6.04 hours: Report from 916th Grenadier Regiment: By 05.45 hours, altogether 140 ships were assembled in the Bay of Vierville. The coastal defenses are subjected to a heavy naval fire.

6.15 hours: Report from 726th Grenadier Regiment: Defense Work No 60 is subjected to particularly heavy artillery fire. In the neighborhood of Defense Work No 37, twenty smaller landing boats are approaching the beaches.

6.17 hours: Report from 726th Grenadier Regiment: Some of the naval units off the coast near Defense Work No 37 turn away to the west.

6.20 hours: Report from 916th Grenadier Division: In the Bay of Vierville, tank landing craft have been clearly observed.

6.25 hours: Ia of the Division informs 352nd Panzerjäger Battalion of the appearance of the first tank landing craft in the Bay of Vierville.

6.26 hours: Report from 352nd Artillery Regiment: The coast between Defense Works Nos 59 and 60 is held under the heaviest artillery fire. Large naval formations lie far away on the high sea. By heavy bombing attacks on 1716th Battery Emplacement, some of the guns were buried by rubble; three of them have been set free again and emplaced anew. At the time the artillery regiment maintains good connections with the observation posts.

6.32 hours: Report from 726th Grenadier Regiment: Landing boats off the coast between Defense Works Nos 59, 61 and 62 and ahead of Asnelles. The enemy is enshrouding sea targets in a mantle of artificial fog and placing a wall of fog before the coast. Up to this time, the companies of the reserve battalion have suffered only a few casualties.

6.37 hours: Report from 726th Grenadier Regiment: The first landing boats are debarking on the beaches ahead of Defense Works Nos 65 and 69. Some of them are tank landing craft.

6.45 hours: Report from 914th Grenadier Regiment: The attack of 2nd Battalion/914th Grenadier Regiment against parachute troops southwest of Brévands is making but slow progress in the terrain not easy to survey. Grandcamp is lying under enemy naval artillery fire.

6.50 hours: Ia of Gen Kdo LXXXIV AK to the Division: According to the testimony of prisoners, one airborne division landed in the Carentan area has the mission to take the town of Carentan. Information by Ia of the Division to Ia of Gen Kdo LXXXIV AK about the newest reports received by the Division on the enemy (see above).

6.57 hours: Report from 914th Grenadier Regiment: Ahead of Defense Work No 92, twenty landing boats are keeping course toward the coast.

7.05 hours: Report from 916th Grenadier Regiment: Near Defense Work No 68, east of Vierville, enemy in the strength of fifty men landed; weaker enemy forces also near Defense Work No 62.

7.06 hours: Report from 726th Grenadier Regiment: Enemy near Defense Work No 60, northeast of Colleville, landed forty men and one tank. Defense Work No 60 engaged in a fire duel.

7.08 hours: Report from 914th Grenadier Regiment: 2nd Battalion/914th Grenadier Regiment, with altogether four companies, is attacking the parachute forces. Against a tenacious resistance of the enemy our attack can gain ground but slowly.

7.20 hours: Report from 726th Grenadier Regiment: Landing of enemy forces on beaches in front of Defense Works Nos 60, 61, and 62, and further to the west. Between Defense Works Nos 61 and 62, enemy in the strength of one company is on the beach, which is under fire from our own artillery. At Defense Work No 61, the 8.8-cm antitank gun was put out of action by a direct hit. In front of Defense Works Nos 37 and 37a on the right divisional boundary line, landing boats are approaching the coast; landing will begin presently. Defense Work No 37 lies under a heavy artillery and rocket fire.

7.25 hours: Report from 726th Grenadier Regiment: One company is attacking in front of Defense Works Nos 60 and 62. Near Defense Work 61, a further four enemy boats have landed; one boat was put to fire by a 5-cm tank gun. The enemy has penetrated into Defense Work No 62, while No 61 is being attacked both from the beach and from the rear. Telephone connections to Port-en-Bessin and to 1 Battalion/726th Grenadier Regiment are disrupted. Inquiry of Ia to 726th Grenadier Regiment: When and by whom is a counterattack to be carried out between Defense Works Nos 61 and 62 to throw back the enemy?

7.30 hours: Report from 352nd Artillery Regiment: At the time there is no connection to the observation post near Colleville. Landing boats between Defense Works Nos 61 and 62 were contended by cones of concentrated fire. From ten to fifteen smaller landing boats are entering the mouth of the River Vire.

7.35 hours: Ia to the Chief of Staff of Gen Kdo LXXXIV AK: Near Arromanches, on the right divisional boundary line, the enemy landing boats are approaching the coast; the landing is bound to begin immediately. Near Defense Works Nos 60–62, northeast of Colleville, enemy forces of from 100 to 200 men have penetrated our lines. In the Bay of Vierville, there are no enemy troops nearby, but a large number of landing boats are quickly approaching. Request one battalion (1/915th) to be assigned from Task Force Meyer for a counterattack in the neighborhood of Defense Works Nos 60–62. The request was granted by Corps HQ.

7.45 hours: Report from 914th Grenadier Regiment: On the sector of our left neighboring 709th Infantry Division, fifteen landing boats lay at the water's edge in the neighborhood of Le Grand Vey.

7.45 hours: Report from 916th Grenadier Regiment: Near Defense Work No 70, northeast of Vierville, three tanks are rolling up the hill; three tanks penetrated into Defense Work No 66; the upper casemate of Defense Work No 62 was put out of action by a direct hit.

7.50 hours: Commander of Division to the Commander of 726th Grenadier Regiment: One battalion from Task Force Meyer is moving to Colleville to launch a counter-attack near the coastal Defense Works Nos 60–62. Will arrive there within one and a half hours.

7.55 hours: Report from 352nd Artillery Regiment: Radio report from 1st Battalion/ 352nd Artillery Regiment, saying that our situation at Defense Work No 60 is uncertain.

7.57 hours: Report from 726th Grenadier Regiment: On the sector of our right neighboring 716th Infantry Division, between Defense Works Nos 35 and 36, thirty tanks have already been landed.

8.01 hours: Report from 916th Grenadier Regiment: Near Defense Work No 68, north of St Laurent, four tanks; near DW No 66, three tanks are already on the beach; at

DW No 65 the situation is still unsettled. The antitank platoon is committed.

8.04 hours: Information from the right neighboring 716th Infantry Division: The Orne bridge near Benouville is in enemy hands. East of the Orne, our counterattack is being launched. 1716th Light Battery is out of action.

8.05 hours: Report from 916th Grenadier Regiment: Weak enemy forces have penetrated into Point du Hoc. One platoon of 9/726th Grenadier Regiment will be committed to launch a counterattack.

8.10 hours: Report from 726th Grenadier Regiment: Situation at Defense Works Nos 61 and 62 unaltered; fighting is going on also at Defense Work No 52.

8.12 hours: Report by Ia to the Chief of Staff of Gen Kdo LXXXIV AK: Transmittance [*sic*] of the newest reports (see above). On the sector of our right neighboring 716th Infantry Division, about 35 tanks are heading via Defense Works Nos 35 and 36 toward Arromanches.

8.19 hours: Report from 916th Grenadier Regiment: Enemy troops have landed near DW No 62. Details are still lacking. A battalion of Task Force Meyer has been committed against the enemy landed north of Colleville. Some tanks have been landed north of Vierville. The enemy ahead of DW Nos 66 and 68 is being attacked by our forces. Near Point du Hoc, the enemy has climbed up the steep coastline (by means of rope ladders falling from the shells); the strongpoint has started fighting.

8.20 hours: Report from 914th Grenadier Regiment: The battle against the parachute troops in the Brévands area waged by 2nd Battalion/914th Grenadier Regiment has not yet come to an end.

8.21 hours: Information from the right neighboring 716th Infantry Division: The thirty tanks on our left wing have turned to the south and are heading to Meuvaines.

8.22 hours: Radio report from 914th Grenadier Regiment: Fifteen landing boats entering the mouth of the River Vire.

8.25 hours: Report from 352nd Artillery Regiment: 3rd Battalion/352nd Artillery Regiment reports: Of the tanks landed near Defense Work No 35, several (about six) have been put to fire or made immobile by antitank and land defense guns.

8.30 hours: Report from 352nd Artillery Regiment: On the sector of 716th Infantry Division, Defense Works Nos 35 and 36 have been overrun. The enemy infantry and thirty-five tanks are lying before Meuvaines. The right-hand division is throwing the 642nd Eastern Battalion to the hill east of Meuvaines. Defense Work No 37 continues fighting. The antiaircraft gun of Defense Work No 40 has shot three or four tanks; besides which, two or three landing boats are burning.

8.31 hours: Ia to 726th Grenadier Regiment: 2nd and 1st Battalions/916th Grenadier Regiment have to prepare for an attack to the right in the direction to Meuvaines. Readiness to be reported.

8.35 hours: Commanding General – Divisional Commander: Gen Kraiss reports: Situation on the right wing near Meuvaines and Asnelles is difficult; Meuvaines is in enemy hands. Ahead of Asnelles, our antiaircraft guns have shot six tanks. Gen

Kraiss proposes to launch an attack by Task Force Meyer (minus one battalion), reinforced by the bulk of 352nd Panzerjäger Battalion, in order to throw back to the coast and into the sea the enemy infantry and tanks penetrating our right wing. Portions of 352nd Panzerjäger Battalion are to be kept in readiness. General Marcks authorizes the committment proposed.

8.40 hours: Ia to 352nd Artillery Regiment: The connection with the observation points is to be established again latest before the tide is coming in again, as it may be presumed that the second wave of enemy forces will try to land then. An artillery liaison detachment of 3rd Battalion has to be held in readiness immediately with the object of supporting the attack of Task Force Meyer.

8.46 hours: Report from 352nd Artillery Regiment: North of St Laurent, Defense Works Nos 65, 66, 67, and 70 have probably been taken by the enemy. Ahead of Defense Work No 68, strong enemy forces are landing, from larger-size boats, an approximate strength of 150 men.

8.55 hours: Report from Telephone Switching Central: Telephone connections to 916th Grenadier Regiment are all disrupted for the time being.

9.05 hours: Report from 726th Grenadier Regiment: Defense Work No 61, northeast of Colleville, is in the hands of the enemy; DW No 62 is firing with but one machine gun; DW No 60 is still intact. Enemy forces are pushing forward between Defense Works 61 and 62 to 63. Further stronger forces are being landed from fifty boats near Defense Work No 62. Reserves of 1st and 4th Companies are being brought up there. Near DW No 52, quiet prevails again. DW No 37 asks for reinforcements. Enemy infantry and tanks are heading to Meuvaines.

9.12 hours: Report from 914th Grenadier Regiment: Ahead of Defense Works Nos 92 and 99, numerous landing boats are entering the Carentan Canal. Debarking has not yet begun. 5th and 6th Battalions/914th Grenadier Regiment are engaged at the Carentan Canal defending against enemy parachute troops.

9.15 hours: Report from 916th Grenadier Regiment: Ahead of Defense Work No 65, northeast of St Laurent, sixty to seventy landing boats are debarking at present. No reports have been received from St P. Point du Hoc. Situation ahead of Grandcamp is unaltered. Defense Works 65–68 and 70 are occupied by the enemy. Further considerable debarkments near Defense Works Nos 65 and 66 have been ascertained.

9.25 hours: 726th Grenadier Regiment reports: Three enemy tanks on the eastern wing of Defense Work No 38; reconnoitring has been started.

9.30 hours: Ia to 916th Grenadier Regiment: The self-propelled company of 352nd Panzerjäger Battalion is subordinated to 916th Grenadier Regiment; the company itself is still at Engreville. 2nd Battalion/916th Grenadier Regiment is to be committed to a counterattack against Defense Works Nos 65–69.

9.35 hours: Report from Ic to Ia: Enemy radio message intercepted reading: To all commanders of the units: Everything is going OK, only a bit too late. Alaska.

(Presumably a request for reinforcements or artillery fire.)

9.45 hours: Report from 914th Grenadier Regiment: On the sector of the right neighboring 709th Infantry Division, tanks are being landed between Defense Works Nos 3 and 5; the Division, having no connection with its superior command, asks for support in the form of armor-piercing antitank weapons.

9.47 hours: Division to Corps HQ: Transmission of the request of the left neighboring regiment for support by antitank weapons against landed enemy tanks, as the Regiment is no longer able to get connection to 709th Infantry Division.

9.55 hours: Ia – Chief of Staff of Gen Kdo LXXXIV AK: Discussion and estimation of the general combat situation.

10.00 hours: Ia to 352nd Artillery Regiment: Information pertaining to the enemy landed near Defense Works Nos 3 and 5 on the left neighboring sector. Commission: With all available guns of 2nd Battalion to contend the enemy between Defense Works Nos 3 and 5 and to intercept his supply lines. Report from 352nd Artillery Regiment: The situation re ammunition with the heavy 4th Battery is very strained.

10.12 hours: Report from 726th: Three auxiliary craft in the harbor of Port-en-Bessin were sunk by direct hits of bombs.

11.00 hours: Radio message of the Division to Task Force Meyer: When are you going to start? In what direction?

11.01 hours: Information from the right neighboring 716th Infantry Division: Out in the bay of the mouth of the River Orne there are thirteen cruisers and a large number of landing boats. On either side of Vaux Château the enemy has succeeded in making a penetration.

11.10 hours: Report from 3rd Battalion/726th Grenadier Regiment: Defense Works Nos 66 and 68 north of St Laurent, contrary to previous reports, are still firmly in our hands. On the other hand, the enemy, with the strength of two companies, has penetrated into St P. Point du Hoc. Reserves, which were available, have been committed against Point du Hoc with the object of restoring the previous situation. From the men-of-war on the high sea the enemy is firing at the steep coastline with special shells from which a rope ladder is falling out, with the help of which the steep slopes can be climbed. The occupational troops of Defense Works Nos 71 and 73 are very weak; the construction pi-units (Bau-Pi-Ernherten) have been brought up for reinforcements.

11.12 hours: Report from 914th Grenadier Regiment: Somewhat to the north of Point du Hoc, twenty bigger naval units on the high seas, including troop transporters, and approximately from two to three hundred landing boats, have been observed.

11.14 hours: Report from 726th Grenadier Regiment: At 11.10 hours, 1st Battalion/916th Grenadier Regiment started an attack against the enemy occupying Hill 22 east of Asnelles. Allegedly, the enemy has taken Asnelles. The situation on the left wing is critical, as the enemy has already advanced up to the church in Colleville. Defense Works Nos 60 and 62 proceed defending themselves gallantly.

11.32 hours: Information from the left neighboring 709th Infantry Division: Further landings are effected along the whole front. The enemy has succeeded in making some breaks.

11.38 hours: Report from the Aviation Report Center Caen: At 11.21 hours, fourteen larger-sized naval units were sighted on the the high seas ahead of Grandcamp.

11.40 hours: Report from 726th Grenadier Regiment: The southwestern exit of Colleville has been taken by the enemy. Further tanks are being debarked ahead of Defense Work No 62. A great number of tanks are congested before the antitank ditch.

11.42 hours: Report from 914th Grenadier Regiment: The enemy is extending his landing place on the sector of our left neighboring 709th Infantry Division spectacularly. On the sea there are at present twenty-two ships with barrage balloons.

11.47 hours: Report from 914th Grenadier Regiment: 1st Battalion/914th Grenadier Regiment has not yet contacted the enemy. In the bay of the River Vire there is a strong enemy concentration with barrage balloons. The attack of 2nd Battalion/914th Grenadier Regiment against the parachute troops in the Brévands area is progressing slowly.

11.48 hours: Information from the left neighboring 709th Infantry Division (inquiry of Ia): There is no connection to Carentan. The situation in the sector of our left neighbor next but one is perfectly quiet.

11.55 hours: Report from 916th Grenadier Regiment: The enemy has occupied the southwestern exit with one platoon. Further landings of tanks are taking place ahead of Defense Work No 62.

12.05 hours: Ia to 914th Grenadier Regiment: Concentrated cones of artillery fire are delivered by 2nd Battalion/352nd Artillery Regiment on Defense Works Nos 3 and 5 on the left neighboring sector, where the enemy is landing in companies. Defense Work No 1 is encircled.

12.20 hours: Information from the left neighboring 709th Infantry Division (inquiry of Ia): The penetration by enemy tanks extends already to a depth of four kilometers. Ahead of Defense Works Nos 3 and 5, there are twenty-two landing boats with barrage balloons. Countermeasures with antitank weapons from the north and from the southwest are under way.

12.25 hours: Ia reports to the Chief of Staff of LXXXIV AK: New report on enemy activities is submitted; see report at 12.20 hours. The occupation troops at St P. Point du Hoc are encircled by two enemy companies. A counterattack with portions of 3rd Battalion/726th Grenadier Regiment has been launched. The Corps HQ will have 30th Mobile Brigade brought up and subordinated to the Division, assuming, probably, the defense of the right wing.

12.35 hours: Report from 726th Grenadier Regiment: Colleville has been reconquered from the enemy. Defense Works Nos 62 and 62b are in our own hands; 61 is still occupied by the enemy, including one tank.

12.48 hours: Ia reports to Grenadier Kdo LXXXIV AK on the successes attained by 2nd

Battalion/915th Grenadier Regiment near Colleville.

12.49 hours: Report from 916th Grenadier Regiment: Defense Works Nos 60, 62, and 62b are in our own hands; at 61 there is still one enemy tank.

13.17 hours: Report from the right neighboring 716th Infantry Division: Artillery reports forty tanks of the heaviest type heading to Ryes.

13.40 hours: Report from 2nd Battalion/915th Grenadier Regiment: On the left wing of the Battalion, the enemy is infiltrating to the south between Defense Works Nos 62a and 62b; the wing is being extended to the south.

13.45 hours: Report from 914th Grenadier Regiment: Two companies from 2nd Battalion/914th Grenadier Regiment have been committed for the defense at the Carentan Canal, one company attacking the parachute troops from Defense Work No 100c to the south and the other one from Villadon.

13.46 hours: Ia of the Division reports to Ia of the Army the estimate of the general combat situation.

13.58 hours: Report from 352nd Artillery Regiment: 1st Battalion reports that Colleville has again been taken by the enemy. The tanks ahead of Asnelles have turned to the east; the beachhead there has grown to be very big already.

14.00 hours: Report from 916th Grenadier Regiment: 5th Company/916th Grenadier Regiment started a counterattack against the enemy, infiltrating between Defense Works Nos 62a, 62b, and 64, and is going to join the attack carried on by 2nd Battalion/916th Grenadier Regiment.

14.05 hours: Report from 726th Grenadier Regiment: The attack of 1st Battalion/916th Grenadier Regiment on Meuvaines had to be turned to the direction of St Côme, as eight tanks with mounted infantry were attacking Defense Works 40a, 40b, and 40c. DW Nos 60 and 620 are in our hands as heretofore.

14.26 hours: Report from 2nd Battalion/915th Grenadier Regiment: Our attack came up against tenacious resistance offered by the enemy, resulting in heavy casualties. Defense Work No 62 is still holding; DW 62c has no mortar ammunition any longer. The enemy, in the vicinity of the church and the Château Colleville, is infiltrating to the south. A counterattack has been started. Order of the Ia to 2nd Battalion/915th Grenadier Regiment: "The enemy at the château must in any case be thrown back again. Defense Works 60 and 62 must remain firmly in our hands."

14.34 hours: Information from the right neighboring 716th Infantry Division (inquiry by Ia): A considerable break has been made by the enemy troops near the mouth of the River Orne. Several defense works west of the Orne are encircled. The troops landed have established contact with the parachute troops in the rear. Near Ryes, forty tanks of the heaviest type are said to be moving to the southwest.

14.55 hours: Report from 914th Grenadier Regiment: 2nd Battalion/914th Grenadier Regiment has been involved in heavy engagements in a hedgerow terrain in the Catz area. At 14.45 hours a further one hundred paratroopers jumped north of Defense Work No 100. Up to this time, twenty-three prisoners have been brought in.

15.50 hours: Report from 915th Grenadier Regiment (Task Force Meyer): We have established contact with 1st Battalion/916th Grenadier Regiment, which is committed left of us. The general direction of the attack is Meuvaines–Asnelles. The assault guns have arrived at the Regiment.

16.00 hours: Report from 915th Grenadier Regiment: The task force is going to attack from a line of departure with its right wing at Villiers-le-Sec, and left wing at Bayernville. Enemy tanks near Creully have pushed through to the south.

16.02 hours: Report from Ic of the Division to Ia: According to a radio message intercepted, the enemy forces in the Meuvaines area have to be estimated as one full division.

16.10 hours: The break at St Laurent has been extended by the enemy; Defense Work 71c and the village of St Laurent are in enemy hands.

16.12 hours: Report from 726th Grenadier Regiment: Defense Work No 39 has been taken by the enemy. DF 38 is encircled, and even DF 40 is being attacked by six tanks and one infantry company. Furthermore, seven tanks are located ahead of Defense Work No 42, and several tanks in front of DW 44. Strong enemy landings are going on ahead of Defense Work No 62.

16.17 hours: Ia of Gen Kdo LXXXIV AK to Ia of the Division: Our left neighboring 709th Infantry Division has great anxiety about the increasing debarkments on the right wing.

16.34 hours: Report from 916th Grenadier Regiment: Between Defense Works Nos 62 and 64, the enemy is removing staggered obstacles with tanks in order to prepare a broader passage for his tank forces.

16.38 hours: Report from 726th Grenadier Regiment: Ryes is in enemy hands.

16.50 hours: Report from 352nd Artillery Regiment: 4th Battalion reports heavy debarkments of tanks and trucks heading landward between Defense Works Nos 62 and 64.

16.58 hours: Report from 352nd Artillery Regiment: Further strong landings of tanks and trucks between Defense Works Nos 67 and 73.

17.10 hours: Report from 2nd Battalion/915th Grenadier Regiment: Battalion has been bypassed by the enemy in the rear near Château Colleville; he has broken through to the south. Wounded cannot be brought back any longer.

17.21 hours: Report from the 4th Battalion/352nd Artillery Regiment: Further strong landings on the coast near Vierville.

17.25 hours: Report from 352nd Artillery Regiment: 2nd Battalion/915th Grenadier Regiment is contained by the enemy.

17.30 hours: Report from 915th Grenadier Regiment (Task Force Meyer): At the time of our movement into the assembly position, the enemy infantry and tanks have taken Villiers-le-Sec and the hill south of it. In face of a superior enemy, the fusilier battalion (on the right wing) had to withdraw to St Gabriel, as the assault guns could not come up against a superior number of enemy tanks. There is no longer any connection to the left 1st Battalion/915th Grenadier Regiment near Bazenville. The Commander, Obstlt Meyer, presumably seriously wounded and made prisoner.

17.43 hours: Report from 726th Grenadier Regiment: The enemy has pushed forward from St Honaire to the south, toward Russy.

17.50 hours: Ia reports to the Chief of Staff of Gen Kdo LXXXIV AK on the whole of the combat situation.

17.50 hours: Report from 916th Grenadier Regiment: The enemy, who is continuously receiving reinforcements, has penetrated into Vierville, Asnières and Louvières. The Commander of the Division, from the command post of 726th Grenadier Regiment to Ia: General information about the situation on the right wing. Southwestern edge of Ryes has been occupied by a fortress pi-company. 1st Battalion/916th Grenadier Regiment is to establish contact to the left; connection to the Battalion, however, has been disrupted for hours.

18.00 hours: Chief of Staff of Gen Kdo LXXXIV AK to Ia of the Division: On the sector of the right neighboring 716th Infantry Division, the enemy has made a particularly deep penetration. 30th Mobile Brigade, subordinate to 352nd Infantry Division, because of lack of heavy infantry weapons, can only be used for sealing purposes.

18.25 hours: Ia of the Division to 352nd Pi-Battalion: Together with the 17th Landes Bau Battalion, 17th Pi-Battalion is to reach the St Laurent area via the command post of 916th Grenadier Regiment.

18.25 hours: The Commander of the Division, from the command post of 916th Grenadier Regiment to Ia: 1st Battalion/914th Grenadier Regiment has the order to clear up the situation at the Point du Hoc strongpoint by a counterattack. A counterattack from the east with detachments from the Le Guy strongpoint has also been started.

18.26 hours: Division to 352nd Field Replacement Battalion: The Field Replacement Battalion and portions of the March Battalion, which have already arrived, have to reach the region south of Mosles.

18.28 hours: Report from 726th Grenadier Regiment: Enemy tanks are forcing their way from Sommervieux to Magny. In order to stave off this thrust, six or seven assault guns are being brought up to the Regiment.

18.40 hours: Division to 32nd Antiaircraft Regiment: One heavy battery on either side east and west of Bayeux is to be committed for the defense of the town against enemy tanks.

19.35 hours: Report from 916th Grenadier Regiment: Fifteen larger transporters and thirty smaller craft at a distance of ten kilometers from the coast, headed to southeast, have been observed. Enemy in Vierville has been reinforced by one company.

19.40 hours: Ia of the Division to Commander of the Division at the command post of 916th Grenadier Regiment: Information concerning Task Force Meyer. Assault guns have been moved from St Gabriel to the west in order to ward off enemy tanks ahead of Bayeux. Divisional Commander to the Ia: The defensive line on the sector of 916th Grenadier Regiment extends from the eastern suburbs of Colleville over 69c, 69 to 71cc. Beginning with Defense Work No 74 to the west, everything is in order. The enemy at St P. Point du Hoc is contained from east and south by 9th Company/726th Grenadier Regiment.

1945 hours: Report from 916th Grenadier Regiment: Parachute troops landing near St P. le Guay.

20.40 hours: Ia of the Division reports to the Chief of Staff of Corps HQ on the combat situation.

20.59 hours: Report from 914th Grenadier Regiment: Fifty troop-carrying gliders have landed west of the Carentan Canal.

21.00 hours: Report from 726th Grenadier Regiment: 1st Battalion/915th Grenadier Regiment reported by radio that it has been pocketed in the neighborhood of Bacenville, and that it has taken prisoner a British general.

21.07 hours: Ia of the Division reports again to Chief of Staff of Corps HQ on the combat situation.

21.12 hours: Report from 726th Grenadier Regiment: Ahead of Port-en-Bessin, fifteen large and thirty small landing boats have been ascertained.

21.35 hours: Report to the Division from Fusilier Battalion 352: Enemy infantry and tanks have taken St Gabriel; remnants of the Battalion are retreating to Brécy.

21.42 hours: Ia of the Division to Chief of Staff of Corps HQ: By prisoners' statements, the 50th British Infantry Division has been ascertained near Sommervieux. The fifteen large and thirty small transporters reported as being at sea are heading [on] course [toward] Port-en-Bessin. The battleships have already proceeded [to fire] broadside[s]. The landing of further strong enemy forces is imminent.

22.10 hours: Ia of the Division to Chief of Staff of Corps HQ: One battalion of 30th Mobile Brigade in the middle sector is to be subordinated to 916th Grenadier Regiment as the situation near Grandcamp is uncertain. The parachutists there have joined with the terrorists [French Underground movement].

22.33 hours: Ia of the Division to 726th Grenadier Regiment: 513th and 518th Battalions of 30th Mobile Brigade will be brought up and subordinated to the Regiment. New defense line has to be built up in the line Brécy–Esquay–Sommervieux–Pouhgny–Tracy.

22.55 hours: Report from 352nd Fusilier Battalion: The strength of the Battalion is but forty men, plus additional fifty men from 1st Battalion/915th Grenadier Regiment; furthermore, there are six assault guns intact. In face of strong enemy pressure, the task force has withdrawn toward Ducy.

23.07 hours: Ia of the Division to 726th Grenadier Regiment: Portions of 94th Bau Pi-Battalion (360 officers and men) will be subordinated to the Regiment.

23.20 hours: Divisional Commander, Gen Kraiss, to Commanding General, General Marcks: Tommorrow the Division will be able with all available forces to offer the same kind of hard resistance to the supreme enemy, as was the case today. Because of the heavy casualties, however, new forces have to be brought up the day after tomorrow. The losses of men and matériel in the islands of resistance are total. By the heaviest kind of bombing and cones of concentrated fire from naval artillery, greater numbers of the guns built in at field strength were buried under rubble and had later to be set free again.

Divisional Commander, Gen Kraiss, to the Commanding General, General Marcks (continued): The occupational troops in the defense works have fought gallantly. Defense Works 74–91, despite the losses they have suffered, are still in full readiness to defend themselves. At the time, 352nd Pi-Battalion, together with 7th Company/916th Grenadier Regiment, is attacking from Formigny Defense Works Nos 68–70. 6th Company/916th Grenadier Regiment regained Defense Work No 65a, but was then entirely covered by heavy enemy naval artillery fire. 2nd Battalion/ 915th Grenadier Regiment, in an energetic attack, captured the defense work north of Colleville, but is now encircled near Colleville and is clamoring for ammunition. Defense Works Nos 37 and 38 have been fighting gallantly and have shot altogether six tanks. On the left wing, the counterattack by 1st Battalion/914th Grenadier Regiment against St P. Point du Hoc is still progressing. The Field Replacement Battalion and the March Battalion have been moved forward in order to defend Formigny and St Laurent against an enemy heading to the south. No news has been received from 3rd Battalion/352nd Artillery Regiment southwest of Ryes. Almost all of the radio stations of advanced observation posts have been put out of action.

Commanding General Marcks to the Division Commander, Gen Kraiss: All reserves available to me have already been moved up. Every inch of the ground has to be defended to the utmost capacity, until new reinforcements can be brought up.

24.00 hours: By prisoners' statements, the following enemy divisions have been ascertained up to the present: 1st American Infantry Division; 29th American Infantry Division; 50th British Infantry Division; 79th British Armoured Division; 101st American Airborne Division.

The 21st Panzer Division on 6 June 1944

by Generalleutnant Edgar Feuchtinger

0030–0130 hours: The 125th Panzer Grenadier Regiment makes the first report of airborne landings near Rauville, Bréville, Escoville, Troarn, Truffreville, Bannerville, and Demcuville.

0035 hours: Third and highest stage of alert ordered for divisions.

Starting at 0100 hours: The 2nd Battalion/125th Panzer Grenadier Regiment leaves shelter, one company at a time, to engage the airborne enemy troops which have landed in the reported localities.

0200–0400 hours: Continually arriving reinforcements for the airborne enemy troops as far as the Dives area reported by 125th Panzer Grenadier Regiment, 716th Division (static division at Caen), 711th Static Division (east of the Orne), Commander of the Caen area, 305th Army AAA Bn (the AAA Battalion of the 21st Panzer Division) in the antiaircraft position north of Caen, on the Caen–Lion-sur-Mer road.

Approximately 0230 hours: 3rd, 9th, 10th Companies, 125th Panzer Grenadier Regiment, and 4th Company of the 200th Assault Gun Battalion (Cagny) put at the disposal of the 125th Panzer Grenadier Regiment. Two companies of the 22nd Panzer Regiment put in readiness north of Maezières. Ever since the first reports concerning enemy landings were received, the Divisional Commander has been in constant telephone communication with the CG of the Seventh Army. Army Group B would not release the Division for commitment.

Approximately 0245 hours: Division takes first prisoners. Confirmation that 6th British Airborne Division is landing east of the Orne (between Orne and Dives).

From 0230 hours on: Continued news of further airborne landings, also west and south of Caen. Later found to be erroneous. Mock landings on Carpiquet airfield and surroundings with explosive dummies.

Approximately 0400 hours: 1st Reconnaissance Battalion/21st Division ordered to investigate reported landings south and west of Caen. From 0500 hours on, reports to the effect that entire area is clear of enemy.

Approximately 0550 hours: Heavy naval artillery fire in the area around Caen. Artillery positions and 305th AAA Battalion positions hit. Six guns disabled. Pattern bombing on MLR along the coast and on rear positions.

Approximately 0640 hours: Reports of landings along the coast north of Caen. Still no orders for the Division to join battle. Situation on the coast increasingly more threatening. The weaker elements of the 125th Panzer Grenadier Regiment in heavy fighting against 6th British Airborne Division.

0730–0800 hours: Independent decision taken by Division to attack 6th British Airborne Division east of the Orne, in order to keep this area open for a further attack across the Orne against the enemy landing from the sea west of the Orne.

The Division was assembling in the woods at Bellegreville and Chicheboville, and was subordinated to the Seventh Army and LXXXIV Corps at St Lô. After the 2nd Battalion/125th Panzer Grenadier Regiment had been involved in hard fighting east of the Orne from 0100 on, 2nd Battalion/192nd Panzer Grenadier Regiment (Hill 61, east of Périers), 1st Battalion/155th Panzer Artillery Regiment (in position in the area Périers–St Aubin–Beuville), and 200th Panzerjäger Battalion (in the area Périers–Plumetot–Gazelle–Beuville) were subordinated to the 716th Division as soon as the landings from the sea began. This was only rescinded during the night of 6 June 1944. The absence of two Panzergrenadier regiments, one artillery battalion, the antitank battalion and the Army AAA battalion, the spreading of the Division over a wide area, and the combat tasks which cropped up on both sides of the Orne, all had a fateful influence on the course of the combat on 6 June 44.

The 711th Infantry Division Encounters the Invasion

by Generalmajor Joseph Reichert

Once during the night a volley could be heard from the sea, which, however, soon died out. Later on, it was reported that a German convoy had encountered an enemy invasion fleet. Otherwise the night was quiet, until about dawn, when the main operation, the landing from the sea, commenced. It began with a sort of heavy barrage lasting for a long time against the coast from the sea and the air, which extended in some places—in the east—as far as Cabourg and to the heights south of Houlgate. The whole horizon appeared to be a sole mass of flames, until the fire, perhaps after the landing of the first elements, was gradually reduced to single-shot fire.

It lasted a little more than an hour until reports came in, according to which the enemy landing had only taken place west of the Orne. Our own positions had suffered very little from the enemy fire; losses in men were very slight, because the main body of the occupying forces had taken shelter during the bombardment.

Thus, we could start with the further mopping up of the hinterland. The two reserve battalions were charged with this task, that is, the reserve battalion of the left regiment had to mop up the sector between the coast and the road St Arnould–Varaville (inclusive) and the other one, of the right regiment, the area between the mentioned road Pont l'Eveque–Troarn (inclusive). At first our main efforts were directed along the roads, so as to render free the lines of communications. Parts of the antitank battalion were subordinated for this purpose. This mopping-up action had more or less been completed by the evening of 6 June.

The parachutists who had landed did not succeed, probably owing to the counter-measures which were immediately taken locally, in forming groups of any considerable fighting strength, so that in most cases only slight resistance was offered, which could be broken very quickly. Most of them kept in hiding and surrendered, offering no resistance. The prisoners taken, who belonged to the 1st (English) and 1st (Canadian) Battalions of the 6th British Airborne Division, made only very meagre statements, from which it could be assumed that they belonged to elements which became lost and scattered. They were to bail out between the Dives and the Orne and had taken the Dives river, claiming it to be the Orne because the former looked much bigger than the latter. One man in particular reported that originally a landing had been envisaged from the sea as far as Cabourg, but that modern obstacles ahead of the beach, the presence of which had been ascertained there, had caused them to abandon this plan. This was to some extent confirmed by British maps, which were found later with the most accurate markings of individual strongpoints and the obstacles ahead of the beaches. A number of the latter ones in the Cabourg sector had been marked with question marks.

The connection—with the neighboring 716th Division directly affected by the landing operation—which, owing to the overloading of the wire net, was achieved there only after considerable time, indicated that along the entire divisional sector and farther to the west the enemy had forced a landing and had penetrated the coastal area to a depth of two to three kilometers. It was blocked up in a preliminary makeshift way. From the noise of battle, which could be heard from the coast, it could be concluded that single strongpoints on the coast were still holding out. Further countermeasures had been taken. With regard to elements of 716th Division to the east of the Orne, I could find out that the coastal strongpoints were being held and that there was contact between the 716th and 711th Divisions on the coast as well as near Varaville.

By noon, the roads in our own divisional sector had already been cleared by fighting to such an extent that I could drive by car to the command post of my left regiment (744th). In the thick brushwood, we were well able to evade the fighter-bombers which occasionally appeared over the sector. On my way to the regimental command IR 744, I saw a number of parachutes hanging from trees and telephone wires. The terrain in the vicinity of the regimental command post was rather shelltorn; the command post itself, however, had not been hit. From the roof of the castle one could see the enemy fleet outside and observe a lively coming and going of boats to and from the coast. The coastal battery near Houlgate fired against the landing enemy near Quistreham west of the Orne. From the regimental command post I drove to the heights east of Brucourt, four kilometers to the south of Cabourg, from where one could take a good view of the terrain between the Orne and the Dives. Here we had more and more proof of the airlanding of the enemy. A hundred meters away from the road there was a shattered four-motor bomber lying on the ground, and damaged and undamaged troop-carrying gliders were scattered about on the fields or caught in clusters of trees. The terrain to the west of the Dives was dotted with yellow points (parachutes). The noise of battle close by could not be heard. Only from the direction of Ouistreham could the weak sound of MG fire be heard, and one could see single artillery impacts.

The Allied Attack:
The 6th Fallschirm Regiment Reacts

by Oberstleutnant Friedrich, Freiherr von der Heydte

Although the authorities were frequently at odds in their estimates as to where and how the Allied invasion would take place, it was nevertheless apparent that since the middle of May commanders as well as troops were agreed in assuming that an invasion was to be expected during the first ten days of June. Consequently, the lower headquarters were astonished when all division commanders and one regimental commander from each division, the corps artillery commanders, and the commanders of corps headquarters reserves were ordered to report to Rennes on 6 June 1944 at 0830 in order to spend the entire day in an army group map exercise. It was rumored that this map exercise had been ordered by the Wehrmacht High Command, although the possibility existed that it was an idea of Rommel, who, in North Africa, liked to issue his orders in the form of map exercises.

The majority of the officers who had been ordered to report left for Rennes on the evening of 5 June and spent the night there. Consequently, about 50 percent of the division commanders and possibly 25 percent of the regimental commanders were not with their troops during the night of 5 June 1944.*

On 4 June there had been increasing signs that the invasion was imminent. The French civilian population openly discussed the fact that an Allied landing was close at hand. On 4 June a cousin of General Leclerc laughingly told me a rumor that the invasion had been planned for the night of 4 June. During that night, all the French-speaking soldiers from Alsace-Lorraine, who had been serving in the regiment as drivers, deserted, with the exception of one who was found shot the next morning. These drivers had presumably been in contact with French Resistance groups and had deserted immediately upon hearing that the invasion was imminent.

Since the middle of May 1944, the 6th FS Regiment had, in accordance with instructions, been distributed over a long line in field type positions in the Lessay–Périers–Raids–Mont Castre area. The regiment was subordinated for tactical purposes to LXXXIV Corps, for supply matters to the 91st Grenadier Division, and for administra-

---

* The map exercise at Rennes had been scheduled by Seventh Army for 1000 on 6 June 1944, not for 0830 as stated by the author. Instructions had been explicit that the departure of the participants for Rennes was to take place after a quiet night and not before the morning of 6 June. It is incomprehensible why some commanders left for Rennes as early as the afternoon of 5 June.—Pemsel.

tion to II FS Corps. As an "LW unit," the parachute troops being considered "LW personnel," the regiment had been linked with the Cherbourg aircraft warning network.

The 91st Grenadier Division, the so-called airlanding division of the Army general reserve, was, at the beginning of 1944, activated as an Army unit at the troop training grounds at Baumholder. Generalleutnant Falley was the division commander and Lieutenant-Colonel Pickel was the operations officer. The division command post was located near Etienville. Originally, the 91st Division had probably been designated for combined parachute and airlanding operations—Operation Tanne (fir tree) or Operation Fichte (pine tree), planned for the beginning of March 1944—in conjunction with the 6th FS Regiment in one of the northern countries, possibly Finland. After this plan was abandoned, the 91st Grenadier Division, like the 6th FS Regiment, was sent to LXXXIV Corps about 1 May 1944. The combat efficiency of this division was poor. On the morning of 6 June 1944, the division commander, who was on his way back from Rennes, was killed in front of his command post either by American paratroopers or by members of the French Resistance. Command of the division was temporarily taken over by one of the regimental commanders, Colonel Klostermeyer, and later by Generalmajor Köhler, the commander of an adjacent division. The division was decimated during the first three days of the invasion; its remnants were for the time being attached to other divisions or withdrawn. The division staff was employed as a special assignments staff for the purpose of reconnoitering and preparing defensive positions behind the invasion front.

However, apart from the disruption of telephone connections, the death of the commander of the 91st Grenadier Division, and the demolition of the railroad tracks south of Périers, there was, during the first days of the invasion, not the slightest sign of any activity by the French Resistance movement in the district of the 6th FS Regiment and its immediate neighbors.

Late in the evening of 5 June, about 2230, the commander of the aircraft warning service in Cherbourg, a lieutenant serving with the signal troops, informed his regimental commander by telephone that Allied ship movements and the concentration of transport aircraft at British airfields seemed to indicate the possibility of an invasion that very night. Soon after, the signal officer of the 6th FS Regiment made the same report, and, from 2300 on, the regimental commander was able to follow the approach of the Allied transports and fleets on the aircraft warning chart. At 2300 the regiment was alerted.*

A few minutes after the alert order had been transmitted to all elements of the 6th FS Regiment, a severe air bombardment began to the north and northwest of the regimental sector, about twenty kilometers from the regimental command post, which was located north of Périers. Shortly after midnight, the 1st Battalion, which was located

---

* It is strange that the Seventh Army knew nothing of the approach of the Allied transports on 5 June, beginning at 2300 hours, as reported by the author.—Pemsel.

in the Raids area, reported the landing of Allied paratroopers, and about 1300 it reported the capture of the first prisoners, Americans, who reported that they belonged to the US 101st Airborne Division.

After midnight the regimental commander made futile attempts to establish telephone contact with the adjacent regiments, the 91st Grenadier Division, and LXXXIV Corps. All German telephone lines in the regimental sector had apparently been cut by French Resistance groups, as had the underground connection with the aircraft warning center in Cherbourg. Linesmen who were sent out were attacked at several locations; darkness made it impossible to ascertain whether they were fired on by isolated American paratroopers or French partisans. By dawn, the 3rd Battalion had captured a few score prisoners and had pushed to the southeast the American paratroopers who had dropped in their sector.

About 0600 on 6 June, the regimental commander succeeded in establishing contact with General Marcks by way of the private telephone of his landlady and the French post office at St Lô. After the regimental commander had informed General Marcks regarding the situation in the regimental sector, he received this order from General Marcks: "Beginning immediately, the 6th FS Regiment will clear the Carentan area of enemy paratroopers and attack from that area the enemy paratroopers who have landed in the region between Carentan and Ste Mère-Église in the rear of the 709th [?] Grenadier Division and destroy them. All German troops still holding out in the combat zone of the regiment will be placed under its command."

Because the regiment was insufficiently motorized, it was no easy task for the battalion commanders to withdraw their units from the widely separated strongpoints and to assemble them in the Meautis area, west of Carentan. South of the Carentan–Périers road, the 3rd Battalion was still engaged in combat with scattered groups of enemy paratroopers who fought stubbornly; to the southeast and east, the battalion covered in that area the assembly of the rest of the regiment. The 1st and 2nd Battalions reached the assembly area in the early afternoon without making contact with the enemy.

The regimental commander had driven to Carentan in the morning in advance of the regiment. He found Carentan free of Allied troops and almost free of German troops; and between 1000 and 1100, without encountering enemy troops, he reached St Côme du Mont, where a German battalion had dug in. There he awaited instructions.*

An overwhelming picture presented itself to the regimental commander from the church tower of St Côme du Mont. Before him lay the coast and the sea. The horizon

---

* The fact that the 6th FS Regiment did not reach its assigned assembly area until the afternoon of 6 June proves that the extensive dispersal of the regiment for immediate protection against enemy air landings in endangered areas, as ordered by Field Marshal Rommel, was not prudent. Even if the enemy air landings had actually taken place in the quartering area of the regiment, assembling the regiment would have been out of the question. It was necessary to keep the regiment quartered closely together as much as possible so that, in case of enemy air landings, the regiment would be able to attack with concentrated force in any direction. In 1944 in Normandy we committed the same error which the British made at Crete in the Spring of 1941 and which was the main reason for their loss of the island.—Pemsel.

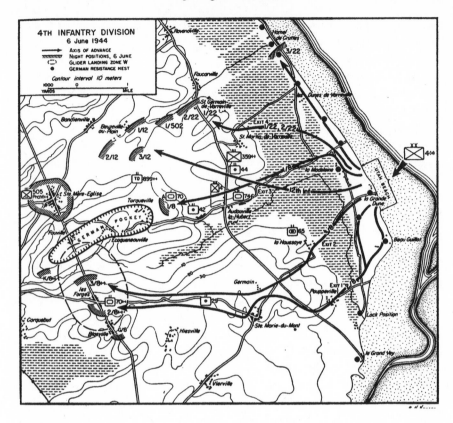

was strewn with hundreds of ships, and countless landing boats and barges were moving back and forth between the ships and the shore, landing troops and tanks. It was an almost peaceful picture; in the combat report which I submitted at the time to the Parachute Army, I wrote that it reminded me of a beautiful summer day on the Wannsee. The noise of battle could not be heard, and from the church tower of St Côme du Mont there was no sign of German defense activities. Only a shot rang out here and there whenever the sentries of the German battalions came in contact with Allied paratroopers.

The regimental commander established his command post in a defile just south of St Côme du Mont and ordered the 1st and 2nd Battalions to be brought forward to the area of St Côme du Mont via the Douve Canal. He issued the following order to the battalion commanders: "The 2nd Battalion will advance on Ste Mère-Église on both sides of the St Côme du Mont–Ste Mère-Église road; it will attack the enemy troops immediately upon contact and annihilate them. The 1st Battalion will cover the regiment on the line of Ste Marie-du-Mont against enemy troops who have landed from the sea. The 13th Company will cover the advance of both battalions."

The 3rd Battalion of the regiment remained in the Carentan area in order to protect the rear and the deep flanks of the regiment; the battalion of the Seventh Army reserve was placed under the control of the 6th FS Regiment and remained in its positions around St Côme du Mont.

At 1900, the 1st and 2nd Battalions advanced from the area of St Côme du Mont. At first, both battalions proceeded rapidly. By nightfall they had not yet come into serious contact with the enemy. Around midnight, the advance elements of the 1st Battalion had arrived at Ste Marie-du-Mont, while the 2nd Battalion had reached a point about 500 meters from the southern edge of Ste Mère-Église. Both battalions sent a number of prisoners back to the regiment.

Some time after midnight (the author can no longer recall exactly when), matters took an unexpected turn. Throughout the entire combat zone of the regiment, American parachute and airlanding units were again descending in large numbers. American paratroopers (members of the 82nd Airborne Division, according to statements by prisoners), who had landed northwest of St Côme du Mont (I have forgotten the name of the exact place), threatened the rear and the deep left flank of the 2nd Battalion; the units which had landed to the north and northeast of St Côme du Mont cut off the 2nd Battalion from the regiment and from the 1st Battalion, while the American paratroopers who had descended east of St Côme du Mont in the very center of the area of the 1st Battalion, which was still advancing, threw this battalion into hopeless confusion.*

---

* During the encirclement of the enemy airlanding forces on the Cotentin peninsula, the German elements in the north, west, and south made the same mistake. While their attempt to attack as soon as possible was commendable, they failed to wait until stronger forces had been assembled for action; the attack was not launched in a coordinated manner; the security measures involved too great a drain of resouces; and, in view of the uncertain situation, they were very soon forced to assume the defensive.—Pemsel.

Invasion

by General der Panzertruppen Leo, Freiherr Geyr von Schweppenburg

In the early morning of 6 June 44, my Chief of Staff informed me of a large-scale enemy landing at the Plateau de Calvados and, to the west, on the Cotentin peninsula. In a few hours, I learned that Army Group D [OB West—Ed.] had ordered the movement to the front of the 12th SS (Hitlerjugend) Panzer Division and, later, Panzer Lehr Division. I personally requested of Genfldm von Rundstedt that Panzer Lehr Division be moved only after darkness because of enemy air action. This request was refused. The Division lost 123 personnel carriers and five trucks in the Panzer Grenadier battalion alone, as soon as it started to march. When the commander of the Panzer Lehr Division received the order to move out at once, he made the same request to Seventh Army to move at night, with the same negative result. Genlt Beverlein, Commander of the Panzer Lehr Division, and Gen Panzer Geyr von Schweppenburg, Commander of Panzer Group West, had experienced for years a considerable amount of stubborn Panzer fighting. Rundstedt, Jodl, and Blumentritt had not. The resulting two schools of thought represented the difference between the tactics of horsedrawn divisions of the Napoleonic Age and the 19th Century and that of mechanized divisions of the 20th Century. The tactical methods of one were hardly understandable to the other.

The decision to move these two Panzer divisions to the front was a very significant one. Hitler had reversed his recent decision (formed after bitter controversy between Rommel and von Geyr, von Rundstedt remaining aloof) and abandoned the idea of a strategic reserve. The Panzer divisions were committed in the same manner as a reserve battalion in 1918 might have been thrown in to take back a segment of a trench captured by the enemy. Since Hitler had the last say, one would have hoped that experts were consulted. This was not the case. Neither Panzer Group West nor Genobst Guderian was asked to express an opinion.

PART FOUR

D-Day: Counterattack

As can be seen from these documents, late on D-Day the German view of the situation varied widely. General Marcks saw that the invasion had indeed succeeded, but to those without his overview (and perception), the American landings seemed to be contained. This left the British forces threatening to drive on Caen as the most important target for the 21st Panzer Division, the only mobile reserve in striking range.

The 21st Panzer Division's counterattack late on D-Day met with strong resistance and naval gunfire, and when darkness fell it had failed to make any gains, even though its point detachment made it to the coast, taking advantage of the gap between the British 3rd Infantry and Canadian 3rd Infantry Divisions. The chance for a counterattack to redeem the situation was aimed at where the Allies were most firmly ashore—and it did not have the weight to dislodge them.

There were German counterattacks throughout Normandy, from the British airborne in the east to the US airborne in the west. Against the US paratroopers, the 709th Infantry Division launched a series on uncoordinated counterattacks at Ste Mère-Église. Elsewhere, however, even "static" divisions and Ost battalions were involved in counterattacks, part of the aggressive German defensive tactics that were to make the Normandy fighting so bitter and prolonged. Evident at all levels, both on D-Day and throughout the campaign, is that the Germans kept up their Great War practice of putting reinforcing units under the control of those forces already engaged, regardless of the chain of command. However, this would often not work well in Normandy, when reinforcing Panzer units were fed in piecemeal to support infantry officers who had no idea how to use them. At a higher level, the Germans attached additional divisions and Kampfgruppen to LXXXIV Corps to the extent that, within a week after D-Day, its headquarters was overloaded, especially after the death of its commander, General Marcks.

D.C.I.

LXXXIV Corps Counterattacks with Local Reserves on the Afternoon of D-Day

by Oberstleutnant Friedrich von Criegern

By 1100 the enemy had been able to establish an almost continuous beachhead as far as Asnelles, with about two kilometers' depth of penetration. There was severe fighting near Asnelles, where the reserve battalion of the 716th Infantry Division launched a counterattack that at first was successful but later was repelled. Thus, Bayeux was endangered by an enemy thrust. Therefore, Corps ordered the reinforced 915th Grenadier Regiment of the 352nd Infantry Division (the Corps reserve)—which had already been put on the march so as to keep open the Vire river crossings east of Carentan—to pivot and attack via Bayeux–Ryes the enemy that had landed near Asnelles and throw him back into the sea.

While the first landing attempt had been repelled east of Grandcamp, the enemy succeeded in establishing a beachhead east of Ste Mère-Église on the eastern coast of Cotentin. Elements of the 709th Infantry and 91st LL Divisions and the 6th FS Regiment had been attacking the airlandings concentrically, in order to annihilate the enemy that had landed from the sea east of Ste Mère-Église. The following units attacked: one Kampfgruppe of the 91st LL Division and elements of the 709th Infantry Division from the north from the Emondeville area, one Kampfgruppe of the 91st LL Division from the west from the area of Pont l' Abbe, and the 6th FS Regiment from the south from the Carentan area.

In spite of the fact that confirmation of their assignment had not arrived as yet, the 243rd Infantry Division, near Cherbourg, received orders to immediately start on the march to Montebourg one reinforced regiment, to be assigned to the 709th Infantry Division.

Strong concentrations of ships were observed offshore along the east coast of the peninsula. The enemy landings, with fighter escort, continued during the course of the whole day.

At 1500, the 12th SS Panzer Division was subordinated to the Corps. But, as it was still in the process of approach, the counterattack by the 21st Panzer Division could not await the arrival. The Commanding General (Marcks), who during the morning had visited the Valognes area to determine countermeasures, returned to 21st Panzer Division at Caen.

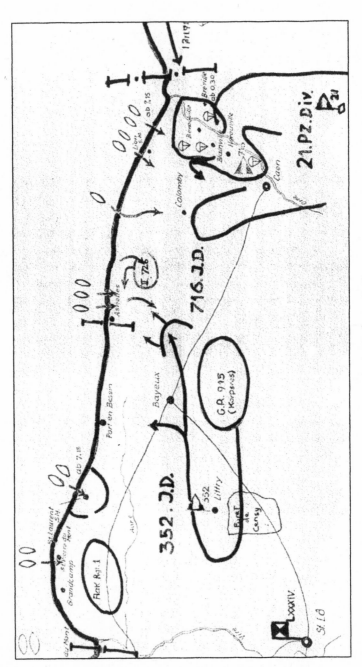

LXXXIV Corps on D-Day

At 1620 the counterattack began. When the general returned in the evening, he reported to Army that the counterattack by the 21st Panzer Division had failed. On one hand, this was due to an enemy airlanding in the rear of the attacking troops; but it was especially true that the attack was not conducted in a concentrated manner by the troops, which had been jumbled together in during previous battles in the commitment east of the Orne river.

The counterattack near Ryes by the 915th Grenadier Regiment of the 352nd Infantry Division also failed. In the evening, the enemy reached the Bayeux–Caen road east of Bayeux.

Counterattacks against the beachhead east of Ste Mère-Église from the north and west were ineffective. The attacking troops were delayed, weakened and partly jumbled on the approach by battles with airlanded enemy forces.

About 1900, the 6th FS Regiment attacked from the southern areas of St Côme du Mont and with one battalion advanced as far as Ste Marie-du-Mont. Another battalion advanced to a point south of Ste Mère-Église. We at least succeeded in annihilating strong elements of the airlanded enemy or pressed them together in the area of Ste Mère-Église.

The result of the first day of the invasion was not very hopeful. It was not possible at any single spot to prevent a landing. The coastal defense was broken through at three points, even though individual islands of resistance still held out inside the points of penetration. The bulk of the coastal artillery was put out of action. Heavy losses were caused by ship artillery. We did not succeed in taking full advantage of the favorable situation, caused by the temporary weakness of the enemy, immediately after the landing. Corps had hoped that it would be possible at that time to mop up the situation with its own forces. The weak reserves were already delayed, and weakened to such an extent by the enemy airborne troops (one division at the Orne river, two divisions west of the Vire river) that, during the day, they were no longer able to carry out a decisive attack.

The success of the invasion is mostly due to the heroic fighting by troops in the first landings of enemy airborne divisions. Decisive, however, was the lack of German Luftwaffe and Navy. Only this made it possible for the enemy to approach unobserved and unharassed and to bring to its full effectiveness during the landing his supremacy in the air and on the sea.

There was little hope of successfully continuing the counterattack with our own forces before the arrival of large reserve. Since Gen Marcks had his doubts that the High Command would take countermeasures in good time, he considered the invasion as already successful on the evening of 6 June.

During the night of 6/7 June, I SS Panzer Corps assumed command in the Caen sector in order to conduct, after the arrival of the 12th SS Panzer Division and together with the 21st Panzer Division, a counterattack west of the Orne river. Thus, the 716th Infantry Division was assigned to I SS Panzer Corps. The former right boundary of the 352nd Infantry Division became the Corps' right boundary

The 21st Panzer Division's Situation (6 June 1944)

by General der Panzertruppen Leo, Freiherr Geyr von Schweppenburg

The first Panzer division to be engaged was the 21st Panzer Division, located in the vicinity of Caen. The disposition of this division on D-Day was a striking example of wretched Panzer tactics and the result of Rommel's orders. Before the invasion started, the division was scattered in four groups and quartered on both sides of the Orne river. The 125th Panzer Grenadier Regiment, northeast of Caen, formed the first group; the 6th Airborne Division (British) jumped into the midst of their billet area. The second group—the division staff and the Panzer regiment, with one artillery battalion and weak elements of the Panzerjäger (antitank) battalion—was in reserve southeast of Caen. The third group, consisting of a battalion of the 192nd Panzer Grenadier Regiment, was on the west bank of the Orne. This battalion was attached to the 716th Infantry Division and was committed in the front-line positions along the coast. Behind it was the bulk of the Panzerjäger battalion. The 193rd Panzer Grenadier Regiment, less a battalion, was located north of Caen.

The main body of the 21st Panzer Division had received strict orders not to move; it was not to be committed without the consent of Genfldm Rommel. Thus it happened that these troops had to stand by as spectators while the enemy paratroops jumped on their comrades. Only after an investigation of the situation by the Ia—who believed in the doctrine of Panzer Group West to attack an airborne enemy without delay—was the main body of the division committed against the British. Thus, this group acted on its own responsibility, against orders. After issuing the attack order, the division commander had left his command post to meet Gen Infantry Marcks, who was at that time Corps Commander [LXXXIV Infantry Corps—Ed.]. The latter officer was at the command post of the 716th Infantry Division in Caen. The meeting took place at about 1000 hours. The Ia, the only man who knew tank warfare, remained behind.

At 1300, just at the time the tank regiment made contact with the enemy, an order was received from Corps to break off this engagement and to attack those forces of the enemy which had reached the heights north of Caen. This entailed crossing the Orne and running the gauntlet of narrow defiles in the town of Caen. By noon, the enemy had established a beachhead between the Orne and the Vire, 25 kilometers wide and five kilometers deep. About this time, Seventh Army subordinated the 21st Panzer Division to the 716th Infantry Division; the latter had ceased to exist as a fighting unit.

236

Before the invasion, when the controversy over the use of Panzer divisions as local tactical reserves was at its height, Panzer Group West had pointed out that the unavoidable consequence would be the subordination of Panzer divisions to commanders who had received no training in the employment of tanks. No decision had been made with regard to this controversy.

Seventh Army, meanwhile, had requested the Luftwaffe to direct its main effort against the beachhead, west of the Orne. In the afternoon of D-Day, the 21st Panzer Division was ordered to continue the attack on the west bank of the river in the direction of Riva-Bella.

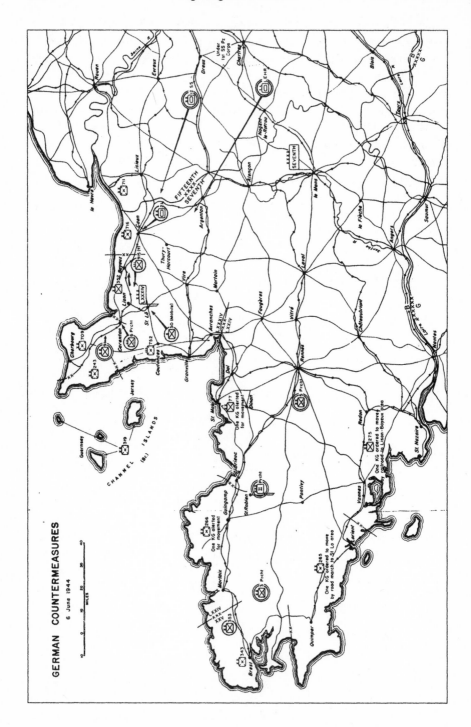

GERMAN COUNTERMEASURES
6 June 1944

Counterattack of the 21st Panzer Division

by Generalleutuant Edgar Feuchtinger

1200 hours: After the assembly of the division, Corps HQ ordered an attack on the enemy who had landed from the sea west of the Orne, north of Caen. All marches in that terrain, which did not boast trees and which was under constant surveillance by enemy planes, had to be made with the units well dispersed. Due to the heavy air activity (constant bombing of the marching columns and attempts to destroy the Orne bridge) and the heavy fire from naval artillery, the march through the narrow places in Caen was still more difficult.

There was only one usable bridge in Caen. A further light bridge was available in Colomoelles. The approaches of the various combat teams had to be fixed correspondingly.

1600 hours: At 1600 hours the division was ready to attack north of Caen with two combat teams:

Armored Combat Team:	22nd Panzer Regiment
	I Bn (light armored halftracks)
	125 Panzer Grena Regiment (less 1st Co)
	1st Co (light armored halftracks)
	220 Panzer Engr Bn
	III Bn, 155th Panzer Art Regiment in the areawest of Heronville—west of 23 [*sic*].
Combat Team:	192nd Panzer Gren Regiment, consisting of:
	192nd Panzer Gren Regiment, less its II Bn
	2nd Co, 220th Panzer Engr Bn
	II Bn, 155th Panzer Art Regiment in the St Contest—Cussy area

The 125th Panzer Grenadier Regiment less its 1st Battalion, the 21st Reconnaissance Battalion, and the 200th Assault Gun Battalion were involved in fighting against the 6th British Airborne Division east of the Orne.

Objectives of the attack:

Armored Group: the coast between the mouth of the Orne and the eastern outskirts of Lion-sur-Mer.

Group 192 Panzer Grenadier Regiment: area around Lion-sur-Mer.

239

The attack by the armored group threw the enemy out of Lebussy and reached the heights north of Lebussy. When it was north of Mathieu–Combes, the group, continuing the attack through Épron, came under heavy fire from tanks and artillery, coming from the direction of Périers and Hill 61.

A number of Mark IV tanks were lost. The British tanks were firing from a distance of approximately 2,000 meters, whereas the fire from the Mark IV tanks on the British tanks, although scoring definite hits, was not effective, as the projectiles had no more power of penetration at that distance. (600 meters was about the greatest distance at which fire on such targets was effective.)

Although it would rob us of a lot of time, it had now become necessary to move the Combat Team to the west in order to evade the fire. This move was made still more complicated by the fact that all radio communications were interrupted by the enemy, and that no orders could be radioed through to the tank crews. Finally, it was possible to carry out the attack on Hill 61 in the direction of Périers under cover from southwest of Gazelle.

At about 1900, there was another heavy enemy airborne landing. On both sides of the Orne, it cut off the fighting groups from each other and isolated them. It was particularly difficult to combat these airborne landings, for the most part consisting of troop-carrying gliders, as the tanks could not fire at targets in the air and the Division AAA Battalion, in position north of Caen, had been destroyed by the British naval artillery. Machine-gun fire from the Panzer Grenadiers accounted for about 26 gliders in the air.

By a local advance through Plumetot, the Combat Team, 192nd Panzer Grenadier Regiment, had reached the coast at Lion-sur-Mer. A heavy tank attack, together with the airborne landing, had meanwhile engaged the left wing of the Combat Team and threatened to destroy it. Despite the airborne landing and the tank attacks, we succeeded in keeping the Combat Team together, but lost a large amount of men and matériel, in particular a number of self-propelled guns and the largest part of the 1st Company/ 192nd Regiment, which was cut off in a signal communications strongpoint near Douvren. This company, although isolated, resisted for eight days, until lack of ammunition and food forced it to surrender. Radio contact with it was maintained until the end.

Under cover of darkness, the division had to be put in some sort of order in the line Havent Wood–south of Escoville–north of Honorine–Blainville (2nd Battalion/192nd Regiment here)–northern outskirts of Herouville–heights north of Leboussy–north of Épron–north of St Contest–Buron. This was carried out successfully. Contact could also be made with the 2nd Battalion/192nd Regiment in Blainville. This battalion gradually fought its way back to the northern outskirts of Herouville and there took over connection with both sides of the Orne.

At approximately 2200 hours, the division was subordinated to I SS Panzer Corps. At approximately 2300 hours, the divisional commander at his advanced command post was in telephone contact with the Commanding General and the Chief of Staff of I SS Panzer Corps, who were at the command post of the 21st Panzer Division.

This evaluation of the situation was given to them:

In the course of 6 June 44 the enemy had succeeded in making his landings on both sides of the Orne from the sea and from the air with strong forces. Opposed to the 21st Panzer Division east of the Orne was the 6th British Airborne Division; west of the Orne were the 3rd British Infantry Division, at least one armored brigade, and parts of the 3rd Canadian Division. The enemy was supported most effectively by his air force and naval artillery.

An attack along the whole front of the division was impossible with the available forces, particularly as the static 716th Division had to be written off. Even now, an attack east of the Orne would hold the greatest promise of success. For this it would be necessary to direct those elements of the 12th SS Division which were only just coming into this sector and to subordinate them to the 21st Panzer Division. From the beginning of the invasion, the division had considered it of paramount importance to recapture this sector, as otherwise

    a.   It would be a standing menace to the division's east wing;

    b.   The enemy would be in a position to reinforce this bridgehead with troops at his convenience;

    c.   It would constantly tie down strong German forces;

    d.   It would, due to the favorable terrain, be the area from which the enemy would carry out his large-scale attacks in the direction of Falaise, after gathering his forces.

On the other hand, to the German Command the recapture of this sector, and the immediate forming of a bridgehead at Ranville, would mean the possession of the eventual starting point for an attack on the east flank of the landed enemy and his supply bases. In the division's opinion, based on the enemy's strength and on personal impressions, an attack with any hopes of success [*sic*] and with the aim of throwing the enemy back into the sea could only hold out any hopes of success if it was carried out on 7 June 1944 with not less than three concentrated Panzer divisions and a guarantee of the corresponding Luftwaffe support needed for dealing with the enemy air force and forces out at sea. These conditions would promise success on either the west or the east of the Orne.

Corps could not agree to these suggestions. Corps stated that the 12th SS Division would take up contact with the 21st Panzer Division during the night, and that both divisions together would attack west of the Orne in the morning of 7 June 1944.

Thus, it never came to a counterattack any more, as only one Panzer Grenadier Regiment and one Panzer Battalion from the 12th SS Division had arrived as neighbor to the 21st Panzer Division by 1600, and these forces were not enough for a combined attack.

I SS Panzer Corps Moves Up to Counterattack, 6 June 1944

by Generalmajor Fritz Krämer

In May of 1944 there were increased signs that an invasion was imminent. The Commander-in-Chief West kept the Corps currently informed of developments. The Channel coast, the Dieppe sector, Caen and the Cotentin peninsula were named as probable landing points. Since mid-May, large-scale troop movements were also carried out. By 1 June, Commander-in-Chief West was keeping the Commanding General or Chief of Staff informed on Hitler's opinions on the invasion, the latest of which presumed that the date would be about mid-June. As OKW reserve, the Corps was directly subordinate to OKW, but the divisions envisaged for commitment were not yet known.

On 6 June 1944, at about 1000 hours, the Chief of Staff was informed by Chief of Staff Panzer Gruppe West of the landing of strong enemy forces near Caen. Still nothing was known concerning the probable commitment of Corps. Nevertheless, orders were given to the staff and troops to be prepared for immediate commitment.

At about 1400, Ia of Seventh Army, Oberst iG Helmdach, telephoned that Corps was assigned to Seventh Army. The Commanding General and Chief of Staff were to come immediately to Seventh Army headquarters at Le Mans for briefing, and Corps troops were to start immediately in the direction of Caen. However, the Chief of Staff I SS Panzer Corps pointed out to Chief of Staff Seventh Army the lively enemy air activity already observed by Corps, and the long distance involved, stated that it was not possible to cover the distance by a Fieseler Storch airplane, and asked for a telephone or written order.

At about 1500 hours, Corps received the following order by phone:

I SS Panzer Corps, subordinated to Seventh Army, will throw the enemy landed near Caen back into the sea. Following units will be subordinated: 21st Panzer Division near Caen, 12th SS Panzer Division, and probably Panzer Lehr Division.

21st Panzer Division is already committed near Caen.

Division CP Caen.

Since 5 June 1944, 12th SS Panzer Division is on march from Dreux area into the Elbeuf area.

To thwart espionage activity, we had been ordered to check the authenticity of every important telephone order a short time after its receipt, by telephoning the headquarters which had issued it. Enquiries by telephone at General of Panzer Troops West and Seventh Army confirmed the correctness of the aforementioned order.

Counterattacks in the Caen-Bayeux Area

Since Corps staff and troops had been alerted on the forenoon of 6 June 1944, the march in the direction of Caen could be started at about 1600 hours along the Nantes–Foreux–Trun–Falaise road. The main road was avoided because of the great danger from the air, and the units moved in extended columns. Already there were burning vehicles of all kinds everywhere on the road. No considerable Flak formations or air forces were available for defense against enemy fighter planes, so these were able to attack as though carrying out exercises. Air attacks had a paralyzing effect on some of our drivers. German soldiers were not accustomed to this type of attack, and it was several days before they became accustomed to it, placed observers in vehicles, and took necessary countermeasures. Whenever enemy fighters approached, the vehicles were raced, if possible, to a house, tree, slope of the road, or other cover, and the crew alighted. High Command soon ordered that march columns and supply vehicles move only at night.

While on the way, the Corps Chief of Staff met the Commander of the 12th SS Panzer Division, who gave some valuable hints about camouflage during marches, and also said that the command post of the 21st Panzer Division was no longer at Caen but at St Pierre-sur-Dives. Sections of wood south of Falaise were the intermediate goal of Corps troops and the main body of the staff. The combat train echelon had been ordered to assemble in a forest about four kilometers north of Falaise. To prevent loss of valuable headquarters radio cars, the echelon had been ordered to keep radio units very small and widely separated during the move.

In a verbal order to its commander, the 12th SS Panzer Division was diverted by way of Elbeuf–Lisieux–Caen. Marching was to start in the early hours of the evening, making full use of the darkness. Guides and persons who were to receive orders had been ordered to proceed to the road junction five kilometers north of St Pierre. At 1800 hours no contact had been established with the Panzer Lehr Division, which had not yet been subordinated.

Apparently, the news about the enemy landing had quickly passed to the civilian population. Groups of civilians were standing before the doors of their houses in towns and villages. Their attitude was not hostile; rather, they showed a strong resentment towards the Allied air attacks, which oftentimes did not discriminate between German motor- and horse-drawn vehicles and French civilian vehicles. Likewise, the civilians were aware that enemy air attacks had almost demolished Falaise.

When Corps arrived at Falaise, it was impossible to pass through the burning town, and we had to detour along a road that the local military police had cleared. This roundabout way was passable for tanks and heavy motor vehicles, so that delay was the only obstacle the air attack created.

At 2000 hours on 6 June 1944, the Commanding General and Chief of Staff met at the command post of the 21st Panzer Division at St Pierre-sur-Dives. Repeated enemy air attacks, detours, and the conversation with the division commander of the 12th SS

Panzer Division had delayed arrival. Already it was apparent that men and vehicles could be saved from destruction only by restricting daytime traffic, and moving at night with dimmed lights. Avoidance of the main roads and use of subsidiary roads were not sufficient, as the enemy fliers also kept the subsidiary roads under observation.

The old maxim of Panzer troops, "It is better for both driver and vehicle to use good roads even if the distance is greater," proved to be true also at night. Troops moving at night arrived at assembly areas in full strength and earlier than if they had moved by day with very great distances between units. Unfortunately, it was a long time before higher headquarters was convinced of this and correctly calculated time and distances.

Upon his arrival at the command post of the 21st Panzer Division on 6 June 1944 at 2000 hours, the Commanding General of I SS Panzer Corps was confronted with the following situation:

1. Only the first general staff officer was present at the command post of the division. As early as the forenoon of 6 June, the 21st Panzer Division had been committed to support of the 716th Infantry Division employed on the coast. The division had not yet attacked compactly, as, for reasons not yet ascertained, it had been committed first on the right and later on the left bank of the Orne. Elements of the division were still on the right bank of the Orne, as the commander of the 719th Infantry Division, employed there, wanted the tanks. The command post had no contact by telephone with the individual combat groups of the division. The division commander was at the command post of the 716th Infantry Division. Telephonic communication with him was frequently interrupted, and audibility was poor at times. He had no contact with his combat groups, except through messengers and special-mission staff officers. He had failed to take a radio set with him. (For a commander of a Panzer or motorized division to leave his headquarters without a radio set was considered tantamount to traveling without his head.)

   The Panzer regiment of the division was committed on the left bank of the Orne and had contacted the enemy. The situation was vague. Approximately 60 tanks (Panzer IV and V) were ready for action. They were adequately equipped with ammunition and fuel.

2. The 12th SS Panzer Division was on the march. We could not expect its arrival before noon on 7 June 1944. (Actually its assembly was not completed until the morning of 8 June.)

3. The 716th Infantry Division, committed at the coast, was split up into several parts, but details of its situation were not available at division headquarters. Some of its elements were employed in individual shelters. In the vicinity of the coast, contact was maintained by radio or telephone.

4. There was delay in establishing telephone contact with Seventh Army at Le Mans, and, when contact was established, audibility frequently was practically nil. The relay station at Falaise was operating under severe difficulties due to the damage to the town by bombing. In a teletype conversation with Seventh Army at about 2400,

Corps requested subordination of the Panzer Lehr Division and reported assumption of control of the 716th Infantry Division, and also that a coordinated attack of Corps units was not expected to take place before 8 June 1944. Further increased support was requested from the Luftwaffe, and the impossibility of daytime marches was pointed out. Seventh Army made it clear that it was essential to carry out a compact attack by Corps as soon as possible.

Reports received by the 21st Panzer Division during the night showed that elements committed on the left bank of the Orne, together with such elements of the 716th Infantry Division as were still capable of action, were on the point of establishling a line of resistance roughly from Blainville (north) to the Caen–Douvres railroad. The divisional sector was opposed by British troops. The enemy had pushed his beachhead inland for about seven or eight kilometers.

Computation of time during the night of 6/7 June made it clear that the most advanced elements of the 12th SS Panzer Division would not arrive south of Caen before early on 7 June. Their assembly could not be completed before the night of 7/8 June. We had to consider delays due to enemy air activity.

The most advanced elements of the Panzer Lehr Division could be expected to arrive at the bridge near Thury-Harcourt on the morning of 7 June.

A Panzer division without supply troops required nine or ten hours to pass a given point, so the assembly of divisions could not be completed before the evening of 7 June. This was only possible if there were no mishaps, an assumption that could not be depended upon. Corps considered that the morning of 8 June was the earliest it could attack.

The only possibility of an earlier attack would have been by the commitment of individual elements of the division within sectors fixed on the map, without awaiting the arrival of artillery, and consequently without artillery support. This would have resulted in splitting up the division, and it could never have been brought together again. The committed elements of the division might have been exterminated by the advancing enemy, had it been called upon to fight against artillery with mere rifles and machine guns. Even if the most favorable results were achieved, the division would be tied up in such a manner as to deprive it of its chief advantage—mobility. Our higher headquarters could have computed this time as well as we, but during the teletype conversation it became evident that they indulged in the desirable but ill-founded hope that the Panzer corps could move mountains.

In this vague situation it was imperative not to lose our nerve. The Commanding General, therefore, decided to prevent an extension of the beachhead by the combined efforts of the 21st Panzer Division and the still-active combat elements of the 716th Infantry Division, in order to launch a compact attack after the approach march and assembly of the other division was completed. During the night of 6/7 June 1944, I SS Panzer Corps issued the following order:

1.   We have to reckon with the extension of enemy beachhead during 7 June 1944.

2. In order to prevent extension of enemy beachhead, I SS Panzer Corps, which on 6 June 1944 assumed control of the Orne sector, inclusive of 716th Infantry Division, will assemble for attack on 7 June 1944, and throw the landed enemy back into the sea. Probable time of attack on 8 June 1944.

Therefore:

    a. 21st Panzer Division will hold the line hitherto reached on either side of Blainville. Elements of 716th Infantry Division employed there will be subordinated.

        The reinforced Panzer regiment will conduct offensive action with limited objectives, in order to simulate the presence of strong Panzer forces. Ground gained has to be occupied immediately. It is not essential to establish a continuous MLR.

        During the night of 6/7 June, the elements of the division which are not employed on the right bank of the Orne have to be moved to the left bank.

    b. 716th Infantry Division will hold its present strongpoints and assemble its scattered elements north of Caen. Caen has to be prepared for tenacious defense. All formations of Army, Navy, and Luftwaffe located there will be subordinated.

        All elements capable of combat located in sector of 21st Panzer Division will be subordinated to this division.

    c. Corps Artillery Commander (Arko I) will move Corps Artillery Battalion to its firing position south of Caen and will support 21st Panzer Division in resistance and attack.

        Artillery of 716th Infantry Division, 21st Panzer Division, and other artillery formations employed at the coast will be incorporated into the plan of fire.

3. 12th SS Panzer Division will go into its jump-off position in the region of Caen (excl.)–Verson–Fleury.

    The assembly of Division has to be accomplished speedily. Further orders will follow.

4. Panzer Lehr Division, placed under control of I SS Panzer Corps immediately, will secure crossing of Division near Thury-Harcourt and assemble in the area around Evrécy. Further orders will follow.

5. Heavy Panzer Battalion/I SS Panzer Corps will reach forest west of Bretteville.

6. CP of 21st Panzer Division to be transferred immediately to the region of Caen.

7. Corps CP will transfer into the May-sur-Orne area. Corps Signal Battalion will establish radio contact with Seventh Army, 84th Artillery Commander (AK), and with subordinate divisions. Telephone connections will be established according to verbal directions.

For Corps Headquarters
Chief of Staff
Signature

The 711th Division Prepares for a Counterattack, 6 June 1944

by Generalleutnant Joseph Reichert

On the evening of 6 June, the impression prevailed that the entire coastal sector of the division, including the sector of the 716th Division to the east of the Orne, was firmly in our hands, that the damage to matériel in the strongpoints affected by the bombardment was only slight, and that the enemy who had airlanded in the individual sector was for the greater part annihilated, with only slight losses on our part. About 300 men were taken prisoner.

A further advance with the two reserve battalions into the neighboring sector would hardly have been possible considering the little time available, but it did not seem advisable, because, in spite of the statement by the prisoners, there was no proof whatsoever that the enemy had not tried to take possession of the heights between Touques and Dives after all, and that we had to prepare for a new airlanding or even a landing from the sea. Apparently, LXXXI Corps was also of the same opinion, and—in the evening—this was confirmed by the bringing up of a regiment of the 346th Division (minus one battalion), one artillery battalion, and one engineer battalion. The task of the division was to advance with these forces toward the bridge near Benouville—which, according to reports made by pilots, was undamaged—and to destroy the bridge and to seal off the enemy landing at the Orne. Besides, the Army coastal artillery was ordered to start immediate harassing fire against the bridge. The portions of the 716th Division which were still located to the east of the Orne were subordinated to the division.

In order to carry out this task, I intended to move into position near Varaville the artillery battalion which had been brought up; to assemble the regiment west of Varaville, and—fully echeloned to the right and to the left, the center advancing via the church at Bréville—to attack the Orne bridge near Benouville. At the same time, the reserve battalion of the 744th Infantry Regiment of the Division was to push forward via Merville–Salenelles, to press in the enemy bridgehead east of the Orne from the north, and to split up the enemy defense. Artillery support by the divisional artillery was possible only as far as the line Franceville–Plage–Bréville; beyond it, only by one battery of the Army coastal artillery. Advance observers were to proceed with both attack columns.

The Regimental Commander of the 346th Infantry Division, who arrived on the night of 6 June, was accordingly instructed. He believed that his troops might arrive at about 1100 hours.

Reaction to the Invasion

by Oberstleutnant Günther Keil

The 1st Battalion of the 919th Infantry Regiment and the Georgian Battalion were destroyed or taken prisoner in the course of 6 June. W 1–13* in the area of the 1st Battalion were obviously in the hands of the enemy, with the exception of W 10, W 10a, W 11 and S 12, which were still holding out.

In the morning of 6 June, the regiment had nothing for the purpose of sealing off and securing toward the south. Since there was still the threat of further landings in the area of the 2nd Battalion of the 919th Infantry Regiment, the 3rd Battalion had to remain in its position behind the 2nd Battalion. To reconnoiter toward the south, the special missions staff officer of the 2nd Battalion, Lt Henrichheld, and eight men were detached. He advanced as far as Marcouf and put 100 Americans to flight.

During 6 June, the 3rd Battalion of the 739th Regiment was assigned and subordinated to the regiment. It was employed in the line from the southern edge of the park of the Fontenay-sur-Mer Castle to the Marcouf naval battery, forming the first defense front toward the south.

On the evening of 6 June, Lt Meidam fought his way from W 10 through W 10a to W 11 and from there to S 12. With the crews of W 10, W 10a, W 11 and S 12, he defended S 12 for several days, until he had to surrender because of lack of food and because more than half of his men were severely wounded and could not be taken care of any more. His AT gun and his antilanding gun in S 12 had been put out of action on 7 June, so that he had defended himself merely with a double-barreled MG in an armored cupola. He surrendered when his strongpoint had been encircled by numerous tanks and leaving his MG pillbox had become impossible. This is a statement of Lt Meidam, who was with me in a prison camp; it is partly confirmed by my own observations.

---

* W = nest of resistance.

The 2nd Panzer Division:
Told to Hold in Place

by General der Panzertruppen Heinrich, Freiherr von Lüttwitz

The Division Commander learned during a telephone conversation to Army Group B (around noon, 6 June), that, at that time, it was still believed that the enemy's major attack was about to occur somewhere along the direction of the Somme estuary; solely for this reason, the division was instructed to remain in its present surroundings.

III Flak Corps: Orders for the Initial Commitment in Normandy

by General der Flakartillerie Wolfgang Pickert

In the afternoon of 6 June 1944, there arrived the preliminary order to get ready to move off in the direction of Normandy via Paris. In the evening of 6 June 1944, the Commanding General verbally received more detailed information regarding the landing in Normandy, as well as the order to go into action: III AA Corps is assigned to Panzer Gruppe West, and ordered to cooperate with this Panzer Gruppe. The Corps remains directly subordinate to the Air Force Administrative Command (Luftflotte) 3, in every respect. It is to move, with all dispatch, into the area west and southwest of Caen, and to support the Army in combat, drastically concentrating its forces. The main mission remains antiaircraft defense, but the Army is to be aided in its ground combat as much as possible. Connections are to be taken up immediately with Panzer Gruppe West (Gen d Panzer Tr Geyr von Schweppenburg) in the area west of Thury-Harcourt (exact locality no longer recalled). The fourth regiment (1st Flaksturm-Regiment), committed in the region of Isigny, is to be extracted as soon as possible.

Index